Young People and Learning Processes in School and Everyday Life

Volume 9

This book series provides analyses of contemporary issues and questions related to being young and becoming an adult in a global educational landscape. It examines education pathways in relation to characteristics of transitional processes that are part of this transformational and developmental process, as well as sociocultural aspects. It investigates areas such as education, everyday life, leisure time, family, subcultural affiliations, medialization, work and intimacy.

The series highlights the following areas:

- Contemporary challenges in education and the educational system.
- Young people's experiences and varying living conditions and its influence on academic performance.
- New emerging social and existential identities in relation to education.
- Challenges for education – Inclusion and exclusion in terms of risk behaviours, psychological distress and social unrest.
- Theoretical renewal and a conceptual adaption to education, and the societal and cultural challenges of contemporary school systems.
- Digitalisation, technology and media in modern education. Educational pathways for specific groups.
- Contextual challenges for educational ambitions, such as poverty, politics, war and exclusion of groups.

The series introduces ground-breaking interdisciplinary works in the area of education, challenging the orthodoxies in this field of research, and publishes works on the globalization of education. Furthermore, it introduces research on youth, thus advancing current knowledge on education in relation to the young person's everyday life, nationalities, socio-economic backgrounds and living conditions. In addition, it presents new methodological and theoretical approaches to this research field.

Margaret E. Robertson
Editor

Youth, Identity, AI and Moral Purpose

Education in a Globally Confused World

Springer

Editor
Margaret E. Robertson
School of Education
La Trobe University
Melbourne, VIC, Australia

ISSN 2522-5642 ISSN 2522-5650 (electronic)
Young People and Learning Processes in School and Everyday Life
ISBN 978-3-032-32478-8 ISBN 978-3-032-32479-5 (eBook)
https://doi.org/10.1007/978-3-032-32479-5

This Springer imprint is published by the registered company Springer Nature Switzerland AG
The registered company address is: Gewerbestrasse 11, 6330 Cham, Switzerland

Preface

Youth, Identity, AI and Moral Purpose is a book about puzzles. Not the kind we associate with parlour games, although they may provide clues. No, Artificial Intelligence, social media and the infinite options they offer are the game changers of our times and therein lies the real conundrum. How do we tame these powerful sources? Do we need to tame their powers? Should society demand some controls, or protocols for the public good? How do we move forward with appropriate societal values and norms? Technology provides clues to 'what' and 'how' to go about daily life both observable and hidden from public gaze. Perhaps this has always been the case. The private and public lives of human existence have been a major driver of philosophy, intellectual discourse and action throughout history. The advent of the print machine bought education to the wider populace. The industrial revolution and rise of public education have disrupted privileged lifestyles. Both have changed the world. However, arguably not with the same effect as digitized knowledge, communication and transactions. From the privileged few in former times, to elected officials, to the powers of one, the digital world has changed the ways in which we live and act both locally and globally. Individuals effectively have an arsenal of tools within their home-based grasp to use, manipulate and disperse information at will. From the advent of Artificial Intelligence to enhanced momentum of Generative Artificial Intelligence the need for human intelligence to meet the ongoing challenges seems unparalleled in history.

The tools of the digital world have changed the guidelines for daily life, human interactions, and importantly, education. School-based curriculums have had a generation of time to adapt their programs to embrace digital technologies. They have also adapted their offerings to be inclusive of identity differences and sympathies. Thus, schools, and governments, in many countries, have reviewed their content and curriculum selection to be more embracive of alternate perspectives. The general view is that this is all morally progressive. We need to live in a world where all its citizens are valued and have a voice in public opinion and action. As a movement, for instance, the identity inclusive momentum has garnered respect and action across the spectrum of daily life including within school education. So too have the voices and cultures of indigenous communities. Both reflect the powers of personal experience and knowing your people. In brief, global education trends appear to have gradually shifted their techniques to utilise computerised technologies and be mindful of students' personal needs.

Such positive movements are applauded. They reflect a maturing population well able to withstand change. So how are our institutions managing AI and its GenAI subset? How are our young people managing AI? How can we sustain the hallmarks of a society when its individuals have access to tools that can manipulate, distort and share confidences at will? These are some of the puzzles of our times. Some major shifts in the ways in which we conduct our daily lives are pending.

In our crazy world of contradictions, making the landscape future appears to be the challenge of our times. Artificial Intelligence is the magnetic force around which traditions, knowledge, skills and creative potential are being shaped, negated, possibly corrupted and undoubtedly augmented. Added to the infinite landscapes possible through AI visions, ubiquitous access to smart technologies completes the smorgasbord challenge facing decision makers, and especially, educators. Old style curriculums and pedagogies simply do not touch the times. Worse still the rapidity of global change, mobility and immediacy of distribution of new developments, notably from GenAI, renders solutions today possibly redundant tomorrow. Predictability seems to be out the window.

A pedagogy for the ages should offer leadership. Society relies on learnt sentiments, including shared boundaries around behaviours and daily activities. Alas, in the design of curriculum and education practices, traditions alone offer little solace. The Anthropocene has morphed into a confused set of challenges. Global, national and local politics reveal discordant spaces in which young people are growing up. Information saturation brings moment by moment events to their fingertips. Social media has neutralised reflective, well researched journalistic reporting in favour of streamed updates of sensational happenings and destructive acts impacting human lives both locally and in far distant locations.

By talking charge of the narrative including each new event, authoritarian rule solves such dilemmas but few who believe in a free democratic world would consider this to be the sustainable option for the Anthropocene. Experience founded on well-grounded principles demands smart voices of big thinkers who can sort the options and guide the leaders. Short term heroics will surely fail, and new directions will need delicate balancing of competing perspectives. Wise voices strive to reflect innovators but need to keep track of next generation interests and cultures. Wisdom speaks volumes.

The chapters following offer multiple perspectives on youth and moral purpose within their AI worlds both present and emerging. Some reflect personal experiences from past times. Morgan's chapter on adolescence reflects the changes in a lifetime. Other writers have based their commentary on the intersection of philosophy and AI. Burston in Chapter 9 considers whether we may be moving towards 'hybridised humanoid facsimiles in the future'. In Chapter 8, Tani and Hilanda connect landscape, young people and place both real and AI. In the final section, Wang and colleagues as well as Cruickshank and Jeana Kriewaldt take the puzzle to the higher education context. Their challenge is to rewrite the intellectual journey in parallel with Generative Artificial Intelligence. Other chapters include references to classical myths, fashion and popular media, socio-cultural inheritance, as well as urban lifestyle dominance, climate and sustainability. The diversity of themes reflects the multidimensional lives of young people. Their lives are complex and holistic approaches work best regardless of context and moments in their journeys. The final chapter attempts to synthesise the content with a call for remaining cool, calm and confident in our evidence based shared pedagogical knowledge and expertise.

Melbourne, Australia Margaret E. Robertson
April 2026

Acknowledgements The contest of ideas is always a collaborative effort. This book is a tribute to enduring friendships across the globe.

Competing Interests The author has no competing interests to declare that are relevant to the content of this manuscript.

Contents

Contributors

Paul Albinson School of Education, University of Tasmania, Launceston, TAS, Australia

Andy Bown School of Education, University of Tasmania, Launceston, TAS, Australia

Mary A. Burston La Trobe University, Melbourne, Australia

Emlyn Cruickshank Faculty of Education, University of Melbourne, Melbourne, VIC, Australia

Si Fan School of Education, University of Tasmania, Launceston, TAS, Australia

Markus Hilander Faculty of Educational Sciences, University of Helsinki, Helsinki, Finland

Anuradha Khara Curriculum Design and Innovation, University of Tasmania, Launceston, TAS, Australia

Jeana Kriewaldt Faculty of Education, University of Melbourne, Melbourne, VIC, Australia

John Morgan University of Auckland, Auckland, New Zealand

Margaret E. Robertson La Trobe University, Melbourne, Australia

Sirpa Tani Faculty of Educational Sciences, University of Helsinki, Helsinki, Finland

Yanjun Wang School of Humanities and Social Sciences, University of Tasmania, Launceston, TAS, Australia

List of Figures

Part I
Culture and Society—Youth in the AI Context

Chapter 1
Pedagogy in the GenAI World

Margaret E. Robertson

Abstract In the face of tumultuous changes in the digital world, this chapter considers the challenges faced by society and how the concept is being disrupted globally. Historical events show that is takes courage and imaginative leadership to shift a seemingly stubborn inertia for change. In the GenAI world of contemporary society the qualities of a good person who needs to balance freewill with citizenship responsibilities is educationally challenging. Analysing time and space relatedness, intellectuals provide diverse ideas and strategies. In brief, ethical pragmatism might be an ideal pathway forward. However, there are no guarantees for society or the developing person.

Keywords Human knowledge · Machine learning · Ontology · Epistemology · Society

1.1 Introduction: Society, AI, GenAI and the Crossroads of History

Great minds offer many wise words and advice which we can well reflect upon in times of crisis. Now is one of those times. First, there was the pandemic. Next came Artificial Intelligence (AI) and now its subset of GenAI. The result, real-world exchanges have leaped towards time and space unknowns. Human endeavour has a history of searching for improvements that enhance on existing human knowledge and related tools. Their impact socially can be minimal. However, these two events have disrupted everyday life and systems globally. In summary, and arguably, the digital space of the past three decades belongs to the user and AI has augmented that power. Algorithmic pattern recognition of AI superseded traditional computing. Then came its subset Generative Artificial Intelligence (GenAI) with creativity capability for design and new outputs. Its existence has an aura of its own. The power and

M. E. Robertson (✉)
La Trobe University, Melbourne, Australia
e-mail: m.robertson@latrobe.edu.au

M. E. Robertson (ed.), *Youth, Identity, AI and Moral Purpose*, Young People and Learning Processes in School and Everyday Life 9,
https://doi.org/10.1007/978-3-032-32479-5_1

capability of GenAI supersede its subaltern predecessors including all social media platforms. Indeed, the rapid rise and roll out of GenAI across systems has caused wonder, excitement and perhaps fear for users and blindsided many. In dealing with such game changing tools, history suggests that social agencies tend to patch their existing systems rather than contemplate a process of renewal. Understanding the new tool(s) will take time. In short, it does not seem too bold to assert that AI and GenAI have created a crossroads in history including a major challenge to the notion of society, its rules and customs (Brunnhuber, 2024; Feher, 2025; Krauss, 2024; Peeters et al., 2021). An emerging social ontology that poses significant challenges for society, learning and knowledge boundaries where pedagogical responses are challenged to be dynamic and adjust to evolutionary changes in their knowledge-based spaces. There is little doubt that ChatGPT and its infinite successors will continue to disrupt the status quo within the knowledge making world. Reality is that the 'old ways' have a fractured foundation. Wiley (2024) captures the significance with the observation that "Artificial Intelligence can therefore be properly defined as the branch of computer science that focuses on emulating cognitive functions typically linked to human intelligence, including but not limited to learning, problem-solving and pattern recognition. This foundational idea propelled AI [and its subsets including GenAI] from purely theoretical research into inventive practical applications that began transforming every aspect of society, securing its place as one of the most significant scientific achievements of the modern era" (p. 57). This chapter provides an overview of AI-related knowledge including implications for everyday lived experience, learning and the possibility of a redefined society. There are no guarantees or definitive answers in this puzzle. More like starting points for informed conversations and a pedagogical framework that may best prepare future citizens to make wise decisions for their personal well-being and social connections. In essence there is virtue in the quest to seek some markers for that process as a working suggestion for a valid epistemological framework.

1.2 The Making of a Good Person

As a starting point, a simple maxim to keep in mind is what it means to be a good person. Therein is a goal to help shape decision making regardless of data source. Real space, imagined space and technological space are sources of stimuli for human interaction and action. Like the magical fragility and reality of the newborn child moments are fixed in place and time. A new life, a new beginning, a new future to unfold. Across cultures and contexts, behavioural responses are guided by experience, knowledge, learned responses, environment and training. The mechanics of shaping the development of the newborn connect with fields of knowledge such as brain-based learning, freewill and human cognition research. They are starting points for finding clues and potential answers to questions related to events such as the intersection of AI and human behaviour. However, and more importantly, the making of each good person is inextricably bound to culture, tradition and society.

By re-examining some of the education theories that have stood the test of time this chapter seeks to identify the key indicators of successful learning programmes. Each of the dimensions which contribute to the identity and character of the developing person is explored as part of the ultimate puzzle faced by educators, parents, and society's decision makers across all endeavours of daily life.

1.3 Freewill, Society, Ontological Upheaval

It's tempting to assume we all have freewill and can exercise this quality anytime and place. Certainly, sociologists have had to consider a person's freewill interactions with their 'scientific' judgments (see Bauman, 2024). Youth cultures have traditionally exercised their right to protest and missions to bring about change. However, if commentators in the popular press are a guide to the tempo of our times, then we are left to wonder if humans have any remaining freewill space. Artificial intelligence (AI) is a 'mind reader', it can 'do thinking for you'; all you need do is 'ask it', and 'it never gets bored with you'. Better than a human friend. In other words, humans need or can play a passive role in tasks by withdrawing from the decision-making process. We might also consider that common habits of watching screens for endless hours or binging on online movie series can be blamed for changing who we think we are. Our choices in what we watch or the online sites with which we engage all have programmed systems or 'cookies' which project selected content and biases. We've become lazy in our thinking and processing of real-world data preferring to use a mobile phone app or ask the computer copilot for solutions and direction. I'm reminded of an instance while passing New York's Trump Tower building. A young woman peering into her mobile phone asked 'where is the Trump building? I'm meeting my friend there and I can't find it on my phone'. Her observation skills appeared to be subsumed by the power of the phone to deliver her to the right location which ironically, she had 'found' and was standing outside its entrance.

The paradox is that human creativity and imagination have got us to this point. The Turing test (see Floyd et al., 2023) which purports to distinguish human responses from machines exists as a turning point in this journey of human endeavour. [Alan Turing is acknowledged as inventing the first version of AI. His legacy is part of the Apple computer symbol. An apple with a bite removed is associated with the apple found near Turing's body on his premature death from suicide.] While research continues to apply the test there is evidence that the gap is lessening. That is, the AI versus human gap in responses is narrowing and GenAI can subsume our human ability to create and innovate. Or can it? Do we sit back and allow the streaming of GenAI to control society and dictate terms for our moral and ethical well-being, or pause, reflect and use the might of our cranial intelligence to maintain our dignity and social identity? Society's existence and substance versus individuals' free choice behaviour is a valid starting point for offering pedagogical directions some tangible criteria for efficacy. In this context, the calamity of the present dynamic can be well served by remaining calm and reviewing our assumptions regarding society, individual freewill and environment.

One of the certainties of radical societal change is the burden of history. Turing's troubled and shortened life reflected the human cost of self-belief and yet today we can look back and celebrate his achievements. Unravelling the workings of the mechanical 'brain' has become a historical marker for current AI events. However, his life journey faced both intellectual and personal backlash from peers and societal rules of the time. From this experience, we can consider that yielding to the hegemonic pressures of accepted philosophy and societal management or adopting a status quo approach may be the current enemy of pedagogical reform. Adopting the evolving ontological argument versus epistemological knowing needs creative thinkers and a willingness to see the world from innovative positions which may well be possible with GenAI outputs. That is, with the caveat that GenAI creativity is underpinned by 'deep learning' from underlying data bases whereas human creativity should have greater claim to authenticity. Human creativity is unique.

Society has entered an ontological space where freewill can be augmented, rewarded and a contributory element of navigating sustainable life skills. Alternatively, the human spirit may well fall on troubled waters if self-confidence weans. Thwarted, punished and unimaginable pain or helped along the journey by pedagogical responses that enable valid decision making and just societal responses. An individual's freewill assumes a learned ethical position which aligns with their cultural and societal heritage. By contrast AI competes for our attention from a different space of stored information. As Ahn et al. (2024) note: "AI is a non-living machine that operates on algorithms meticulously crafted by human developers or operators. Consequently, AI, in theory, lacks freewill and ethical responsibility" (p. 848). The sour note to be acknowledged on this conclusion is that GenAI usurps this hurdle with powers to operate outside human direction.

1.4 Philosophical Foundations: Montaigne, Rousseau and the Voyage Metaphor

A useful starting point has been to think of the development of ideas and critical thinking from the perspective of being a traveller. Using travel as the metaphor, Van Den Abbeele (1991) considers a voyage though the French enlightenment and philosophy including an analysis of the essays of Michael de Montaigne and Jean-Jacques Rousseau's. He connects the voyage of these intellectual movements with the development of Western culture from Hellenic times onwards (p. xv).

> It would seem, moreover, that the very banality or banalizing of travel to be found in literature both veils and unveils its importance for Western culture. The voyage is undoubtedly one of the most cherished institutions of that civilization, and banal as it may be, travel is persistently perceived as exciting and interesting, as liberating, and as what "opens up new horizons." The dearest notions of the West nearly all appeal to the motif of the voyage: progress, the quest for knowledge, freedom as freedom to move, self-awareness as an Odyssean enterprise,

> salvation as a destination to be attained by following a prescribed pathway (typically straight and narrow). Yet if there is such a great cultural investment in the voyage, that locus of investment is nonetheless one whose possibility of appropriation also implies the threat of an expropriation. The voyage endangers as much as it is supposed to assure these cultural values: something can always go wrong. The "place" of the voyage cannot be a stable one.

The enduring influence of Montaigne and Rousseau[1] is noteworthy. Montaigne's early education shaped his curiosity and self-reflection. Rousseau expressed his views on education through his writings. Significantly both critical thinkers were concerned with the discovery of knowledge through experience rather than as a body of predetermined facts and information stored in books and drip fed to pupils by teachers and tutors. Know thyself is the wisdom noted in their writings.

Born of aristocratic French parentage in 1533 Montaigne's father guided the child's education with experiences of life and living beyond the secure space of the family chateau. The pedagogical plan was to bring him closer to the people and their daily challenges. In early childhood he was sent to live for an extended time with a peasant family. Latin was encouraged as his first language at home. From childhood he was emersed in conversation and activities that expanded his knowledge of Greek and Italian literature and arts. A renaissance man who captured attention with his focus on individualised learning whereby the tutor becomes the guide and learning needs to flow from experience. A delight in discovery rather than the rote memorisation of texts that typified education from tutors of the time. Now translated for global readers his ideas on education and life are captured in his essays on travel and journal letters (Frame, 2003). The essays regain contemporary appeal for their conversational style and connection with the everyday interactions that might take place between friends or in personal musings on events and activities. On education Montaigne wrote:

> This great world, which some multiply further as being only a species under one genus, is the mirror in which we must look at ourselves from the proper angle. In short, I want to be the book of my own student. So many humors, sects, judgments, opinions, laws, customs teach us to judge sanely of our own, and teach our judgement to recognise its own imperfection and natural weakness, which is no small lesson. (Montaigne, circa 1579, in Frame, 2003, p. 141)

The focus on self-reliance as a guiding principle for life's decisions seems fundamental for child development including how we choose to exercise freewill. In the current context of AI and open boundaries to the world's knowledge and its applications, personal strengths in decision making are of paramount importance. Educators in schools and higher education are not only baffled by the powers of AI and its effectiveness to 'do' the work of students but scramble for responses that will maintain the integrity of the curriculum content and lead to valid and reliable assessment processes. Montaigne would respond to this dilemma by questioning the pedagogical practices that bureaucratic and centralised management systems seem reluctant to disrupt. Alas, this power and control approach to education must be the starting

[1] Many other great thinkers and philosophers can be included and could be explored. For example, Goethe, Dante, Descartes.

point for change. Students, their worlds and their preferences for learning are the logical starting points for bridging the teaching and learning gap. Once again, the wisdom of Montaigne is truth telling.

> If, as is our custom, the teachers undertake to regulate many minds of such different capacities and forms with the same lesson and a similar measure of guidance, it is no wonder if in the whole race of children they find barely two or three who reap any proper fruit from their teaching. (Montaigne, circa 1579, in Frame, 2003, p. 134)

Jean-Jacques Rousseau, born in Geneva in 1712 during the Enlightenment and on the cusp of industrial Europe, also experienced life beyond his middle-class upbringing. Educated as a scientist his observations of the political and economic changes reflected in his writings on the labour market were controversial. His concerns are documented in *The Social Contract* which was first published in 1762. In this he considers the tension between individual freedoms and society including mandated authority to legislate. Considered his major work, *Émile, ou De l'éducation,* his views on education inspired revolutionary changes in France and revised views on civics and citizenship education across borders. Novelistic in style the development of *Émile* reveals the importance of experiences of the natural world and what exists. A treatise against what he perceived to be a corrupt society including religious dominance, his views were widely rejected by the ruling parties of the times. Ironically, his courage and virtue regarding inequality survived the conservative voices and are qualities worthy of revisiting. As Tully and Scott (2020) note:

> Jean-Jacques Rousseau's passionate attack on inequalities political, social, and economic, his critique of reigning governments in the name of democracy, and his questioning of the authority of science or philosophy in defence of moral virtue shook the century of Enlightenment and the aftershocks are still felt today. (p. 184)

Indeed, it could be said little has changed. Inequalities remain a vexing question in society. What we can conclude is that the legacy of Montaigne and Rousseau set in motion a continuing debate and contest of ideas about education and how best to shape the development of the child with pedagogical practices embedded in experience. The metaphor of the traveller who is encouraged to look around their environment and make decisions based on moral virtue and individual needs assumes a social commitment and responsibility for personal growth. All very well in theory. However, the reality of our globalised free flowing open access to information world poses layers of systems all competing for individual attention and often in conflict with one another. At best the past can offer warning signs and indicators for forward thinking decision making. With AI's impact being equated with the impact (but much faster) of the Industrial Revolution and the arrival of the Gutenberg press which brought print to the masses, patches on existing systems will not work. AI's copilots and chatbots personify unlimited freewill. The question is how humans can manage AI intrusions in their decision making so that whatever decisions they may make represent an outcome of personal freewill and not the robotic responses of the AI software. It is the dilemma of our times and no amount of posturing related to old thinking will be adequate. Revolutionary thinkers like Montaigne, Rousseau and Turing are needed. Humans need to find their relationship with the technology in ways that maintain their integrity and commitment to a sustainable and virtuous future for forthcoming generations. Rather than be alarmed by predictions of job losses and lifestyle threats, epistemological responses are to be found in positive steps towards new and different enterprises. Freewill is to be celebrated and encouraged, albeit with caveats for meeting the needs of civil society.

1.5 Intellectual Landscape, History and Social Theory: A Brief Overview

Adding to the context influential twentieth-century thinkers such as John Dewey (1916), Michel Foucault (see Ball 1990), Alfred North Whitehead (1938), Bertrand Russell, (1932), Roland Barthes (2000) and Zygmunt Bauman (2024), among others, have shaped debates on education, knowledge and society. Bauman's concept of "liquid modernity" is particularly noted for describing the fluid and uncertain nature of contemporary social identities and responsibilities. In Bauman's words: "Human life…is a continuous search for strategic responses adequate to perceived situational challenges, and a similarly continuous recycling of perception by the strategies selected and put in to operation" (2024, pp. 153–154). Hence, "Living in a liquid-modern setting calls for, and ultimately consists of, an incessant flow of reflexivity" (p. 154). Such is the social state which resonates with the challenges posed by AI and digital culture.

Questioning the stability of structures and meanings, including classical and Hellenic traditions French poststructuralism became a critical social and philosophical movement of the late twentieth century. Key figures like Jacques Derrida, and Michel Foucault challenged traditional binaries and emphasised the role of power in knowledge production and in Miller's view "…whether in literature, fashion, or kinship patterns–the poststructuralists consistently refused to endorse any form of totalization, preferring to concentrate on the local and the particular" (1998, p. 206). Their influence on educational thinking has undoubtedly been significant. At the same time in Miller's analysis the works of both can be shown to have links to the past with the suggestion that the footprint remains in our cognitive and reflective memory albeit continually disrupted by real events and new knowledge such as technology affords. Perhaps this contradiction is best understood in the writings associated with new historicism which as an approach has been gathering renewed literary interest. Attributed to American scholar Stephen Greenblatt, his essay 'Towards a poetics of culture' (1989) the approach seeks to reanalyse the interplay between literature and culture. The new historicism view is that the power dynamics and textuality of history help shape the narrative embedded in our cultural traditions. For example, Marxist traditions associate specific economic, political and social outcomes with capitalism and identity. The antithesis of this view can be to take Derrida's perspective on deconstruction and to critically review early Marxist literature as a means of understanding localised injustices and ethics within a contemporary context.

The context of ideas in the twenty-first century underscores an acceptance of difference and responsiveness to the momentum gathered around perceived intrusions from multiple directions including digital sources. Take, for example, Slavoj Žižek's (1997)* ideological fantasies, pop culture, philosophy and a whole lot of worldly influences that have blown open many of the traditional norms of philosophy. In addition, post-colonial accounts of Homi Bhabha (1994) and Edward Said (1979) have helped raise awareness of eastern culture and challenged Western assumptions. More recently gender and identity studies (including bell hooks, 2009) have introduced a new wave of culture wars designed to pave the difficult terrain for inclusive policies and curricula (e.g. see Sotirakopoulos, 2021).

1.6 Space, Place and 'Being' in the Geopolitical Landscape

So far, this chapter has attempted to show that philosophers and intellectuals help shape our collective memory including ideas and responses to new challenges. There is a kind of cumulative wisdom that guides our thinking. Nevertheless, as AI is tightening its grip on daily life the old ways may not be enough. They trip up as reality takes an unexpected turn. However, anchoring the many twists and turns of ideas over time and recorded history is always the reality of place and context (see Peters, 2011). The traveller's journey continues. History records past events but to quote from Hartley's (1953) novel *The go-between*, 'the past is a foreign land'. The landscape of now is dynamic and ever changing. An important parallel research tradition to that of historians, sociologists and philosophers has followed developments in personal mobility, global migration and the increasing concentration of populations in mega-cities. While this dimension is more closely dealt with in Chapter Two there is a realisation in the geopolitical landscape that brings to the fore the spatial turn first noted by scholars including Edward Soja (1996) and Doreen Massey (2005).

Soja's construct of *Thirdspace* partly derived from Henri LeFevbre's (1991) critique of everyday life and the writings of Michel Foucault. Soja seeks to prioritise space over time. He recognises 'other spaces' that complicate the everyday. The spatial imagination is material and mental but is also a product of "the creation of another mode of thinking …well beyond them in scope, substance and meaning" (p. 11). Real and imagined space in this 'thirding' construct draws upon LeFebvre's constructs of 'perceived, conceived and lived space' as well as bell hook's (2009) views on marginalism and being on the edge. Developing this reordering of space over time, Massey's book titled *For Space* (2005) urges an awakening of our imagination about how we think about space and how we identify and develop a sense of place. She challenges the 'subordination of space over time' (p. 21) notably by nineteenth-century philosophers. Exploring these ideas further in a subsequent book titled *World City* (2007), Massey provides contemporary context to the geospatial dynamic through reference to the global shift of populations towards megacities.

London is her research focus for illustrating how megacity population concentrations are creating new geographies and reordering the financial, commercial and regulatory frameworks away from local connections to global transactions, communications and communities. More than half of the world's people (World Bank, 2026) now live in urban settings and while acknowledged as places of excitement and likely to be highly stimulating they are also likely to be places of extremes in wealth, access to lifestyle benefits and causes of poverty and social alienation. The biggest megacities show the rapid growth and concentration in Asia including Tokyo, Delhi, Shanghai, Dhaka, Osaka and Karachi. Within these evolving spaces individuals must find their identity and purpose. There is no doubt that digital media and AI advances will help shape personal identity in urban spaces and provide affordance for making self-enhancing connections with compatible communities. Free market neoliberal contexts are opportunities for innovative enterprises. Places where creative and smart thinking individuals can succeed. In a paper titled *Cities and states in geohistory*, Soja (2010) synthesises the case for public discourse to understand and include reference to the spatial dynamic involved in all forms of human endeavour. He writes:

> The need for such spatialization of even the best historical writings arises from what can be described as the Great Ontological Distortion that took place in Western scholarship in the last half of the nineteenth century. Almost entirely unnoticed in the mainstream literature was an intellectual fixation on temporal and historical perspectives that would inject a socio-historical bias into the then emerging social sciences as well as into Marx's historical materialism. Foregrounding historical interpretations of social relations, social will, and societal development, while decidedly insightful, essentially subordinated space to time, geography to history, creating an ontological predisposition that would carry over to affect epistemological debate, theory formation, and empirical analysis in all the human sciences. Cities and states, for example, came to be studied literally and figuratively "through history" while their geography or spatiality was reduced to a neutral background environment, a container of social life and history, a stage for a social drama unfolding primarily across time and only incidentally across place and space. One of the few to recognize this ontological distortion was Michel Foucault (1986), who quizzically asked why is it that we have come to think of time as dynamic, process, movement, development, dialectic while space tends to be seen as fixed, dead, extra-social background, or environment. (p. 362)

The essential element of this argument is that space and time interact and further to this recognition is the view that compression of interactions and transactions have direct links with technology and mobility advances. Paul Virilio's construct of dromology (2000) offers a contested view of the process which not all observers are prepared to accept. However, there is general acceptance of the change in pace of life and the time–space eclectic associated with the arrival of modern late nineteenth- and twentieth-century transport including rail, motorised vehicles and air travel. More recent is warfare using drones which appears to add a further complicating dimension to the time–space equation. The time–space dynamic has taken on a configuration or juxtaposition of parallel versions of actions and behaviours each of which is accessible for human interaction. Real time–space and virtual time–space and how the interplay of all elements are connecting suggest a new ontological reality as the basis of epistemological knowing. Revisions of pedagogy and curriculum documents are undoubtedly the challenge of the age in which we live.

1.7 Learning, Creating and Ethical Imagination

While not trying to predict any future directions it does seem that different cultures adopt similar time-honoured strategies which are worthy of reiterating as starting points for new conversations related to the world of now. In European states the questioning technique attributed to Socrates in Hellenic times survives as does the role of the guru or 'master' associated within Asian cultures. Both are methods for developing the abilities of the individual learner to acquire wisdom and achieve independence and a good life. Likewise in the arts the birth of the apprenticeship system in Renaissance times enabled the novice to observe and learn at the 'foot' of the master. The Renaissance artists including Michelangelo, Leonardo da Vince, Albrecht Dürer, Botticelli and later Rembrandt all relied on their apprentices to complete commissions which in turn passed on their skills and techniques. The master-pupil relationship remains at the core of learning and each of these systems retain their integrity as tools for learning. The expert master, or guru facilitates the transmission of knowledge and teaches the novice. Hence, the teacher as the pedagogue takes on the role as guide and mentor and it can be expected that a relationship of trust between the student or novice and expert is one of the preconditions for successful learning outcomes. Individualising the approach taken in the learning space is viewed as the optimum strategy for bridging the gap between learner's abilities and curriculum content. The implication is that instruction is best served through dialogue, conversation and active participation in the process.

Nowadays, formal education exists in some form in most of the world's nations. Authoritarian systems are more likely to retain a preference for subject centred didactics. Where authority is less centralised and less regulated or based on a distributed system there is more likelihood of discovery regarding content, teaching style and expectations. Regardless of policy each student will make their own journey and develop understandings of the curriculum that best 'fit' with their personal skills, abilities and interests. Hence, learning outcomes will differ for each learner and herein lies the opportunity for creative and imaginative responses to flourish—provided the pedagogical environment is flexible and enabling. Whatever the personal circumstances the child may inherit there is always the possibility of a distinguished future where opportunities are laid bare and open for engagement. An eye for talent and how best to steer that potential is foundational for educational leadership across the spectrum of cognitive and emotional abilities. Early identification of excellence within a specific learning domain can be lifechanging. Alan Turing, for instance, was one of a group of gifted mathematicians who studied at the University of Cambridge and who was subsequently chosen to work on the code deciphering that we regard as the beginnings of computer science.

Within the current world of AI there is need of similar imaginative, curious and determined intellect to steer an ethical and sustainable path forward. Specialists, however, will need to be identified in all our social, commercial and economic fields of endeavour. AI has gained a ubiquitous status across all fields of activity with the potential for discordant decision making and chaotic outcomes unless experts work together. Interoperability between society's divisions assumes the need to find ways to collaborate and build connections across boundaries. For the benefit of society there is also the hope that the nature of such cooperation and enterprise has an ethical and globally responsible set of principles for action. Such skills are best learnt during the development phases of young people's education.

Listening with purpose is often key to locating the right triggers for learning and guiding young people's thinking for success in adult life. Expert teachers are recognised for having that talent. Like the sports 'spotters' at junior sporting events the keen eye can identify talent beyond the technical ability and that talent is invariably linked with imaginative and creative thinking. Kieran Egan's theory of education offers valuable guidance for practitioners caught up in the current systems. Acknowledging the ideas of Dewey (2016) on education and Russian psychologist Vygotsky's (1994) theory of language development Kieran Egan's theory of an educated mind notes three discrete education goals for schooling (1997).

1. A socialisation goal to give students the same understandings and habits to help them succeed in society (see Montaigne).
2. An academic goal to give students an understanding of truth, allowing them to change society (see Plato).
3. A psychological goal to give students the chance to develop their own understandings and skills through a process of self-discovery, allowing them to create themselves as individuals (see Rousseau).

The cognitive tools associated with these domains he identifies as: somatic, mythic, romantic, philosophic and ironic (see Egan, 1997). That is, tools the child develops in their learning process towards adulthood. In brief, the somatic tool relates to how we understand the world from the perspective of our bodies. It's a 'pre-linguistic take' on the world. Next comes oral language which helps us recognise binary opposites. "we predominantly use the logic of metaphor, making sense of things in terms of other things which is the source of our imaginative lives and creativity". The third tool acquired is literacy which links us to the world around us, to heroes and what he terms romantic associations with the world. The fourth tool links us with constructs of society and moral systems. "The mind seeks the truth in general schemes". The last tool to acquire is the 'ironic' or that which relates to "a better sense of where we end and the world begins" Like Piaget's developmental stages each tool involves a step in cognitive development allowing an element of imaginative thinking and growth in individual knowing which in turn allows for the creative mind to develop and embed the cultural norms of society. Weible's (2015) detailed analysis of Dewey's writings and the more recent writings of Egan reminds us of the visionary thinking of these theorists in terms of their valuing of the 'cultural store'. There is agreement that imagination is essential for ethics (p. 90). This is an important reminder for the current AI challenges. While much more could be interpreted from their works the essential ideas are stated here for a reminder of what educational theorists know to be important in curriculum development within education settings.

1.8 Next Steps—The Next Generation Points the Direction

In this opening discussion great thinkers and enduring legacies are valued as starting points for developing a theory of education for the complex world of AI and its place within the cultural 'store' of knowledge. While it is not the purpose of this chapter to provide detailed analysis of the works of any of the great thinkers noted the pointers serve as reminders of the power of great minds to discover new knowledge and make a difference for the whole of society. We still refer to John Dewey's (1916) writings today after more than a century. There must be a reason for this. His legacy is enduring because of the relevance of his ideas—pragmatism, experience and imaginative action-based education. If these have been basic tenets for education for over a century, then surely, they can rollover into the key elements of an AI pedagogy. This is a question to come back to time and again as authorities in education and wider society find paths to navigate ways forward with their digital copilots alongside.

To end this chapter, some glimpses are offered into the imaginative worlds of young people and how their entrepreneurial skills are inspirational guides for what is possible within the regulatory frameworks of existing social systems. They show courage and fascinating links between imagination, and creative innovation which have some uncannily similar connections to past times.

> *Fashion, the twenty-first century flâneur*: First identified in nineteenth-century Paris by Baudelaire and then developed as a concept by Benjamin in the twentieth century the flâneur is associated with strolling through urban spaces, capturing moments connected with modern city life (see Cutcher & Irwin, 2018). Being part of but separate from the crowds, shops and arcades. Stylish, fashionable and urban. Kishik's (2015) *Manhattan Project* associates these ideas with the streets of New York. More recently the association of participant and observer has captured renewed attention in fashion, assemblages in AI and youth culture. The aesthetics of the cities are rich spaces for artistic expression and multi-media installations which youth cultures embrace. Clothing fashion, personal appearance including body tattoos are the makeup of the contemporary 'flâneur'. Social media is the 'fashion store' for reference cues and deciding where and how to 'fit' as both street observer and participant. More extreme is the culture of make believe linking the flâneur with AI in a video streamed installation.
>
> In Flâneur, the walker is no longer fully human: AI-generated, fragmented, automated, and dissolved into a stream of data. Visitors enter a virtual gallery where visuals and soundscapes shift in response to their movements. Visitors move, influence the appearance of the space and the soundscape, watching the figure dissolve into clouds of particles.[2]

[2] See online at Flaneur - Interactive Installation (https://www.infratonal.com/flaneur_interactive_ai_installation.html).

Medieval games: Live action replay is a popular pedagogical tool that taps into our fantasy images. Youth cultures (and in fact all generations) globally appear to have a fascination with medieval games and related battles. Fair gatherings and re-enactment activities have heavily invested followings. Often located in city parks and recreation grounds with space to move there is an element of the surreal for the observing public. Humans in full character dress bound for such events can appear to be of another world. In fact the followers of this 'sport' invest heavily. Devotees can build their collections of appropriate garments and adornments from online and local retail outlets. Replica buttons, fasteners, slippers, amulets, jewellery, etc. all match the chosen character of the past. Social media offers the perfect opportunity for streaming live action and displays of collections. These games or tournaments from medieval times appear to reenact power relations and showcase social hierarchies. As such they serve as sources of cultural identity within real time and space reality. Added to the creative elements within this process AI can augment the imaginative dimension of the dramas and enrich their event sequences.

Both examples rely on an aesthetic or practice belonging to past lives. Their reinvention now adds to the cultural 'store' of contemporary times. They act as exemplars of how the cultural norms and ethics are passed on to the next generations and with the added dimension of digital tools old ways can be modified and enriched. Relevance is maintained and new ideas can be explored. The critical element is capturing the imagination of the participant and making connections with communities of like-minded individuals who can in turn provide the reference group for individuals to develop their identity and societal conscience. Self-expression within safe spaces has the dual role of conforming to a shared set of values and allows new ideas to be take shape, be both tested and expressed.

1.9 Conclusion

Optimism within youth cultures should encourage collaborative decision making in curriculum decisions and curriculum making. Poised on the edge of the cliff of societal change both from AI and geopolitical conflict decision makers could do well to review the wisdom of great minds both past and present. More importantly, the skills of young people and their emersion in digital media can be the critical resource for moving towards a new ontological basis of knowing. The key point here is that their lived experience is both culturally connected in time and place and has evolved with the rollout of the technologies. How to maintain ethical and responsible decision making during the developmental process of hopefully becoming a 'good person' is the critical question. As a guiding principle it is worth remembering that history shows that epochal change times tend to have a limited use by time. Well-entrenched societal values provide the foundation upon which we all rely for staying connected in sustainable ways.

References

Ahn, J., Kim, J., & Sung, Y. (2024). The role of perceived freewill in crises of human-AI interaction: The mediating role of ethical responsibility of AI. *International Journal of Advertising, 43*(5), 847–873.

Ball, S. J. (1990). *Foucault and education.* Routledge.

Barthes, R. (2000). *A Roland Barthes reader* (S. Sontag, Ed.). Vintage.

Bauman, Z. (2024). *Theory and society. selected writings* (Vol. 3). Polity Press.

Bhabha, H. (1994). *The Location of culture.* Routledge.

Brunnhuber, S. (2024). *The third culture: The impact of ai on knowledge, society and consciousness in the 21st century.* Springer International Publishing.

Cutcher, A., & Irwin, R. (2018). (Eds). *The flâneur and education research a metaphor for knowing, being ethical and new data collection.* Springer Nature. Palgrave. https://doi.org/10.1007/978-3-319-72838-4

Dewey, J. (1916). *Democracy and education.* Macmillan.

Egan, K. (1997/1998 June). The educated mind: How cognitive tools shape our understanding. *Canadian Journal of Education/Revue canadienne de l education.* https://doi.org/10.2307/1585992

Feher, K. (2025). *Generative AI, media, and society.* Routledge.

Floyd, J., et al. (2023). Revisiting the Turing test: Humans, machines, and phraseology. In J. Katz (Ed.), *Nudging choices through media* (pp. 75–113). Palgrave Macmillan.

Greenblatt, S. (1989). Towards a poetics of culture. In H. Veeser (Ed.), *The new historicism* (1st ed.). Routledge.

Hartley, L. P. (1953). *The go-between.* Penguin Books.

hooks, b. (2009). *Belonging a culture of place.* Routledge.

Kishik, D. (2015). *The Manhattan project.* Stanford University Press.

Krauss, P. (2024). *Artificial intelligence and brain research: Neural networks, deep learning and the future of cognition.* Springer Berlin.

Lefebvre, H. (1991). *The Production of Space.* Blackwell.

Massey, D. (2005). *For space.* Sage.

Massey, D. (2007). *World city.* Polity.

Miller, P. (1998). The classical roots of poststructuralism: Lacan, Derrida, and Foucault. *International Journal of the Classical Tradition, 5*(2), 204–225.

Montaigne, M. (2003). *The complete works. everyman's Library* (D. Frame, Trans.). Stanford University Press.

Peeters, M., van Diggelen, J., van den Bosch, K., Bronkhorst, A., Neerincx, M. M., Schraagen, J., & Raaijmakers, S. (2021). Hybrid collective intelligence in a human–AI society. *AI & Society, 36*, 217–238.

Russell, B. (1932). *Education and the social order.* Routledge.

Peters, M. (2011). Critical historiographies in educational theory: Retemporalizing experience 'after' the spatial turn. *Geopolitics, History, and International Relations, 3*(2), 48–66.

Said, E. (1979). *Orientalism.* Vintage.

Soja, E. (1996). *Thirdspace.* Blackwell.

Soja, E. (2010). Cities and states in geohistory. *Theory and Society, 39*(3/4), 361–376.

Sotirakopoulos, N. (2021). *Identity politics and tribalism: The new culture wars.* Imprint Academic.

The World Bank. (2026). See https://www.worldbank.org/

Tully, K. A., & Scott, J. T. (2020) Rousseau's observations on inequality and the causes of moral corruption. *Political Research Quarterly, 73*(1), 184–195.

Van Den Abbeele, G. (1991). *Travel as metaphor: From Montaigne to Rousseau.* University of Minnesota Press.

Virilio, P. (2000). *Polar inertia.* Sage.

Vygotsky, L. (1994). *Thought and language.* The MIT Press.

Weible, D. (2015). Getting it right from the beginning: Imagination and education in John Dewey and Kieran Egan. *Education and Culture, 31*(2), 81–112.
Whitehead, A. N. (1938). *Modes of thought*. The Free Press.
Wiley, R. (2024). Artificial intelligence and psyche: The trickster and our moral compass. *Psychological Perspectives, 67*(1–2), 55–65.
Žižek, S. (1997). *The plague of fantasies*. Verso.

Margaret E. Robertson is Emeritus Professor of Education, La Trobe University, Melbourne, Australia. Research interests include cultural geography, youth studies and innovative pedagogy.

Chapter 2
Culture Versus Nature: AI Reinventing Place

Margaret E. Robertson

Abstract An important paradox of our times is the disconnect of populations from nature. Globally the world's people have been progressively migrating to large urban concentrations both as foreign citizens and/or relocating from rural hinterlands. Built urban lifestyles create cultures that distance people from their nature-based survival needs. Young people the world over show their concern for climate change and an apparent longing to reengage with leisure-based nature pursuits. Their lifestyles, however, are often contributors to global survival problems. Could technology, and specifically AI, provide a pathway back to lower density living and harmony with nature? The major challenge is to discover the cultural foundations for what appears to be a new intellectual enlightenment.

Keywords Urban · Ethnic diversity · New enlightenment · Cultural heritage

2.1 Introduction

Close to 90 percent of the population in high income countries is living in urban locations[1]. As centres of commerce, culture and governance, towns and cities the world over are the acknowledged places for decision making and exchanges of ideas. Machines, including AI have minimised traditional jobs in rural locations and new jobs are increasingly linked with business, commerce, technology and urban-based activities. Although this is a mobility pattern that has been taking place since the beginnings of Industrialisation more recent advances in food production have minimised labour needs to the point where remote farm management using AI and Wi-Fi provides tools that replace manual labour. It is possible to run and

[1] For data see Urban population (% of total population) | Data (https://data.worldbank.org/indicator/SP.URB.TOTL.IN.ZS)

M. E. Robertson (✉)
La Trobe University, Melbourne, Australia
e-mail: m.robertson@latrobe.edu.au

M. E. Robertson (ed.), *Youth, Identity, AI and Moral Purpose*, Young People and Learning Processes in School and Everyday Life 9,
https://doi.org/10.1007/978-3-032-32479-5_2

operate farms from remote locations most likely located in towns and cities. Added to these centripetal rural-urban migration movements the population profile of large cities located in wealthy nations continues to diversify with foreign migrants either displaced from their homelands or in search of better lives. This urban and ethnically diverse reshaping of high-income nations contrasts markedly with poor nations including the central African region where drought, poverty and famine are enduring enemies of improved lifestyles and strong motivation for refugee relief in high income nations. Rural to urban movements of people and foreign arrivals create changes in society that continue to reshape local cultures and shared beliefs. The result is that the culture and the episteme dynamic is a complex and evolving web of diversity, exchanges, negotiation and consensus building. One major outcome is the increasing disconnect between large urban populations and their surrounding landscapes. In highly urbanised contexts speculative comment might be that nature appears to be an object for leisure and exploration rather than lived space for survival. This chapter seeks to review current trends in cultural migration and survival including a synopsis of the status quo as well as a look back at the meanings of culture, how it evolves and potential pathways towards harmony and ultimately the survival mortar for the Anthropocene within an AI dominated world.

2.2 Changing Societal Profile—A Study of Now

Using Australia as an example the trends are informative of the population dynamic and cultural changes that follow from foreign migration. A major change has been the ethnic diversity of new arrivals. As a guide the Australian Bureau of Statistics (ABS) define ethnicity as a demographic with:

1. a long-shared history, the memory of which is kept alive
2. a cultural tradition, including family and social customs, sometimes religiously based
3. a common geographic origin
4. a common language (but not necessarily limited to that group)
5. a common literature (written or oral)
6. a common religion
7. being a minority (often with a sense of being oppressed)
8. being racially conspicuous.[2]

Australia's population has grown steadily since its late seventeenth-century colonial roots with strong connections between urban and rural communities. Its vast territorial lands have been shaped by a federal and state government system not dissimilar to the United States. For the first two hundred years of colonial and post-colonial rule the population growth was dominated by British migration and post-World War II

[2] See Cultural diversity of Australia | Australian Bureau of Statistics (https://www.abs.gov.au/articles/cultural-diversity-australia)

relocation of families mainly of European origin, most notably Italy. Italian migrants and lesser numbers of displaced Europeans were to boost the skill base of the population on large infrastructure projects notably hydroelectric schemes. Their skills added to the existing knowledge base and perhaps more importantly enriched the local communities where they settled. Notwithstanding the terrible injustices experienced by the indigenous population throughout this period the new arrivals brought new ways of thinking to the nation. Languages other than English, cultures of refined cuisine and lifestyle diversity helped change the local values and gradually assimilate over time to become part of the fabric of Australian culture.

More recent foreign migration has resulted in greater diversity. A shift away from traditional English-speaking nations and their strong European connections Census figures[3] indicate that while England remains the leading country of origin, the largest increase in numbers are arrivals from India followed by China, New Zealand and the Philippines. The Vietnam war brought increased numbers of permanent arrivals from China, Vietnam and Cambodia. These twenty-first-century movements have sharply changed the demographics of some urban census districts: "In 2021, the SA3 [statistical area] with the highest number of countries of birth was Sydney Inner City. Almost half (47.9%) of the population of 218,000 was born overseas and came from 183 different countries"[4]. Within the Sydney metropolitan area: "The area with the highest proportion of overseas-born population in Australia was Auburn in western Sydney. In 2021, 61.7% of the population was born overseas, this was an increase from 60.0% in 2016". Large numbers of these arrivals are Arabic speaking and of Muslim faith both of which are significant cultural shifts from earlier migration waves. To summarise, the 2021 data show that 27.6% of the nation's population was born overseas and highlight the way in which ethnic diversity is altering the nation's identity. The other significant issue to note is that foreign migration mostly gravitates to the major metropolitan areas where there is less likelihood of contact with rural locations. Rural locations offer fewer employment opportunities and are less attractive for newcomers. This suggests a new rift or divide between the large cities and their hinterlands. Newcomers are permanent urban dwellers. In essence the figures suggest less assimilation and more cellular cultural communities which should enrich the national narrative but can harden uncompromising attitudes and fracture cultural norms.

Nevertheless, navigating such culturally divergent landscapes can be rewarding and history will record the events and outcomes. However, the changes in population backgrounds pose significant challenges for government authorities and educators whose role it is to convey the knowledge and shared values, existing and emergent, of the Australian nation. Core values are based on democratic principles of inclusion, social justice and acceptance of diversity and as the population becomes more diverse in background the governance becomes increasingly messy. Adjusting policy takes

[3] See Cultural diversity of Australia | Australian Bureau of Statistics (https://www.abs.gov.au/articles/cultural-diversity-australia)

[4] See Cultural diversity of Australia | Australian Bureau of Statistics (https://www.abs.gov.au/articles/cultural-diversity-australia)

time. Capacity building relies on creative and collaborative decision making within local communities including schools, health and welfare institutions. It's a stepped process. To illustrate, one such example is happening within the USA with a gathering of intelligent young people for policy makers to hear their opinions and suggestions from a lived perspective. Exploring *21st Century Democracy in Practice* the report of this activity noted the breadth of the challenge in the Bulletin of the American Academy of Arts and Sciences:

> Nearly 250 years ago, the nation's founders came together to build a functioning democracy. But today, the U.S. population has grown exponentially to nearly 330 million people, distributed over an area nearly nine times larger than the thirteen original colonies. The nation is more diverse and larger than ever. Given these immense changes, how can we make a system that was created almost 250 years ago still work? The Commission on the Practice of Democratic Citizenship was created to answer this question. (2020, p. 9)

2.3 Urban Identities Reconnecting with 'Other' and Universal Values

The consequence of urban expansion is that the experience base of most twenty-first-century citizens now is exclusively urban-based living, especially those who belong to the AI generation. It is a sobering thought to consider the impact of this reality on the knowledge and experience base of urban citizens. However, perhaps herein lies a contemporary irony that appears to refute or mollify the trends noted. There are, perhaps, small signs of a post-pandemic centrifugal pull away from the large cities. The cost of real estate and housing in the big cities has escalated to the tipping point of being unaffordable for younger people and there is now an alternative made possible with AI and the internet. The pragmatics of this reality may yet bring about a much-needed renaissance with nature connected relationships. Like the concept of society itself, nature has many meanings (Macnaghton & Urry, 1998) and cultural linkages.

Theoretically AI and internet access are a source of personal freedom and can be the lifestyle stimulus for choosing to live away from large urban concentrations. The knowledge workplace tools provide access to information anywhere and place freeing the worker from their collective workplace. Not surprisingly, the other topical element to consider is that working from home since the pandemic has gained appeal with many workers choosing this option over commuting often long distances from suburban residences to inner city workplaces. Precipitated by the pandemic the disruptive pressure has enabled workers to gain leverage for their employment and negotiate flexible working hours and places of working.

In brief, the Anthropocene can be viewed as the period when human freewill and knowledge-based learning became less dependent on its 'real estate' base. Its full effect now is recognised in the significant changes to the earth's climate and ecosystems (see Castree, 2021). We could argue that human enterprise has gone through a process of altering earthly surroundings and so freeing populations from their subsistence base to enter a world reshaped for their personal wealth generating purposes. Getting to this stage in the human and planetary relationship has changed who we think we are as individuals and what we view as society. The question is how our collective thinking can shape what is to come without losing connection with the bottom-line reality of our biological survival. There is a serious concern that AI generations may lose connection with their planetary reality. Such a catastrophic prognosis should be a wakeup call for education authorities to review and update both the content and strategies used in their pedagogical practices.

A brief look back at a nation's heritage and cultural development provides a reminder of how its values and culture have evolved. They provide clues to the institutional fabric that underpins the shared beliefs of Western nations and can provide the intellectual hooks for carving out what might be called the 'new enlightenment' for complex and culturally diverse contexts. The next section seeks to explore some of the puzzles of our times by briefly reviewing what we know from the past and how that knowledge can help us to better understand where we are now and possibly help predict safe futures including some fundamental values which we must preserve and ensure the next generation understands.

2.4 Change and Culture Survival

Törnberg and Uitermark (2024) provide a useful contribution to this complex field of change. "While industrial modernity saw society as a machinery to be designed according to detailed blueprints, digital modernity views society as organic and alive, to be herded and nudged through digital infrastructures, AI, and algorithms" (p. i). As a starting point, this story has much earlier beginnings and if we are to understand the impact of contemporary societal changes it seems logical to question the fundamentals of what it is to be human including obvious human frailties. So, from the future back to cave sites as a beginning. Succinctly summarised Martin Puchner's (2023) *Culture a New World History* makes the obvious but important point related to human know-how. He states "know-how concerns tools, science and technology, the ability to manipulate the natural world. The story of know-why concerns the history of culture as a meaning-making activity. It is the domain of humanities" (p. iv). The Chauvet Cave located in south-east France might be one such starting point for identifying key elements of human modernity, and its separation from other species. Discovered in 1994 and named after one of the speleologists, Jean-Marie Chauvet, the site is UNESCO heritage listed and regarded as globally significant for its paleolithic links to human development. Hidden by landslides for thousands of years radiocarbon dates the cave drawings back more than 30,000 years. There is also evidence of a second human group entering the cave. As Puchner notes this group came from a different cultural view and perhaps mystified by their discovery made their own contribution to the cave art, like a palimpsest, before a second landslide 'sealed' the cave until its recent discovery. Puchner notes how the cave's wall images suggest some form of religious meaning or art form, with hints of myths and legends other than their hunter and gatherer subsistence. Meaning making about the world of survival outside demanded some form of spiritual support. Archaeologists exploring the famously named skull chamber (see Montelle, 2022) propose there is evidence of spatial arrangement, possibly a theatre. The other instructive element of these discoveries relates to cultural continuity. As Puchner notes the second group of humans who entered the cave came from "a different culture, with different myths, stories, rituals, symbols, and ways of understanding the world" (2023, p. iv). They as "latecomers were probably as mystified by the elaborate paintings made by their distant predecessors as we are" (p. iv). The important point made is that culture requires continuity and if landslides occur in the metaphorical sense this continuity is lost.

The Chauvet Cave story is a tangible reminder of time capturing artefacts of human history repeated in geographical locations scattered across the globe. However, there is another side to this story which relates to long held oral cultures. Illustrative are the many indigenous communities who claim to be original inhabitants of the land in which they have lived and survived. The Australian Aboriginals, for example, are regarded as perhaps the oldest continuously hunter and gathering humans to have survived and retained their cultural ties, practices and rituals. Cave paintings and artworks link the present to the past. Added to these, it is the telling of the culture and re-enactment of the rituals which provide the glue that guarantees the survival of their cultures in the present times. Australia is a vast country and continent. Aboriginal settlement across the lands embraced a nomadic lifestyle and developed bonds with their territories that have largely provided for their families and withstood climatic events including floods, fire and winds for thousands of years. Nevertheless, for most Aboriginal Australians that harmony with nature was to change forever with the advent of British colonisation in the late eighteenth century. Confrontations resulted in killings and forced removal from their lands often to distant and inhospitable locations or resettlement in built communities. The loss of identity for Aboriginal people across the continent has been palpable. Like the Chauvet Cave story this was the landslide event that could have sealed away the existence of Aboriginal culture for ever. History, perhaps ironically, has provided some insurance against this fate. The vast lands of Australia and widely dispersed spread of Aboriginal cultures and languages have acted as a friend. Remarkably, and illustrating the point, more remote inland tribal groups located in the Gibson desert region of Western Australia somehow escaped connection with relatives and European settlement until the 1960s. Connection was made for the first time by Pintupi speaking relatives in 1984 of the Pintupi Nine 'lost tribe' who had escaped contact with European colonisers until this relatively recent time. Nevertheless, it is widely acknowledged that Aboriginal people share a story of wrongdoing by others and now more than two hundred years on there remains a significant chasm between the realities perceived by Aboriginal people, their descendants and their collective desire to secure their cultural heritage. Fortunately, and not to diminish the acts of the past there is an enduring legacy of Aboriginal culture through storytelling, language revival projects and festivals such as the annual Garma Festival held annually in Arnhem Land.

Natural disasters such as landslides, earthquakes, fire and floods as well as land invasions can cover up and often destroy historical human occupancy. Such was the case with Chauvet Cave and Aboriginal Australians. Likewise, volcanoes can destroy communities. Such was the case with Mount Vesuvius erupting and covering the city of Pompei in Roman times. There are many examples. More recently natural disasters have been occurring near coastal regions, including threats to Pacific Islands from global warming and sea rise. History has also shown that human rights and property can be taken forcibly by military backed dictatorships and ideologues with fanatical beliefs such as Adolf Hitler. Sovereign power gained by treachery or perhaps inherited monarchical dynasties, can be the almighty hegemony for a period. Mostly, however, dominant powers slip into oblivion as is well demonstrated by the history of lost Empires including the Greek and Roman Empires in European history; Khmer Buddhism and Ming dynasties in Asia; Incas of South America and lost kingdoms of Africa including the Sudanese Kingdom of Kush. In brief, both natural causes and human made events and actions can precipitate loss of property, belongings and purpose leaving those humans who survive to ask questions with difficult or unsatisfying answers. Arguably, oral cultures such as the Pintupi Aboriginals who retain their long-held stories of who they are and where they belong can offer role models for what makes a sustainable future. They carry their artworks and values in memory and through direct contact and rituals pass on their survival codes of behaviour. Likewise, the world's religions provide a referential code of living for all who practice their faith. Alternatively, the collective stories that signify the cultural views of a collective community can be passed on to the next generation via artefacts including art, literature and music as well as landscape aesthetics and governance. Reference sources provide directions for the path taken for everyday living and gain purpose for humanity from a sense of belonging to a community.

Regardless of change from any of the localised environmental, technological and societal sources of the times, the concept of cultural continuity is important and gathers new meaning in the context of global issues. Major events include technological dominance, displaced populations, wars, dissenting politics and the many ongoing and unexpected natural disasters. Current evidence suggests there are many such hostile signs of cultural disruption globally. Linked with the changing nature of human occupancy and survival the direct consequence of major events in time is that place meaning is a dynamic and needs to be understood for the current generation and those to follow. As history has shown this can be a fraught process unless smartly managed and core values are retained. Our next generation will inherit this set of problems unless wise decisions are taken and implemented sooner rather than as patches to broken systems and inevitable outcomes of events taking place now.

2.5 Culture Changes—From Ignorance to Knowledge

If we are to understand the current change period, the evolution of Western discourse to the present day has a lineage or continuity along with periods of darkness that needs to be reiterated. Greek scholars including Aristotle brought an intellectual reasoning to their processing of observations that relied on evidence rather than a divine or religious meaning. His surviving works indicate he was the voice of the ancient period of Enlightenment with messages that retain relevance. Makolkin (2015) writes:

> Aristotle wrote the following profound lines: One sign causes Belief, another Knowledge" (1984, vol. 2: 2287). This was his formula of the entire cultural production which included history, science, pseudoscience, divine mythology, politics and economics. There is not a single area of human activity, public or private that is not governed by this principal dichotomy, covering all basic concepts of Fact and Fiction. ... The idea of a belief-producing sign, elegantly covering the etiology of all human misconceptions, subtly contained the critique of the reductionist myth and false explanation of the mysterious Cosmos. (p. 73)

Aristotle records how those citizens with wealth and power invested in grand buildings which served as meeting points for social gathering and rituals to be enacted. No doubt these were spaces for knowledge transmission by educators who could pass on the regulatory epistemology (Roberts & Wood, 2007) or shared beliefs and understandings of the times. The essential distinction is made between personal beliefs and facts which can be observed. Importantly, his ethical writings[5] have survived long periods of isolation from the early and late Middle Ages through to the modern era possibly given their most prominent relaunch with the invention of the printing press by fifteenth-century German blacksmith Johannes Gutenberg. The production of books, articles and newspapers created incentives for learning and literacy which spread knowledge beyond the boundaries of nobles and wealthy. The social momentum had begun the shift towards the period of the Enlightenment with scholars gaining influence for valuing reason and empiricism and the spread of the scientific method. Rene Descartes (1596–1650) regarded as the 'father' of modern philosophy is recognised for advocating mathematical reasoning and an epistemology based on reason or secular argument rather than religious belief. Many great thinkers joined this movement including Isaac Newton (1642–1727) famed for his advocacy of the scientific method involving hypothesis testing, data gathering and analysis. As the momentum grew so did the expansion of platforms for scholars to share their ideas and develop their thinking that would lead to discoveries that have carved out much that is now taken for granted in the twenty-first century.

The Enlightenment is generally regarded as the contributor to modern economic growth and wealth. European Scholars including Descartes, Galileo, Locke and Francis Bacon triggered the quest for knowledge about the universe that would lead to the Industrial Revolution. In this sense the Enlightenment is recognised as the beginnings of scientific thinking and economic growth. Mokyr's (2005) analysis of

[5] See Aristotle, D P Chase translator (2019) Nicomachean Ethics. Great Britain: Lightning source inc.

the intellectual origins of economic development links this period to a time when that which was considered useful knowledge came under scrutiny. "Modern scholars seem agreed: Bacon was the most influential mind to regard knowledge as an entity that continuously expands and adds to itself" (p. 291). In essence:

> I have termed the Industrial Enlightenment a belief in the possibility and desirability of economic progress and growth through knowledge. The idea of improvement involved much more than economic growth or technological change; it included moral and social improvement, alleviating the suffering of the poor and the unfortunate, and more generally such matters as justice and freedom. (Mokyr, 2005, p. 291)

The Bacon method of inductive reasoning connects with empiricism and gathering of data for useful and informed knowledge. Along with his followers the intellectual strategies developed provided the groundwork for knowledge expansion and pragmatic applications that continued to bring about material and cultural changes in beliefs and customs. Mechanical efficiencies including the advent of the steam engine and rail networks were instrumental in changing landscapes and linking rural communities with factories and new distribution points. The momentum 'at home' extended to sea voyages of discovery such as those of Charles Darwin and Alexander Von Humboldt (see Rawding, 2017). Their research and discoveries were to generate charts and maps for maritime exploration to 'new' lands that would irrevocably alter their socio-cultural landscapes. After centuries of long distance trading between nations along land routes what was to come via sea routes resulted in an avalanche of European dominance and Empire building in distant locations. Land acquisitions suppressed local cultures and juxtaposed European values in the Americas, mineral rich African nations, Australasia and the Pacific. The eighteenth and nineteenth centuries became the golden period for exploitative trade in distant commodities for the European markets. While each of these events could be and are the subject for scholars and descendants of first nations peoples their mention in the context of how culture is shaped and may be changing today is of more general interest, notably how culture is made.

Applying the Bacon method required organisation and capabilities for practical and useful knowledge rather than for erudition and natural philosophy. Thus, the birth of scientific academies including Britain's Royal Society. Granted royal charter by King Charle's 11, the Society's online website today states:

> The Royal Society's motto 'Nullius in verba' was adopted in its First Charter in 1662. is taken to mean 'take nobody's word for it'. It is an expression of the determination of Fellows to withstand the domination of authority and to verify all statements by an appeal to facts determined by experiment.... Natural philosophers of this period were products of their society [and male]. They were drawn from the professional and aristocratic classes and were exclusively male. They were not professional scientists; but lawyers, merchants, physicians, aristocrats, and landowners, who were brought together by a common interest at the Royal Society's weekly meetings[6].

Within European nations The Society and others like it marked a shift in recognised authority from the church and religion to a more secular worldview with economic

---

[6] https://royalsociety.org/about-us/who-we-are/history

wealth that rewarded effort rather than inheritance. Inevitably, that early transition from religion to secular decision making generally rewarded those who already had wealth. The real long-term benefit was to improve living and working conditions that would benefit poor people and begin the journey towards access to education and opportunities to share the wealth. Aided by the growth in public education today the Society supports scientists of all genders and from the world over. It is the oldest continuously meeting 'scientific community' in existence (Howes, 2021) and noted for its organisational ability for social reform and the capacity to adapt its mission to the changing times. The survival of this organisation and its branches globally is testament to the continuing interest in knowledge creation and discovery, and in this century, activities have switched to big data and the affordances of smart technologies that support AI. In this digital information context, there remains a significant commitment to science education.

> Our digital world offers many exciting opportunities but also presents major challenges. Tomorrow's citizens will need to separate fact from fiction and be confident to choose trusted sources of information over others.[7]

The message is clearly stated:

> A good science education helps young people to acquire knowledge and skills, but also demonstrates how science is done. Science is based around evidence that can be trusted, tested and reproduced. In an age of misinformation and disinformation, young people need to be confident curators of knowledge and capable users of data.

And,

> Establishing scientific literacy is vital for our democracy since it helps people make informed choices about themselves and their society. ... It will also be vital in helping people to understand the often, hard choices they will face as the world tries to tackle global challenges.

In brief, the voices of the scientific community and immanent scholars seem clear. If we are to manage the tumultuous impact of AI within our communities, we need to prepare our young people to be wary and be prepared. Strong cultural values such as those noted in long surviving cultures will be tested and need to weather considerable storms from possibly unknown directions both natural and digital. Placing these cautionary words of wisdom within the context of home, community and ethnical diverse frames of reference creates a minefield of future challenges.

2.6 Soft Power Threats and Counter Threats

There seems little doubt in acknowledging the power of social media and all its various platforms. This century has witnessed a shift in 'news' accessibility from newsprint, radio and television to personal 'news' feeds to mobile devices including smart phones, watches and an increasing presence of e-vehicles. Each device enables

[7] See https://royalsociety.org/current-topics/education-skills

the owner or user to obtain firsthand knowledge of events and potentially participate in exchanges of information which bypass recognised or official channels. Separating fact from fiction has become more difficult and within our communities should cause us to question the meaning of society within the AI world. Power-knowledge relationships are assumed to be both formal and informal in structures. Hence, the imperative of preserving and vigorously supporting the collective voices of well-respected organisations as reference groups for navigating sustainable pathways forward. This reality raises the matter of social power.

Making the valuable distinction between 'power to' and 'power over' Castree's (2014) observation of social power raises relevant issues for the current debate. If you consider the authoritative power of governments or groups or individuals to control others, then this is 'power over'. There is a control element which may or may not force the outcome. In the social power space of young people such equivalence can be found in gang cultures and sadly they can have links with associated criminal 'warlords'. 'Power to' is more likely to be relational such as within families and indeed within education settings where teachers have the power to make a difference in the lives of their students. Along with 'power within' ethnically diverse neighbourhoods it seems possible to observe both kinds of social power. Noted as redefining social power and observing the shift from 'hard' to 'soft' Foucault's (1994) analysis of the power-knowledge change beyond the recognised institutional hegemonies of state and church identified the powers of the Enlightenment. Fast track these ideas to the present influence of digital power and the idea of a new Enlightenment there is evidence of both positive and negative influences over individuals and their communities. Castree's analysis highlights the complexities associated with social power.

> On the one hand, we can accept that social power may take several different forms whose nature and precise modes of operation are still subject to debate…. We don't look for the 'right' conception because ideas about social power, like all ideas, knowledge or information, are being judged according to the effects they seek to engender. (2014, p. 193)

There is much that could be interpreted from such observations and within the context of digital media and AI in particular there would appear to be infinite directions open for debate. The fact that the morphology of the AI world is unravelling in real time is likely to impact the course of scholarly debate for decades to come. Soft power within the knowledge-power construct seems to have limitless pathways and potential effects. Certainty is not a given and appears fragilely balanced between multiple power relations including socio-cultural, societal, ethnic, economic and geopolitical influences.

2.7 Making Sense of It All

The twenty-first century appears as a tumultuous shift away from the rhythms of past daily life. Digital technology and AI have changed the game for the Anthropocene. Like an untrained child or untamed animal there is this aura now that exists mainly outside any human control. If we pause to consider the full consequences, then there will be good reason to be fearful of what might or can happen in future decades. As this chapter has briefly outlined history shows how ruling hegemonies come and go or become buried in natural events. In pragmatic terms the domiciling habits of the majority of the world's people in large cities may be the most vulnerable reality of our times. Reliable food chains sustain urban communities. They rely on transportation links with often distantly located producers along with accessible distribution outlets for consumers. As high-density small land area sovereign states like Singapore know this reality can require imaginative and resourceful food production strategies. One alternative to nature providing food supplies is artificial sources or manufactured food supplements. However, like AI, all of these sources require energy which raises the question of sustainability long term and brings the argument full circle to our connections and relationship with nature spaces.

2.8 Messages From the Tech Giants

Rather than become too alarmed there is much to celebrate with these human achievements. In all aspects of life, notably health, AI is already making a positive difference for humans. Nevertheless, being awestruck by the capabilities of AI could well be to the detriment of humankind. The human mind created AI and the human mind needs to be trained to manage AI rather than the reverse. According to Bill Gates (2025), the windows software founder "Yet, while AI could eventually provide scalable, individualized learning, it can't replicate human connection, mentorship, empathy, and the ethos of a wise teacher". As if to remind us of our humanity Gates and other tech giants including Elon Musk have shown societal leadership in this current technological phase by investing in environmental sustainability projects aimed at responding to climate change and ultimately human survival. Political leadership appears to run in parallel with these tumultuous changes. Reality can appear to have dual authorities—one connected with the sovereignty of a nation and the other connected with the 'free' powers of technology.

2.9 Conclusion

The Enlightenment provided the intellectual, philosophical and social preconditions for the Industrial Revolution. Its emphasis on reason, empiricism, individualism, and secularism fostered a culture of innovation, entrepreneurship and scientific inquiry that was essential for the technological breakthroughs of the eighteenth and nineteenth centuries. The intertwined nature of these two historical periods demonstrates the profound impact of intellectual and social movements on technological progress. Where ethical considerations, social equity and the responsible use of technology are paramount, understanding this relationship is crucial for navigating the complexities of technological development in the twenty-first century. Just as the Enlightenment shaped the trajectory of the Industrial Revolution, our current philosophical and ethical frameworks will determine the future of technological innovation. The new Enlightenment is set within the global realities of predominantly urban lifestyles and economies along with hegemonic struggles between competing political powers that seem far from settled. Understandably, pedagogical responsibility within all education contexts will have difficulty determining curriculum directions. The power-knowledge dynamic is turbulent. Being proactive with tuition within the traditional disciplines will connect learners with their cultural heritage. However, the citizenship futures of young people will need practical guidance on decision making that will make them smart thinkers within a context of competing and often inalienable negative interests.

References

21st Century Democracy in Practice Source. (2020). *Bulletin of the American Academy of Arts and Sciences, 73*(3), 7–9.

Castree, N. (2014). *Making sense of nature.* Routledge.

Castree, N. (2021). Framing, deframing and reframing the Anthropocene. *Ambio, 50*, 1788–1792. https://doi.org/10.1007/s13280-020-01437-2

Foucault, M. (1994). *The order of things.* Vintage Books.

Gates, B. (2025, February 4). Bill Gates on AI and innovation. *University News.* https://www.harvardmagazine.com/2025/02/harvard-bill-gates-ai-and-innovation

Howes, A. (2021). *Arts and minds: How the royal society of arts changed a nation.* Princeton Scholarship Online.

Macnaghton, P., & Urry, J. (1998). *Contested natures.* Safe Publications.

Makolkin, A. (2015). TDR. Aristotle's views on religion and his idea of secularism. *Electronic Journal for Philosophy, 22*(2), 71–79.

Mokyr, J. (2005). The intellectual origins of modern economic growth. *The Journal of Economic History, 65*(2), 286–351.

Montelle, Y. (2022). *Tdr/drama Review, 66*(2), 10–26.

Puchner, M. (2023). *Culture a new world history.* Ithaka Press.

Rawding, C. (2017). 'Nature' and the legacy of Alexander von Humboldt. *Geography, 102*(2), 95–98.

Roberts, R. C., & Wood, W. J. (2007). *Intellectual virtues.* Oxford University Press.

Törnberg, P., & Uitermark, J. (2024). *Seeing like a platform: an inquiry into the condition of digital modernity*. Taylor & Francis Group.

Margaret E. Robertson is Emeritus Professor of Education, La Trobe University, Melbourne, Australia. Research interests include cultural geography, youth studies and innovative pedagogy.

Chapter 3
Generational Change Versus Inertia: The Dynamic Interplay of Ideas, Thinking and Inventions

Margaret E. Robertson

Abstract Generations are custodians of past values and customs. Nevertheless, the idea that history encourages inertia is contested. Societal advances rely on questioning insight, and young people are the carriers of new ideas into the future. In classrooms and places of learning globally unless the pedagogical approaches are under constant review, there is a risk of falling behind the technological advances of the time. AI is a global game changer. Young people are adept learners of technology and can provide the solutions to problems faced by their adult mentors—provided they have the intellectual space to contribute and be valued for their efforts.

Keywords Friendships · Fandom · Archetypes · Ideas · New thinking · Place and space

3.1 In the Beginning

The lessons learnt at school ought to provide the catalyst for developing lifelong intellectual and social skills. Friendships formed can spark collaborative futures including the confidence to take risks and branch forth with innovative and imaginative projects. Enough said about the visions of Mark Zuckerberg, founder of Facebook who along with the Microsoft empire of Bill Gates and co this chapter tries to explore the minds of young people through other edgy examples of their creative successes. Although the powers of educators can augment talents of individuals within their care, personal achievements can arise from secret skills and strengths developed in parallel with formal education. The challenge for pedagogues has to be observing and listening to learners so that wisdom infuses the activities of their students and ensures their formal and informal activities remain within the bounds of social morality and legality.

M. E. Robertson (✉)
La Trobe University, Melbourne, Australia
e-mail: m.robertson@latrobe.edu.au

M. E. Robertson (ed.), *Youth, Identity, AI and Moral Purpose*, Young People and Learning Processes in School and Everyday Life 9,
https://doi.org/10.1007/978-3-032-32479-5_3

A New York bestseller sits on my bookcase and provided you enjoy being led into weird spaces the book is a gripping read. Its images and text reveal the world of teenage fandom, popularity and multi-media success. Alexander Hirsch is the author and screenwriter of The *Book of Bill* (2024) and its earlier equally successful television series *Gravity Falls*. Born in 1985 in California of Jewish parentage, Hirsch and his twin sister spent many of their holidays in the countryside log cabin of their great aunt Lolo. These times are thought to have provided the inspiration for the characters he invented. Seymore's (2024) review provides a summary:

> "Gravity Falls" … follows twins Dipper and Mabel Pines, who are sent to the mysterious town of Gravity Falls, Oregon, to stay with their Great-Uncle "Grunkle" Stan (Alex Hirsch) at his tourist trap known as the Mystery Shack. While there, Dipper finds a journal proving the town's infamous legends might be real after all. … During the show's first season, Dipper and Mabel try to identify the author of the cryptic journal while learning more about the town's bizarre history. Along the way, they fight mythical creatures such as evil gnomes, ghosts, zombie-like creatures called "The Undead," cursed wax figures and even a unicorn. …"Gravity Falls" was a passion project for Hirsch, who also voiced other characters such as Soos and Bill Cipher. Hirsch felt inspired by his relationship with his twin sister and their summer vacations in Oregon. The show amassed a huge fan base due to its technical excellence, writing, creative themes and rich storyline. …After two short seasons, the series finale of "Gravity Falls," titled "Weirdmageddon 4: Somewhere in the Woods," aired on Disney Channel in 2016. The finale made for a conclusive end to the series, in which Mabel and Dipper save Gravity Falls, send Bill back to his Nightmare Realm and leave for the summer to return home to California. (p. 1)

Hirsch maintained that was the end of the show. However, fans hoped for a return. The show was hugely popular and the winner of multiple media awards. Importantly, it attracted a significant viewership and following from young people, including teenagers and young adults. Its humour, writing and animations underpin the size and passion of its fandom which is evident in the variety and popularity of related merchandise (see, e.g., Fig. 3.1).

That was not going to happen until the 2024 release of the *Book of Bill* which reignited the passion of fans. Seymore notes:

> "The Book of Bill" follows Bill's perspective about how he left the second dimension and terrorized Gravity Falls along with some puzzles and riddles for readers to crack, including missing pages from the infamous journal from the original series. In an interview with "Polygon," Hirsch talked about the legacy of "Gravity Falls," and what it was like returning to the series through the psyche of Bill Cypher. … After the book's release, there was some discussion surrounding it and its mature content. Unlike the original series, the book is marketed toward adults and contains dark and violent themes and profanity. "The Book of Bill" is currently No. 1 on the Amazon best-sellers list, and the book's release brought attention back to the show and reignited its popularity. Many fans are discussing the show's theories on TikTok, hoping Hirsch will bring back the show for another season. Whether Hirsch creates the highly anticipated third season of "Gravity Falls" or leaves the show as it is, "The Book of Bill" helped the series reach a new audience, and reignited the show's fandom after its finale eight years ago. (Seymore, 2024, pp. 1–2; See Figure 3.2)

Fig. 3.1 Gravity falls examples of merchandise: Cake topper and tote bag[1]

Bill Cipher is worth analysing. The fandom wiki provides an overview of Bill's origins[2] and complicated character.

> Over one trillion years prior to the events of the series, Bill Cipher was born. He originated from a two-dimensional universe known as Euclydia. When he was born, he had Velcro shoes that squeaked when he ran and was beloved by everyone so much that the mayor declared his birthday a national holiday. On his birthday, Bill gave out free knives to everyone as a gift. In spite of this, however, Bill despised living there, describing it as a dimension of "flat minds in a flat world with flat dreams." There was one other thing about him that was different; he had a mutation that gave him an abnormally large eye that allowed him to see the third dimension. With that, he had the ability to see a direction known as "up," something all others of his dimension could not see. Despite talk of a "third" dimension was illegal in his world, Bill was unable to think of anything else but being able to join it.

American psychologist Philip Zimbardo[3] characterises Bill Cipher as an 'ironic protagonist' who appears in the television series of Gravity Falls. "Bill is depicted as a powerful, malevolent, and enigmatic entity embodying chaos and manipulation. His design—a one-eyed, triangular figure reminiscent of the Eye of Providence—serves as a visual metaphor for omniscience and conspiracy, reinforcing his role as a sinister force lurking behind the scenes". Although a fictional character Zimbardo notes how Bill is complex. "His behaviors, motivations, and interactions reflect deep-seated archetypes and psychological themes that resonate with viewers and scholars alike. His portrayal taps into universal fears of chaos, the unknown, and the corrupting influence of power…". "His initial portrayal as a chaotic trickster evolves into a more focused pursuit of ultimate power, culminating in his attempt to reshape reality". In Zimbardo's analysis "Ultimately, Bill Cipher's character offers a compelling

[1] See Amazon.com.au/Gravity Falls merchandise.

[2] See http://gravityfalls.fandom.com/wiki/Bill_Cipher.

[3] See https://www.zimbardo.com/the-psychology-behind-bill-cipher-from-gravity-falls.

Fig. 3.2 The *Book of Bill* book cover

exploration of the shadow side of human nature, reminding us that understanding our darker impulses is essential for achieving psychological integration and societal harmony". The use of textual games and riddles grip the reader with twists and turns both up and down the moral ladder and make for compelling reading.

Taking a less focussed character view and in a series analysis of Gravity Falls, Piatti-Farnell (2014) seeks to uncover the hidden elements of the narrative and makes comparisons with Gothic intertextuality. Of the animations and text Piatti-Farnell writes: "This visual text provides an example of the reach of the Gothic within popular culture, where intersecting hideous creatures and interconnected narrative structures, although simple and "for children" on the surface, reveal the presence of a dense and intertextual Gothic network" (p. 859). In further commenting on the series relevance to viewers and perhaps in part helping explain the attraction of the program, Piatti-Farnell concludes: "Those interlacings are, of course, never disconnected from the wider cultural framework, and clearly occupy an important part in unravelling the insidious aspects of human nature, from the difficulties of finding "oneself" to the loneliness of the everyday" (p. 859).

The twins provide the anchor with reality and Bill evokes our imaginative and 'at risk' personality traits. Bill states in the *Book of Bill* "After all "Bill Cipher" is imaginary…but are you so sure of that?" Then "After all, you're mortal. One day, you'll be dust. But I'm an idea. And an idea can't be killed" (2024). Bill may be brutal and make hurtful comments but how powerful is that? Mythology, morality, imagination and suspense all rolled in to a gripping narrative kept alive and dynamic with social media feeds to the devotees of Bill. As the creator of these ever so popular real and imaginary characters Hirsch taps the interfaces between popular culture and tradition, religious beliefs and secular lifestyles, power and submission, simple versus intricate realities, and so the list of dualities expands. The formula is one for the times and worthy of considerable respect.

3.2 Then There Was AI

If there is to be a next series after the *Book of Bill* then Artificial Intelligence will be a winning addition and likely source of unleashing more of Bill's friends long lost in the missing journal pages. The dangers are likely to multiply if Bill Chipher is contacted and released in a third series. Bill claims: "Do you realise what I can do in here [your head] if I want. I can flip a switch that makes every neuron burn with pain beyond imagination. …I can delete memories randomly just for fun…. who are you anyway?" (Hirsch, 2024). In the *Book of Bill*, Mabel and Dipper Pines have the last say. Mabel makes it clear that it is time for Bill to move on. Dipper is more direct: "Bill if you're somehow reading this from whatever quantum afterlife you wormed your way into, listen up, …You tried to kill my sister. If I ever see you again outside of my nightmares, there is no force in the universe that will stop me from putting you in the ground. …I defeated zombies., out sleuthed Sherlock Holmes, and survived the start of puberty" (Hirsch, 2024). However, there is doubt that the twins or the dreaded Ciphers have any way of preventing their annexation by AI with reports of the scripts being used to train AI and embellish its data base. Acknowledging this dimension links media popularity with technology advances that are altering the human/computer interface. The generational tide of change may have to deal with more than repressed memories.

The development and increasing information base of AI has a history which is well documented in the published research of Ray Kurzweil. His most recent book *The Singularity is Nearer* (2024) outlines the machine intelligence journey. Starting with Alan Turing's research in the 1950s the question asked is can a computer machine think intelligently and match the thinking of humans. The Turing test is a legacy of his work. First called the *Imitation Game* the test involves a human evaluator who judges a text transcript of a conversation between a human and a machine. If the evaluator cannot clearly distinguish the difference the machine passes the test. Kurzweil includes this step in what he describes as the evolution of intelligence in stages. We are at a point in Kurzweil's view "with our technology already producing results that exceed what we can understand for some tasks" (p. 9). His prediction is that by the 2030s "we will directly merge biological human cognition with the speed and power of digital technology" (p. 8). The future of intelligence is an expanded mind, a'singularity of intelligence' whereby human brains are "no longer shackled to what genetics provide" (p. 11).

Transhumanism predicted as the outcome of a human and technological mergence or ontological change has attracted scrutiny and respect. In Oliver Krüger's critique (2021):

> According to the cosmologists Roger Penrose and Stephen Hawking, singularities (in the plural) denote the special conditions of space and time, such as those created by black holes. These are moments when matter or its precursors are concentrated at a single point and space and light become infinitely curved. The beginning of the universe – the Big Bang – was marked by a singularity. The common understanding of singularity as well as the popular reception of the term in literature and television series usually refer to the fantastic space and time effects of black holes, to which the Penrose-Hawking singularity theorem is applied. (p. 22)

The computer singularity of our times appears to be heading humanity along an irreversible path from which future generations will be both beneficiaries, guardians and critical umpires. Science fiction pre-empts many of the moves. Citing examples from Western cultural media Krüger (2021) concludes: "It seems obvious that the prophecy of singularity is strongly influenced by cultural and religious ideas. The assumption of laws of progress, as well as the steady acceleration of progress claiming universal validity for the entire history of humankind, can all be traced back to an Enlightenment striving for perfection". As opposed to an endless frontier of development, the view of an "absolute and impenetrable limit to this progress: the singularity as the last frontier" (p. 22). Some will argue this as a doomsday sell out. Others like Kurzweil are optimistic about the future. Life is becoming progressively better for all humans. While some will argue the contrary, the impact on health indicators, life expectancy, education, personal mobility and access to knowledge and its inventions are all on the plus side of global measures. Kurzweil is also optimistic about jobs concluding:

> The convergence technologies of the next two decades will create enormous prosperity and material abundance around the world. But those same forces will also unsettle the global economy, forcing society to adapt at an unprecedented pace. (p. 195)

Widely cited, Kurzweil is not without critics who are perhaps less enthusiastic about the future with technology. Berkowitz (2018) explores the argument based on Hannah Arendt's *The Human Condition* or what it means to be human. The loss of 'human plurality' to 'technological singularity' is the threat to human existence as we have known. For instance, "since humans are conditioned beings, the change from living as split beings—earthly in our subjection to fate and worldly in our human capacity to create our own humanly built world—to living uniformly in a fully artificial and alienated world threatens to transform humanity itself" (p. 354). Gomez-Marin (2024) seems to offer a somewhat more cynical and incisive view of Kurzweil's predictions. He maintains:

> The futurist imagines a technology capable of replacing each bit of the brain with a digital copy. Kurzweil does not entertain the role of uncertainty-ridden quantum processes, I suspect, because non-computational mechanisms would upend his paradigm and agenda. He also

> foretells that nanobots will soon dive into people's brains and copy all their memories and personalities, and store them "in the cloud". But would such a "complete computerized replica" still be you? As a functionalist, Kurzweil thinks that doing trumps being. So, if an AI chat bot acts exactly like you, then it is you. The copy matches the original and then supersedes it. I strongly disagree. Reality is not a simulacrum, nor is consciousness a computer function.

Gomez-Marin's review offers a refreshing fact checker within the otherwise somewhat scaremongering literature. He continues:

> Kurzweil's hyperbolic technological fetishism does not stop in 'the cloud'. Apparently, the soul is digital and the body is mechanical. And so, the litany of fiction science, as I call it, goes on: the hype is squared as AI meets nanoengineering, in a revolution that "will enable us to redesign and rebuild — molecule by molecule — our bodies and brains and the worlds with which we interact". He also argues that diligent people will achieve "longevity escape velocity", living for much longer than we do now, by 2030.

Finally in his review Gomez-Marin states:

> Kurzweil's motto is 'merge thy self' (with AI) — we can, we will and we must. Techno-utopian pseudo-religions of this kind can easily get out of hand, but he confidently reassures us that "nothing is being taken away. There will be a great deal added". If I may be forgiven, it seems to me that Kurzweil's understanding of humanity and nature is so bizarrely deficient that his augury is more of a curse than a blessing. His spiritual quest is devoid of spirit. The singularity betrays what is singularly human. (p. 498)

Key points emerge. First, the future with technology is unfolding at a rate few could have predicted. Second, human labour and interactions with their surroundings are evolving beyond Cartesian reasoning. Third, some philosophers and commentators will spin the existential crisis narrative. Finally, and hopefully, common sense retains some leverage and ability to caution irreparable damage. There are stoppable paths to technology gaining the upper hand. They include earth's available resources to supply the basic needs for data banks to exist. Training the AI programmes and handling of AI requests along with demand for computing technology in cars, smart phones, home and workplace machines has caused an explosion in the need for microchips which are the basis of modern computing (Wang, 2023). They require resourcing and this places long term pressure on the sustainability of the underlying hardware supply to meet economic and personal demand. Silicon conducting linked with microprocessor functions are synonymous with technology research centres now scattered around the globe. Some concerns relate to supply versus demand. For the moment we roll on within the technology bubble. Perhaps the next series of Gravity Falls will find good news within the lost journal pages with the Bill Cipher next generation.

3.3 Ideas, 'Space' and Consciousness

So far, this chapter has highlighted two significant facts about the world of now. First, imagination is important and helps capture the attention of audiences of all ages, and can sway politics, sustain religion and influence education. Second, digital technology is ubiquitous, invasive and considered to be a data coloniser of human life. Neither of these are chance actions. They need the right 'climate' to develop an idea into an outcome along with a marketing plan to 'sell' the product. In the current intellectual space, a key argument relates to the intersection between the humanities as traditionally accepted and promoted within cultures and the evolving and rapidly changing digital humanities (Gardiner & Musto, 2015). The latter is deservedly attracting attention. However, in pursuing this argument, it is also worth reminding ourselves that the digital resource relies on algorithms.

Hence, a point of difference from older research is needed here when considering psychological mindsets and how they operate within the digital space. In the 1960s Lynch (1960) and others (Gould & White, 1993; Holmén, 2020) developed the mental map construct. In this earlier research data were often collected from personal sketch maps or linguistic prompts that could be compared for analysis and understanding of the subjective relationship between place and people. The approach appeared to be reminiscent of the theory put forward by Humboldt in the nineteenth century that linked descriptions of nature-based place with social interactions. The dynamic he noticed is co-relational, a theory that appeared to get lost with the dominance of positivism and growth in strength of empirically based psychology. However, more recent conceptual framing of mental mapping offers an empirical base for exploring the connections between historical consciousness in place and mental perspectives. Nowadays, with digital tools such as Geographical Information Systems (GIS) the spatial patterns base on place memory and perceptions can display human behaviours (see Dammann & Kremer, 2024; de Alba, 2025). The software can also provide an intersection with AI 'thought' processing. Imagery can be accessed from cognitive responses and actual place-based data stored within the AI algorithms. This research has the capability of capturing the enhanced complexity of mental mapping because of population mobility, community diversity along with media access to people and places locally and digitally anywhere or place. A layering effect on mental mapping can be detected and more accurately represent the unique elements of an individual's consciousness. The ontological shift, therefore, is away from historically perceived certainty and the need for a pedagogy based on change reflecting local place and space-based reality.

Another dimension to this renewed interest appears to be making use of AI the tool in a collaboration or work in progress related to use of algorithms that link space and literary studies. Researchers in this field argue that adding data to the AI base is inadequate without consideration of the 'ontology used' (see Menon et al., 2024). The challenge for AI is captured by Krzanowski and Polak (2022) who compare machine learning with human learning as a race for the former to mirror the processing of the latter. To act and respond like humans has already developed significantly in the short time AI and now GenAI has entered the digital world. Nevertheless, there are some sureties associated with the operation of machine intelligence to make ethical and moral choices that are ontologically a match with the knowledge choices of humans. Krzanowski and Polak observe: "They [machine learning systems] partially replicate three aspects of the human cognition of "being in the world"; namely, concrete action, situatedness, and interactionism. Nevertheless, the outside world still does not matter to them as it matters to us, because their grounding in reality is inconsequential to them" (p. 1). They conclude: "We have begun developing AI under Descartes' shadow, with Descartes' views about reality being composed and presented to us in clear, logical, distinct ideas". But, "Knowledge is not a finite set of prescribed, deterministic, static rules, complex or otherwise". So, "AI must satisfy two criteria: empirical (i.e., technical) and conceptual (i.e., philosophical)". Hence, for machine learning to mimic human processing and reach that singularity zenith there remains, thankfully, an ontological gap, between cognitive sciences and AI technology. The question remains how close this next step is from reality.

An ability to think is a key element of the human consciousness. Assuming ideas are at the core of human progress and development of AI or machine-based learning (ML) then the argument can be made that humans can, or should be able to, control the future. A warning red light for society ought to be flagged as a means of slowing or controlling the shifts in what is ultimately power to control. Forces for change then are double-edged swords. They can promote societal good. As already noted, many institutions are beneficiaries. Advances to singularity, however, can be cause to wonder who or what is in control (see Winkler & Hoffjann, 2025). Bew's (2016) revised view of Realpolitik seems relevant as a reminder of the pragmatism needed for this journey. "Real *Realpolitik* emphasised the importance of thinking synthetically and holistically, based on an assessment of all the information before us" (p. 304). So, where does the power lie? In Calzati's (2020) analysis of the digital ecology we are reminded of the reality of multiple actors all competing for power. Superpowers China and the United States, along with Google, Amazon, and Facebook in the west and Alibaba in China (among others) are all players present within the data colonisation space. There is an 'ever temporary' realpolitik that "informs today's networked ecology" (p. 926). Bew advises: "What is important is the ability to identify where power, socioeconomic conditions, and ideas overlap and converge" (p. 304).

These are inevitably complex questions and made all the more difficult with the rapidity of change that surrounds us. Ideas can seem both a curse and a blessing.

3.4 Critical Thinking—Managing Ideas

Observe, listen and think are steps that are often associated with teaching and learning. Simple truths that are sound starting points for renewal and considering next steps. Citing the inevitable dangers of the persuasiveness of AI and at the same time its vulnerability to making mistakes UNESCO has a current call for action by all nations.

The campaign for digital literacy involves developing critical thinking beyond the realpolitik of change. The call is for "Minds Over AI – MIL in Digital Spaces," and "An invitation to reclaim agency in an AI-driven world.... To remember that while artificial intelligence can process information at superhuman speeds, human wisdom, judgment, and critical thinking remain irreplaceable. ...Because AI can make mistakes. But we don't have to believe them".[4]

Pedagogy has to respond to change and in the context of viable responses to incessant inroads on personal space from digital sources the reminders from UNESCO are worthy of being turned into classroom billboards. The ontological mismatch provides the pedagogical space for constructive dialogue between learner and instructor. Calzati (2020, p. 926) summarise, "it is crucial to promote digital tech literacies—at all levels of education—that combine skills and know-how in computer sciences, critical thinking and governance". This requires leading "new generations to reshape the human-data-environment ensemble as a whole and by remaining within— reimagining—the networked ecology". The focus needs to be on "Curricula that put interdisciplinary techno-cultural competences and values (competences evolve, values remain) at the center of attention". The aim is so that "well-informed children and other individuals will create a solid foundation for responsible and positive uses of AI systems and digital technologies more generally, and strengthen their personal skills on cognitive, social and cultural levels".

Capturing the imagination of learners and citizens is at the heart of successful education. In this chapter, a few of the challenges have been introduced along with what we know about human interests and consciousness. Understanding the basics of how the digital tools or machine-based learning operate can be our best first step for refining interests and knowledge to live sustainably with technology. Innovative approaches will help this process. One example that captures the interest is the digital agora (see Hognogi et al., 2023). Ironic, that the concept harks back to the ancient Greeks. It is also heartening to consider taking the concept and embedding its form within the technology as a way of marrying the digital with the reality of daily life. Within the digital agora or 'commons' questions can be posed and responses debated with inputs from multiple sources almost and often in real time. The rapid time digital metaphor is reminiscent of the library of old where hours of time could be spent searching manually through card-based catalogues and then requesting articles and or books for library staff to locate and deliver to front desks from library shelving 'stacks'. The digital space provides fast delivery of data and cross referencing and the opportunity for educators to nurture learner citizenry for our times.

---

[4] See https://www.unesco.org/en/articles/ai-can-make-mistakes-why-media-literacy-matters-more-ever.

3.5 The Digital Agora Is the Place to Meet

The digital agora is an example of exposing learners to the powers of the technology within a framework of guided learning. The wisdom of this approach is that younger learners are provided with strategies for navigating the world of uncertainty and rather than acting in a haphazard way are being encouraged to think as well as observe and listen. In the face of rapid change balancing risk versus the need for action is a challenge for governing institutions. History provides a seemingly infinite number of examples of the progress that was or could have been under different forms of governance (see Spiegelhalter, 2024). Probabilities based on numbers in Spiegelhalter's analysis might be reasonable guides to what may or could occur in the future although the wise conclusion is: "We need to be on our guard against both those who make overclaims and, at the other extreme, deliberately try to sow misunderstanding by unduly exaggerating uncertainty" (p. 428). The counterbalancing argument is the need to be mindful of what captures the imagination of young people. The Book of Bill highlights the powers of memory, place affiliation and connections.

References

Berkowitz, R. (2018). The singularity and the human condition. *Philosophy Today, 62*(2), 337–355.

Bew, J. (2016). *Realpolitik*. Oxford University Press.

Calzati, S. (2020). Decolonising "data colonialism" propositions for investigating the realpolitik of today's networked ecology. *Television & New Media, 22*(8), 914–929. https://doi.org/10.1177/1527476420957267

Dammann, F., & Kremer, D. (2024). Spatial concepts, approaches and methods for digital humanities—An introduction to the book. In F. Dammann & D. Kremer (Eds.), *Geographical research in the digital humanities: Spatial concepts, approaches and methods* (1st ed., pp. 7–12). transcript Verlag. http://www.jstor.org/stable/jj.13083323.3

de Alba, M. (2025). Collective memories of urban spaces through mental maps. *Current Opinion in Psychology, 66*, 102151. https://doi.org/10.1016/j.copsyc.2025.102151

Gardiner, E., & Musto, R. G. (2015). *The digital humanities*. Cambridge.

Gomez-Marin, A. (2024). The Stairway to Transhumanist Heaven. *Nature (London), 632*(8025), 497–498.

Gould, P., & White, R. (1993). *Mental maps*. Routledge.

Hirsch, A. (2024). *The book of Bill*. Disney Enterprises, Inc.

Hognogi, G. G., Meltzer, M., Alexandrescu, F., et al. (2023). The role of citizen science mobile apps in facilitating a contemporary digital agora. *Humanities and Social Sciences Communications, 10*, 863.

Holmén, J. (2020). Time and space in time and space: Mapping the conceptual history of mental maps and historical consciousness. *Contributions to the History of Concepts, 15*(2), 105–129. https://doi.org/10.3167/choc.2020.150206

Krüger, O. (2021). The Singularity is near!" visions of artificial intelligence in posthumanism and transhumanism. *International Journal of Interactive Multimedia and Artificial Intelligence, 7*(1), 16–23.

Krzanowski, R., & Polak, P. (2022). Ontology and AI paradigms. *Proceedings, 81*, 119. https://doi.org/10.3390/proceedings2022081119

Kurzweil, R. (2024). *The singularity is nearer*. Random House.

Lynch, K. (1960). *The image of the city*. MIT Press.
Menon, S., Todariya, S., & Agerwala, T. (Eds.). (2024). *AI, consciousness and the new humanism fundamental reflections on minds and machine*. Springer Nature.
Piatti-Farnell, L. (2014). What's hidden in gravity falls: Strange creatures and the gothic intertext. *M/C Journal, 17*(4). https://doi.org/10.5204/mcj.859
Seymore, C. (2024). 'The Book of Bill' reignites 'Gravity Falls' fandom. *University Wire*. https://www.proquest.com/wire-feeds/book-bill-reignites-gravity-falls-fandom/docview/3102363428/se-2
Wang, H. (2023). Analog chip paves the way for sustainable AI. *Nature, 620*(24), 731–732.
Winkler, P., & Hoffjann, O. (2025). On ideologies, micropolitics, and realpolitik—Toward a political perspective on integration in corporate communications. *Corporate Communications: An International Journal, 30*(7), 79–94. https://doi.org/10.1108/CCIJ-12-2024-0221

Margaret E. Robertson is Emeritus Professor of Education, La Trobe University, Melbourne, Australia. Research interests include cultural geography, youth studies and innovative pedagogy.

Chapter 4
Youth Opportunities, Affordances and Perils: Infinite Opportunities to Forge New Futures in the AI Era

Mary A. Burston

Abstract AI challenges our understanding of human intelligence, creativity and innovation. Despite pessimistic predictions that AI will make human intelligence redundant, autonomy to think is the critical foundation for building new ways of thinking and doing. We have the building blocks now but not the technological skills required of a technologically focused future. This chapter examines claims about AI's capacities and effects as well as issues that may have implications for young people and society including a review of national policies. Young people need to take, not wait, to develop entrepreneurial skills for their technological, environmental, civic and economic futures. Education needs to be action-and-forward focussed with intelligence, thinking and creativity needing to be re-imagined for young people to take agency in the digital age.

Keywords Autonomy · Artificial intelligence · AI technologies · AI curriculum · New imaginaries

4.1 Introduction

In anticipating that young people will be the beneficiaries and creators of the future, it is necessary to examine claims about AI's capacities and effects as well as issues that may have implications for young people and society. Following this discussion, specific attention is given to curriculum responses to AI. In the rapidly moving world of technological invention and multi-app development, there is insufficient time to evaluate the impacts of AI across all educational sectors. The field of research is open to hypothesis, speculation and unexamined theories of provability. Yet, governments, global policy institutes, national and international educators and curriculum designers put faith in techno conglomerates' projections about AI's capacities to reshape how

M. A. Burston (✉)
La Trobe University, Melbourne, Australia
e-mail: M.Burston@latrobe.edu.au

M. E. Robertson (ed.), *Youth, Identity, AI and Moral Purpose*, Young People and Learning Processes in School and Everyday Life 9,
https://doi.org/10.1007/978-3-032-32479-5_4

current and future populations will learn, think, adapt to, work and use AI across the life span.

The emergence of AI in contemporary society is deeply embedded in the human imaginary and in the mechanisation of human activities. Machines, automatons and non-human intelligence are common themes from ancient times to contemporary sci-fi and futuristic fiction, media and computer games (Hudson et al., 2023). The contemporary equivalent is the real or perceived threat that digital automatons will take over the world. The cyborgs are at the gate and there appears to be no stopping them (Bridle, 2018; Cave & Dihal, 2019). AI is designed to autonomously replicate human cognitive and intellectual processes through self-generated digital 'genes' that can function and self-replicate with minimal human input or oversight (Janssen et al., 2019; Sharov & Tønnessen, 2021; Williams et al., 2021).

Institutional rhetoric, technological hyperbole, media and social discourses promote the inevitability of AI-generated intelligence technologies whose genesis is attributed to Da Vinci, Boole, Turing and McCarthy's ideations of a machine capable of 'artificial intelligence' (Benko & Lányi, 2009). The rapidity of the growth and development of AI since the 1990s is accelerated by advances in micro-chip design and miniaturised applications that combine neural network pathways, natural language processes, text and facial recognition, and machine learning. Significant global investment in AI systems has boosted rapid growth and acceptance of AI technologies as a normal evolution in human-technological relations. As a ubiquitous technological-social-communications and information system, AI is not confined to science laboratories, systems designers and commercial companies. Everyone connected to the Internet uses AI regardless of age, socio-economic and cultural demographic.

AI disrupts our understanding of human intelligence, creativity and innovation. It can manipulate and reinvent human skills and the knowledge capital used in industrial, academic, legal, financial, health and educational fields. Aspirations to develop self-authored, self-governed and autonomous 'beings' are not reserved for future development. Emotionally intelligent AI humanoids are already developed. More sophisticated versions aim to incorporate human-based ethical values as well as produce AI-generated facsimiles displaying independence and 'freewill'.

AI simultaneously produces fake information and images and deploys algorithms that act as proxy censors of speech and visual content. Whether an ethically appropriate technology for young users or whether it enhances or negatively impacts learning, social and cognitive development are currently debated issues which will continue into the future. Opinion and literature are divided on whether AI is good or bad for society, whether appropriate for educational purposes, for young people, for reconfiguring human intelligence or a threat to human agency.

Not only is AI an inventive phenomenon, its cultural, social, educational, economic and political reach is yet to be measured. As a central figure in AI development, Suleyman is troubled by society's unpreparedness to cope with the potential threat that a 'techno-authoritarian dystopia' could lead to an imbalanced and unequal redistribution of power affecting all aspects of society (2025, p. 10). The current inabilities of legislation and government inaction to constrain or regulate AI's rapacious progression add further concerns about the public interest and how democratic ideals of equality will be impacted. Wajcman observes an apparent lack of concern about the inherent biases that "powerful elite...male white Silicon Valley engineers" hold over the shape of technological systems and how these will influence cultural, social and institutional practices and values (2008, p. 4). AI's relatively recent dissemination as a revolutionary technology raises questions how human agency, learning, cognition and decision-making will be conceptualised.

4.2 What Are We Dealing with?

Fundamental changes to temporal-spatial relations are occurring in the AI era. Perceptions of digital age time are radically different to pre-Internet analogical constructs. The technological efficiencies of mechanisation and automation have led to beliefs that time represents a transactional commodity or a future bank to borrow from and redistribute. Behaviour modification and monitoring are integral to AI's progression and to the ways that AI-generated stimuli affect temporality (Hassabis et al., 2017). Wajcman's profile of use patterns suggests that:

> The 'surfer' figure embraces ICTs in a purpose-oriented and functional approach...to save time; the 'sceptic' views technologies as causing time pressure and thus limits technology usage; and the 'gambler' operates the new technologies to increase time flexibility and juggle different time frames (2008, p. 72).

Paradoxically, an opposite effect of time compression has occurred. The affordances of technologies generate possibilities of being able to do more. Time spent on technologies reduces time for undertaking other tasks in life. AI projects possibilities of releasing humans from the messiness of work, thinking and learning. We want the instantaneity of information and communication technologies that will give us more time. Our wants drive the need for technologies to make our lives better, reduce labour time to complete activities, push for new inventions. How time is allocated is a critical issue since time itself governs all aspects of society, educational development, natural biology, and, planetary environments that are foundational to how we organise ourselves. AI designers leverage the utility of digital technologies and educational, personal, social and cultural habits to present a relationship that appears seamless and normal. Normality disguises subtle changes resulting from technological use. High engagement with social media and the Internet suggests habituation to technology that in turn helps to develop digital literacy competence and skills. Contained in the questions—'what comes first'—machine or human?—are two propositions about automation and autonomy.

Concepts of automation either are framed by either solutionist perspectives or belief in human reasoning to overcome functional issues associated with technologies such as mechanising tools to speed up the manufacture and social, communication, industrial, financial and commercial activities (Nof, 2009). Technological solutionists promote the capacities of technologies to resolve specific industrial, environmental, social and technological problems (Saetra & Selinge, 2024). For an automated object to function, complex cognitive and problem-solving negotiations are going on for technology to perform to expectation. Object-relations theorists draw attention to complex psycho-dynamic interactions between an object (physical or technological) and an internalised sense of the self. From an anthropological / cultural perspective, the simplest to the most complex object can potentially alter "the nature of relationships between humans and their environments" (Malafouris, 2020, p. 41). Human cognition is inextricably linked to material artefacts and to cognitive ecologies that enable us to make sense of the world[s] we are located in (Malafouris, 2013). Material engagement theorists propose that objects are not passive nor neutral. Objects represent mental matrices in which identity, autonomy and agency are mirrored in transactions between an object, its tangible characteristics, and its material and mechanical use and function (Alessandroni & Malafouris, 2022).

Putting full trust in automated technologies does not mean that automated solutions are always accurate or correct despite an almost complete belief that automated technologies are consistently better or preferred than human input. Automation does not always simplify tasks. It increases cognitive complexity as greater demands are placed on technological systems and on human capacities to improve designs or invent technological alternatives. With complexity an operational criterion of AI, greater cognitive attention is required since users need to understand how "knowledge must be organized… [as well as having the] … skills or know-how … [to know what to do] … and [how it applies] …in particular situations" (Dreyfus, 1992, p. xvii). While there are many recommendations for using AI in education, it is not entirely clear whether it works and how it works (Holmes & Tuomi, 2022).

The inherent unevenness between technological domains, application fields, systems and users obscures the unseen impacts of how different domains may or can interact and vary across time and space. Networks are characteristically partial and uneven. Links between technological domains are not fully synchronous especially if it is assumed that automation allows each domain within a system to seamlessly connect with each and other systems and social, institutional and technological structures (May & Thrift, 2001). While the notion of automation might look simple and uncomplicated, it disguises the complexities of cognitive and subjective work needing to be performed so that the automated object (technology) can function in that context, according to that application, at that, and a future time.

4.3 Considering Autonomy and Implications of Autonomous AI

Autonomy is generally perceived as a manifestation of an individual's actions and decision-making competence. Autonomy implies a right to exercise a decision without duress as well as representing qualities attributed to a person (Shell, 2009).

Autonomy holds status in constitutional and rights legislation designed to protect the inviolability of personal decision-making. It has deep reach in moral, ethical and political philosophies and in liberalist ideations of democratic equality and legal precepts applied to actions of reasoning. Medical, educational and research ethics theorists emphasise the need for any individual to have full autonomy and competence, and, understand and agree to proposals and procedures (Bracken-Roche et al., 2017). In the main, the reference is how an individual negotiates, evaluates and decides on the appropriateness of action according to that individual's perspective. Autonomy may be considered a self-attributed agency but making an autonomous decision is not taken in isolation from other factors.

> When we make practical, rather than epistemic, claims on one another… we presuppose the freedom to act on reasons that are grounded, not in our respective relations to something independent of us, but in irreducibly second-personal authority relations that hold between us…our respective perspectives are not simply standpoints on an independent something (Darwall, 2006, p. 280).

Autonomy could be thought of as a decision-making chain involving considerations, impact and effect on others. It is structured and structural and located within a hierarchy of independent and collective decision-making options governed by conditions permitting or restricting the full expression of autonomy in every situation and context. If autonomy is believed to be the expression of a distinctive sense of self, it not universally or democratically applied. American case laws suggest that autonomy has deleterious effects for women and marginalised people (Boone, 2016).

Another interpretation is an 'ought' system or a warning for considering if an action may contravene moral and ethical duties and responsibilities (Taylor, 2005). If practical reason is assumed to represent the ultimate expression of autonomy and the exercise of freewill, contemporary theorists acknowledge the variability of psychological, socio-cultural and contextual factors involved in decision-making as well as the multi-functional and multidimensional characteristics embedded in concepts of autonomy. Autonomy can be arbitrary and capricious, neither predictive nor uniform, heterogeneous and not an enclosed system. Autonomy could be considered as:

1. A domain of knowledge—as autonomy requires us to work out *for ourselves* what is right to do;
2. Motivation—we want to do the right thing *because* it is right;
3. Metaphysical—not just motivation or reason but the concept of freedom that makes things carry the weight they do;
4. Normative ethics—the moral content given by the notion of law (*nomos*) and the demand to think of oneself in relation to others under shared laws (Deligiorgio, 2012, pp. 3–4).

In August 2025 Meta CEO Mark Zuckerberg proclaimed that their current artificial intelligence models are moving towards superintelligent autonomous capacities able to self-correct, modify their own algorithms and "process information thousands of times faster and identify patterns…[that]… humans cannot perceive". META's superintelligent AI is likely to be launched in 2029 (Jackson, 2025). Zuckerberg's predictions about the advent of a superintelligent autonomous and automated technological system suggest that it will resolve the relatively slow pace of human problem-solving (Huckins, 2025). Although technologically autonomous, such a superintelligent thinking technological deity will continue to rely on human input to generate coding systems and modelling responses as its operational viability is human dependant.

McFarland considers that "a software entity is autonomous when it possesses both an 'intent' (an encoded representation of a goal, a purpose, or a task to be completed) and an ability to act to achieve that goal" (2021, p. 4). The end-use and purpose of computerised systems are to run endlessly repeated programmes and software. Autonomy is anticipated. McFarland's analysis is located in military appropriations of autonomous weaponry technologies where autonomy, responsibilities and actions require legal and moral scrutiny. Technological autonomy is not a sovereign entity to itself but a property of human-system collaborations, technological and operational actions. Establishing legal equivalence requires an assessment of how "human and software behaviours that are the signature of autonomous operations… [can be] … subject to legal regulation" (2021, p. 20).

Human autonomy in the AI age is derivative and applicable to operational agendas to produce a competitive product for consumption in the AI market. Although autonomous technologies generate fears about the complete suppression of human autonomy, it represents a field of possible actions conjoined by autonomous technologies *and* human agents (Formosa, 2021). The more complex the conditions and possible actions inputted into technological systems such as AI, the higher the likelihood of technological autonomy becoming enhanced. The ability to bypass certain functions through replicated 'learning' gives rise to perceptions of autonomous self-operation as intelligent AI technologies can bypass coding and logic steps that human agents feed into them.

By delegating certain actions to autonomous technologies, humans forego some aspects of autonomy. Deferral to technological autonomy can affect human agency by eliminating or narrowing down decision-options and choices. To Prunkl (2024), autonomy includes *internal authenticity* (being true to oneself and values); *external / environmental dimensions* affecting *capacity* and *agency*; *adaptive preference* in cases of limited options. Compromises to individual autonomy can arise through technological manipulation and where autonomous technologies are intentionally programmed and designed to control agency. Because autonomy intersects ethical and moral values and principles, there are expectations that technological companies and users are held accountable to societal and ethical standards. Building trust in 'the machine' of AI technologies requires all actors to follow ethical guidelines on full disclosure of benefits, harms and risks (Thiebes et al., 2021). It also raises questions about the governance of ethical standards, which regulations, which jurisdictional guidelines and regulation of technological inventions will be conceded or implemented.

4.4 Curriculum Responses to AI—the Autonomy of Learning and Teaching

The sociality of learning is perceived to be changing in relation to alignments with learning and data analytics conceptualised by computer scientists and software engineers (Linderoth & Stenberg, 2025). The suggestion is that learning and teaching autonomy diminish as data informatics become legitimised in pedagogy and curriculum. Educational practices, including teachers' and students' roles as learners are increasingly brought into the orbit of datafication. A problem for society, educators and young people is whether to concede partial or total learning and teaching autonomy to AI (Walsh et al., 2021). Caution needs to be taken when conceptualising learner autonomy (Rödl, 2016). It can be partial, curriculum guided, developmental, individual and contextually appropriate. In the educational sense, autonomy is an aspirational state and a teaching/learning practice designed to enable students to become independent learners (Boud, 2012). From Platonic times, autonomy features in a triadic relationship between developmental, pedagogic and curriculum processes designed to produce or induce faculties of critical reasoning, knowledge and citizenship qualities. For summary purposes, educational understandings of autonomy include:

1. Teacher autonomy—pedagogical and curriculum implications;
2. School and community level autonomy—participatory rights, limitations and entitlements;
3. Individual autonomy—rights, freedoms, decision-choices, actions;
4. Pedagogical autonomy—content, focus areas of learning, instructional methods, professional judgement;
5. Curriculum autonomy—policy objectives, philosophical orientations and
6. Student autonomy—developmental competence, independence, reasoning abilities, technical skills, knowledge acquisition and application capacities (Wermke & Salokangas, 2015).

As young people will be the beneficiaries and creators of a future likely to be saturated with superintelligent autonomous AI, how are curricula of the present responding and preparing them to enact their autonomy in a different future?

4.5 Southern Hemisphere Digital Literacy Curriculum—Australia

Curriculum development, design and regulation is a joint enterprise between the Australian Curriculum, Assessment and Reporting Authority (ACARA) and individual states. ACARA sets out what Australian students should learn and be taught. It advises the federal government on the state of schooling, undertakes national testing, reviews teacher workforce projections, monitors and reports on areas requiring attention and updates the Australian national curriculum where needed (Clarke, 2023). The Australian National Curriculum is a three-dimensional composition of eight learning areas; seven general capabilities and cross-curriculum priorities incorporated into the content of the learning areas and general capabilities frameworks. Each state and territory is responsible for funding school sectors and providing a world-class standard of education for all students. States and territories determine how they will deliver their curriculum in conjunction with the national curriculum and agreement with the *Mparntwe Declaration* (Australian Government, 2019). Principles informing Australia's educational approach to digital literacy are described in the *Australian Framework for Generative Artificial Intelligence (AA) in Schools* (2023). Guideline values are:

1. Transparency: understanding how school communities use AI, know how it works, and its impact;
2. Fairness: AI tools are accessible, fair and respectful;
3. Accountability: human agency and accountability for decisions and
4. Privacy, Security and Safety: all school users have protection of privacy and data (pp. 6–7).

National and state curricula facilitate the analysis of core concepts and real-world problems as well as extracting and representing information from data, systems information, consideration of ethical and social implications and providing solutions.

Using the State of Victoria as an example, progressive knowledge and skills described in Version 2 of *Victorian Curriculum F–10 Digital Technologies* are guided by ethical design principles outlined by *Universal Design Australia* (2025b). Digital literacy is interpreted in the Victorian curriculum as a learning continuum from Foundation to Year 10 encompassing literacy and numeracy skills and knowledge about how to safely and ethically use digital technologies in educational, communications and social contexts. It is organised into four elements; practising digital safety and well-being; investigating; creating and exchanging; and, managing and operating. Each element is organised into three sub-elements. These twelve sub-elements are further allocated to sets of sub-elements according to year level and anticipated development of skills, knowledge and learning outcomes. Instructional intentions are leveraged to enhancing digital literacy in relation to national agendas on employability and knowledge skills of the future. Subsequent year levels explore the digital curriculum in conjunction with learning areas, general capabilities and curriculum strands.

Policy guidelines set out requirements for schools, students and school communities for the safe use of digital technologies (digital hardware, software and resources) and intended purposes for supporting learning. Schools are responsible for producing, updating *Acceptable Use Agreement (AUA)* every two years and publicising behaviour expectations. Schools and teachers are encouraged to judicially balance "teaching and learning with and without digital technologies". Schools are responsible for ensuring that all students have equitable access to digital technologies. Core concepts indicated in the national curriculum generally correspond with the Victorian curriculum in the areas of abstraction, data acquisition, specification, algorithms, digital systems and privacy and security. Attributed meanings of AI processes and concepts elaborated in the Victorian curriculum are of particular relevance given how Version 2.0 of the Victorian Curriculum (2024) is to be fully implemented in 2025. Descriptive meanings need to be continually updated in reference to the development and enhancement of AI terminologies. Explainable AI intelligence (XAI) is one example. Philosophical, legal and ethical features are to be added to the technological functionality of 'black box' algorithmics. The aim is to build AI systems incorporating trustworthiness, accountability and transparency (Tuhin, 2025). *Explainability* is a purposefully designed phase in AI development to convince organisations, society and institutions of technological trustworthiness and accuracy (IBM, 2025).

Despite curriculum ambitions for Australian students to be equipped with digital literacy skills and knowledge, the *National Assessment Program in ICT Literacy (NAP- ICTL)* survey (2022) finds:

1. A significant drop in ICT literacy for Year 10 students since 2017;
2. Declining Year 10 achievement in three out of six states;
3. No difference in achievement from 2017 with Year 6 students;
4. Female students have higher levels of ICT literacy than Year 6 and 10 male students;
5. Significant gaps between Indigenous and non-Indigenous students and
6. Level of ICT literacy differs between metropolitan, regional students and parental occupation (see Friedman et al., 2023, p. 67).

Although characterised as the 'digital native' generation having exemplary knowledge about digital technologies, this generation does not have fully developed digital literacy skills. NAP-ICTL (2022) data show bare pass proficiency at Year 6 (55%) and lower at Year 10 (46%). 13% of Year 6 and 5% of Year 10 students cannot open emails, copy and paste on a spreadsheet and find information on a webpage. Digital literacy is deteriorating although digital technologies are ubiquitous for communicating, working, living and learning. There is no digital competency framework for teachers although one is designed for Australian workplaces. Teacher efficacy and the value they place on using digital technologies are critical factors for promoting and motivating students to develop digital literacy competence.

Evidential gaps exist in Australian schools' progress in the education of digital literacy 13.2% of Australian schools are at early-stage; 53.9% use dual learning (text and digital) and 32% are highly tech enabled. Government schools lag behind non-government schools at early years (2.7%) and at dual learning (3.00%) stages. Both sectors even out at highly tech enabled. 78.0% of secondary schools use AI for education and administrative purposes with the remainder intending to implement AI within two years. AI is not fully used for educational purposes. (Campion Education, 2025).

Multiple digital competence models are proposed to assist Australian teachers and students to develop knowledge, skills and competence in these and other areas of learning. In 2012, Eshet wrote that "digital literacy is more than…a technical ability to operate devices properly", p. 268). The then proposed model consisted of photo-visual, metaphoric, information, socio-emotional and real-time skills. A tendency in educational approaches is to focus on the instrumental uses of digital technologies. This overlooks the thinking demands of digital literacy including multitasking, collective intelligence, transmedia navigation, networking and negotiation of systems and data (Iordache et al., 2017). Digital literacy incorporates emotional intelligibility, critical and global thinking attributes. Along with emotional intelligibility, natural and epistemic curiosity are prioritised. In this typology:

1. *Diversive curiosity* is where the hunt for knowledge begins although slow and frustrating;
2. *Empathetic curiosity* is when you see the world from others' perspectives—and *why* they think and do things and
3. *Epistemic curiosity* represents the 'more disciplined, and effortful type of curiosity' (Leslie, 2014, p. 190).

Young people need highly developed semantic analysis skills to interpret information and communication. Semantic knowledge requires a sophisticated understanding of literal and inferential meanings of natural and machine language forms that constitute coding maps and computer logic in relation to:

1. *Namability*—meanings and how the literality of words and names are categorised and transposed into binary codes. Numeric transposition offers infinite reconstructions and replications of computer language without the nuances and ambiguities of natural language;
2. *Calculability*—algorithmic manipulation and how reductive constructions of empirical diversity are presented as concrete realities;
3. *Measurability*—reality and experience and how measured, named and identified by mathematic calculations and assumed to be statistically valid, true and correct, and
4. *Representability*—meanings materialised in texts, imagery, sound, speech and how digitally manufactured criteria reduce room for 'thinking' through the semantic logic of AI intelligence systems (Cope et al., 2021, pp. 1229–1231).

Integral to future-oriented curricula are digital literacy, critical thinking, analysis and problem-solving skills collectively attributed as digital competencies. Educators offer digital literacy in curriculum and subjects but knowledge and skills gaps remain.

4.6 Ambitions, Agendas and Achievement—Northern Hemisphere

The European Union *Digital Education Action Plan (DEAP) (2021–2027)* is a policy initiative for developing and providing "quality and inclusive digital learning" for European-member states. The COVID crisis identified problems and limitations within educational systems, uneven access to the internet, inequity and compromised opportunities to engage with digital technologies. The provision of digital education in the EU is complicated by varying country of origin approaches, slow adoption and development of a common digital literacy curriculum within EU member states. Building from action intentions in the 2018 plan; the 2021–2027 plan identifies the need for structural reform and a coherent policy framework to bring together all stakeholders involved in the transformation to a digital society. Of strategic importance is fostering a high-performing digital education for enhancing digital skills and competences. The tasks are to:

1. Establish a common vocabulary and terminology for building a shared understanding of digital education content;
2. Develop quality digital education content in terms of its utility, trustworthiness, accessibility, interoperability and sustainability;
3. Generate guidelines for helping stakeholders to apply quality criteria for the creation, selection, use a DREnd evaluation of digital education content;
4. Promote digital literacy and skills for digital education content design and use (*DEAP*, 2024, p. 3).

Since a uniformly agreed digital curriculum is to be ratified, the remaining option is to examine the current state of digital literacy in two national contexts—The Netherlands and the UK.

4.6.1 The Netherlands

The autonomous nature of Dutch schooling systems, sectors, curriculum content and pedagogy distinguishes it from the centralised state and federal models of Australian schooling. There is no national curriculum. School autonomy and educational freedom are embedded in the 1917 Constitution. Autonomy, authority and accountability are finely balanced in Holland's private and public educational sectors. While schools have the authority to choose their pedagogical agendas, governance systems ensure that professional standards, quality of teaching and learning, assessment and other processes are met. School boards hold key decision roles over teacher/workforce allocation, the internal organisation of schools, curriculum and assessment (Neeleman, 2019; Stevenson et al., 2021).

Dutch school curriculum is undergoing reform in response to the aims of the OECD's multidimensional learning framework (OECD Learning Compass for 2030, 2019a). A mapping analysis of Dutch curriculum and OECD cross-curricular themes and skills finds variable responses to 2030 goals. Mindful of OECD interpretations of Dutch curriculum nomenclature, digital literacy is not identified as a specific subject. Digital literacy is found in technology and home economics but not specifically in mathematics, technology and science learning areas. Computational thinking/coding/programming rank lower (35%) in the Dutch curriculum than 46% of OECD counterparts (Education 2030 Curriculum Content Mapping, 2019b, pp. 35–41). The OECD finds high correspondence with global themes of sustainability, health and globalisation but less with technology and the specific goals of digital literacy. Overt differences can be identified with respective curriculum designs. One is autonomous and distributed (The Netherlands) whereas the EU is collectively systemised for implementation in all EU schools and educational curricula.

In 2024, a digital literacy curriculum was implemented for years K-8 schools in The Netherlands and organised into three domain groups—"(A) Practical knowledge and skills, (B) Designing and making, and (C) Interaction between digital, technology, digital, media, people and the society" (Grgurina & Tolboom, 2024, p. 30). The implementation of K-8 digital literacy curriculum in The Netherlands is an ongoing project. The OECD made further amendments to the AI digital literacy framework in 2025 (*New AI Literacy Framework,* 2025c). The updated intentions are to integrate AI literacy with mathematics, history, social sciences and computer sciences curricula. Ongoing revision and republication of EU and OECD policy directives contextualise continuous movement of content and application in response to new AI applications and pedagogical recommendations. Although the introduction of a Dutch K-8 digital literacy curriculum is relatively recent, a snapshot finds that 82.7% of the Netherlands' population have basic digital literacy skills compared to the EU at 55.6% (Kralj, 2023). The positive policy environment for building digital literacy skills for a broader population demographic in the Netherlands, not only through schooling, is considered instrumental for achieving the nation's digital development goals.

4.6.2 Digital Literacy Curriculum in the UK

While the term national curriculum is a generic reference for compulsory and elective subjects in the UK, Scotland, Wales, Northern Ireland and England have devolved jurisdiction of their curriculum. Maisuria's (2023) research briefing to the House of Commons (Westminster) explains the governance structure of each curriculum jurisdiction and how it applies to state/council schools and other schooling sectors. All school sectors have compulsory, elective subjects and digital literacy areas but devolved jurisdictions differ in approaches to national culture and language components, and curriculum settings. Ofsted (UK) has a broad approach to digital literacy and describes attributes, values and skills, skills of planning and creation, communication and collaboration, problem solving, digital safety, well-being and intellectual property associated with media and technological uses. Ofsted also oversees hardware/software compatibility and technological standards needed to functionally deliver a digital curriculum in schools (GOV.UK, 2019, 2020, 2022a, 2022b).

UK's digital literacy curriculum references the *Education for a Connected World Framework* (EfCW) framework for developing healthy habits and well-being; building relationships and communication; considering digital footprint and identity; problem-solving issues of cyberbullying and online harms, information and media literacy. These focus areas align with eight *Common Sense Education's Digital Citizenship* strands. There is no specific subject or curriculum on digital literacy. The closest is computing. Research into the state of digital literacy education in the UK finds variable pedagogical applications and curricula designs. What and who determines the concept of digital literacy appears to be a complication for deciding whether digital literacy is part of media literacy, mathematics, science, technology or a separate learning area/subject in the curriculum (Francis, 2025; Polizzi, 2020). An authentic digital literacy curriculum needs experienced teachers who understand how AI, social media and other digital programmes and apps that can be pedagogically productive (McFarlane, 2019).

Following their evaluation of *Common Sense Digital Citizenship* learning strands, Abades-Barclay and Banaji (2024) argue for a specific digital citizenship curriculum for addressing and resolving the digital divide in UK schools. Phippens (2024) knowledge mapping analysis of primary students' digital literacy knowledge is backgrounded by the EfCW framework. Their analysis of UK primary school students' digital literacy skills finds higher engagement with EfCW learning strands for online relationships, self-image and identity and managing online information. Students' knowledge was less secure on privacy and security and online reputation strands. Average scores of 3.6 out of 5 indicate a general good understanding at primary school level. Despite initiatives for improving digital literacy education, 43% of fourteen-years old students do not have basic computer literacy skills, well below the EU target of 15% by 2030 (EU International Computer and Information Literacy Study (ICILS), 2023). EU performance scores are declining (Fig. 1: Country Averages and Distribution for CIL, p. 18). Data disprove the mythology that "being born in a digital world automatically makes one digitally competent". A serious complication in the UK is the evidence of lower numbers of GSCE students taking Design and Technology, Computer Science and Information Technology subjects. Trend data show participation at 20% or below between 2018 and 2024 (Francis, 2025, p. 14).

4.7 Towards an Authentic Curriculum

Education technologies can transform how students learn because they offer opportunities to explore complex phenomena and create digital representations of their ideas. An ongoing assessment of students' digital literacy skills is being undertaken by PISA (2025). An analysis of responses to tasks and digital literacy competencies should provide evidence of how learning technologies develop in relation to:

1. self-regulated learning—the monitoring and control of metacognitive, cognitive, behavioural, motivational and affective processes while learning; and
2. computational and scientific inquiry practices—referring to the capacity to use digital tools to explore systems, represent ideas and solve problems with computational logic (OECD, 2025b, PISA, *Learning in the Digital World*, p. 10).

The acquisition of digital literacy skills has significant school and post-school implications. By 2050, 60% of all jobs will be eliminated or reconfigured by AI (World

Economic Forum, 2025, 6–9). Between half to one third of EU workers have inadequate digital literacy skills. 61% of Australian workers do not know nor are trained in using AI; 46% use AI inappropriately; 59% make errors in their work due to AI; 44% contravene policies and guidelines; 57% never evaluate AI's accuracy and 51% pass off AI-generated content as their own (Gillespie et al., 2025, p. 50). Deconstructing and redesigning curriculum for an AI 'knowledge economy' are complex. From Yuksel et al.'s (2017) analysis, sixth-generation knowledge is more likely to be shaped by:

1. Netocracies—global actors with the power of technological advantages and networking skills;
2. Netocrats—who can harness information networks, communications, control finance and legislation and shape different form of government, and
3. Netizens—anyone contributing to the development of the Net (Yuksel et al., p. 229).

With the acceleration of AI development, a time lag is inherently an issue for a digital literacy curriculum. Where curriculum meets technological invention, a formal curriculum cannot keep pace with the emergence of novel and autonomous AI applications. A synopsis of employability skills for the digital future includes researching independently; understanding basic technology; adapting to changing technological requirements; using collaboration tools and teaching others about technology. Inferred in future skills agendas is the criticality of autonomy for learning how to build mental models, use multiple intelligences, including appropriate ethical use and the development of ethical standards of practice. A disruptive mind-set is needed to recreate new ways of doing things. IQ alone will not define future employability skills. As workplace cultures and practices adjust to AI environments, young people will need to be global thinkers with the abilities to 'see' the world differently from standard curriculum-focused content and knowledge. Emotional, ethical and social intelligence will be critical employability characteristics for mediating human, social and technological needs (Kolbjørnsrud et al., 2016).

Next phase AI will incorporate explainability to extend autonomous intelligence (XAI). It is designed to build trust and confidence in how AI algorithms work and how results and outcomes are arrived at (IBM, 2025). Being able to examine the reasoning of algorithmic models, biases and erroneous data, hypothetically assists designers and users to identify and correct system errors and gain trust in XAI's reliability. While health-care, financial institutions and legal sectors are identified as primary users, there is interest in developing learner-centred XAI applications for schools and higher education programmes (Khosravi et al., 2022). Conceptual and practical issues remain about how XAI can be used in educational contexts. A core concern about XAI explainability in education is whether teachers and students will defer to technological accuracy in preference to human-cognitive explainability. Explainability is deeply sedimented in historical, epistemological, ontological and philosophical theories concerning validity, confidence, probability, accuracy, causality and predictability (Ruben, 2015). When considering explainability as an operational function of AI intelligence, questions are raised about what and who have autonomy to determine the *explainability* of that content; what explanatory proofs will be needed; what will *explainability* look like in educational settings if human thinking autonomy is ceded to AI super intelligence (Ruben, 2015, p. 9). A digital literacy curriculum will need to invest in human autonomy, agency and explainability to revision an action-and-forward focussed curriculum where thinking and creativity are prioritised so that young people can participate in their digital futures.

4.8 Conclusion

This chapter intersects epistemic, pedagogical and curriculum moments that bring to mind Schumpeter's notion of 'creative destruction'. Existing knowledge and ways of doing things are not immutable to change but are continually re-invented and re-imagined. Algorithmically derived knowledge systems interweave chronological, philosophical and epistemological pasts. AI represents a digitised diorama of our present world. It is our reality now. Young people are no longer constrained by formal educational boundaries and have autonomy to roam the internet for instructional materials and guidance on many subjects. Young people's inherent curiosity, intelligence, creativity and entrepreneurialism *will* reconstruct the dioramas of *their* futures.

References

Abades-Barclay, F., & Banaji, S. (2024). *LSE – Common sense digital citizenship curriculum evaluation.* Department of Media and Communications, LSE, UK. 4–101 PDF Dedicated digital citizen curriculum needed to help pupils navigate online dangers and tackle 'digital divide' – LSE

Alessandroni, N., & Malafouris, L. (2022). Blurring ontological boundaries: The transactional nature of material engagement. *Adaptive Behavior, 31*(2), 127–131.

Australian Government, Department of Education (DoE), Canberra, ACT. (2019). *The Alice springs (Mparntwe) education declaration* (2019). https://www.education.gov.au/indigenous-education/resources/alice-springs-mparntwe-education-declaration

Australian Government, Department of Education (DoE), Canberra, ACT. (2023). *Australian framework for generative Artificial Intelligence (AI) in schools.* https://www.education.gov.au/schooling/resources/australian-framework-generative-artificial-intelligence-ai-schools

Australian Curriculum, Assessment and Reporting Authority (ACARA), Canberra ACT. (2025). *Australian curriculum.* https://acara.edu.au/curriculum

Benko, A., & Lányi, C. (2009). History of artificial intelligence. 1758–1762. In *Encyclopedia of information science and technology* (2nd ed). IGI Global.

Boone, M. (2016). The autonomy hierarchy. *Texas Journal on CL & CR, 22*(1), 1–48.

Boud, D. (2012). *Developing student autonomy in learning.* Routledge.

Bracken-Roche, D., Bell, E., Macdonald, M., & Racine, E. (2017). The concept of 'vulnerability' in research ethics: An in-depth analysis of policies and guidelines. *Health Research Policy and Systems, 15*(1), 8.

Bridle, J. (2018). *New dark age: Technology and the end of the future.* Verso Books.

Campion Education. (2025). *Digital landscapes in Australian schools.* Digital-Landscapes-in-Aus-Schools-2025.pdf

Cave, S., & Dihal, K. (2019). Hopes and fears for intelligent machines in fiction and reality. *Nature Machine Intelligence, 1*(2), 74–78.

Clarke, S. (2023). *School education: A quick guide.* https://www.aph.gov.au/About_Parliament/Parliamentary_departments/Parliamentary_Library/Research/Quick_Guides/2022-2023/SchoolEducation

Cope, B., Kalantzis, M., & Searsmith, D. (2021). Artificial intelligence for education: Knowledge and its assessment in AI-enabled learning ecologies. *Educational Philosophy and Theory, 53*(12), 1229–1245.

Darwall, S. (2006). The value of autonomy and autonomy of the will. *Ethics, 116*(2), 263–284.

Deligiorgio, K. (2012). *The scope of autonomy: Kant and the morality of freedom.* University Press.

Dreyfus, H. L. (1992). *What computers still can't do: A critique of artificial Reason.* MIT Press.

Dung, L. (2023). Current cases of AI misalignment and their implications for future risks. *Synthese, 202*(5), 138.

Eshet, Y. (2012). Thinking in the digital era: A revised mode of digital thinking. In Cohen, E. B. (Ed.), *Issues in informing science and technology* (pp. 267–276). Informing Science Press.

European Union (EU). (2024). *Digital Education Action Plan (DEAP) (2021–2027).* https://education.ec.europa.eu/focus-topics/digital-education/plan

European Union (EU). (2023). *International Computer and Information Literacy Study (ICILS) in Europe, 2023: Main findings and educational policy implications.* Publications Office of the European Union. https://data.europa.eu/doi/10.2766/5221263

Formosa, P. (2021). Robot autonomy vs. human autonomy: Social robots, artificial intelligence (AI), and the nature of autonomy. *Minds and Machines, 31*(4), 595–616.

Francis, B. (2025). *Curriculum and assessment review,* 1–45 PDF Curriculum and Assessment Review: interim report - GOV.UK

Friedman, T., O'Malley, K., Osborne, K., Ockwell, L., Helou, L., Watts, Z. (2023, Oct 18). *National assessment program: ICT literacy 2022: Public report.* Australian curriculum, assessment and reporting authority. https://research.acer.edu.au/ict_literacy/24

Gillespie, N., Lockey, S., Ward, T., Macdade, A., & Hassed, G. (2025). *Trust, attitudes and use of artificial intelligence: A global study 2025.* The University of Melbourne and KPMG, Melbourne 2–110. https://kpmg.com/xx/en/our-insights/ai-and-technology/trust-attitudes-and-use-of-ai.html

GOV.UK. (2019). *Commonsense digital citizenship.* Common Sense Media—written evidence (MLI0011)

GOV.UK. (2020). *Education for a connected world.* Education for a Connected World - GOV.UK

GOV.UK. (2022a). *Ofsted strategy 2022–2027.* https://www.gov.uk/government/publications/ofsted-strategy-2022-to-2027/ofsted-strategy-2022-27

GOV.UK. (2022b). *Meeting digital and technology standards in schools and colleges.* Updates - Meeting digital and technology standards in schools and colleges - Guidance - GOV.UK

Grgurina, N., & Tolboom, J. (2024). K-8 digital literacy curriculum in the Netherlands. In *International Conference on Informatics in Schools: Situation, Evolution, and Perspectives,* October 8, 2024. (pp. 30–43). Springer Nature.

Hassabis, D., Kumaran, D., Summerfield, C., & Botvinick, M. (2017). Neuroscience-inspired artificial intelligence. *Neuron, 95*(2), 245–258.

Holmes, W., & Tuomi, I. (2022). State of the art and practice in AI in education. *European Journal of Education, 57*(4), 542–570.

Huckins, G. (2025). *Five ways that AI is learning to improve itself.* Grace Huckinsarchive page https://www.technologyreview.com/2025/08/06/1121193/five-ways-that-ai-is-learning-to-improve-itself/

Hudson, A. D., Finn, E., & Wylie, R. (2023). What can science fiction tell us about the future of artificial intelligence policy? *AI & SOCIETY, 38*(1), 197–211.

IBM. (2025). *What is explainable AI (XAI)?* What is Explainable AI (XAI)? | IBM

Iordache, C., Mariën, I., & Baelden, D. (2017). Developing digital skills and competences: A quick scan analysis of 13 digital literacy models. *Italian Journal of Sociology of Education, 9*(1), 6–30.
Jackson, V. (2025). *Meta's AI shows self-learning breakthrough, Zuckerberg calls it a step toward superintelligence.* https://www.amworldgroup.com/blog/meta-ai-takes-first-step-to-superintelligence
Janssen, C. P., Donker, S. F., Brumby, D. P., & Kun, A. L. (2019). History and future of human-automation interaction. *International Journal of Human-Computer Studies, 131*, 99–107.
Khosravi, H., Shum, S. B., Chen, G., Conati, C., Tsai, Y. S., Kay, J., & Gašević, D. (2022). Explainable artificial intelligence in education. *Computers and Education: Artificial Intelligence, 3*, Article 100074.
Kolbjørnsrud, V., Amico, R., & Thomas, R. J. (2016). How artificial intelligence will redefine management. *Harvard Business Review, 2*(1), 3–10.
Kralj, L. (2023). *The Netherlands: A snapshot of digital skills.* https://digital-skills-jobs.europa.eu/en/latest/briefs/netherlands-snapshot-digital-skills
Leslie, I. (2014). *Curious: The desire to know and why your future depends on it.* Basic Books.
Li, F., Cheng, L., Wang, X., Shen, L., Ma, Y., & Islam, A. Y. M. (2025). The causal relationship between digital literacy and students' academic achievement: A meta-analysis. *Humanities and Social Sciences Communications, 12*(1), 1–12.
Linderoth, C., & Stenberg, C. (2025). Welcome to class. *Confero: Essays on Education, Philosophy and Politics*, 20–36.
Maisuria, A. (2023). *Comparing the school curriculum across the UK* 2023-comparing-curriculum-across-uk.pdf
Malafouris, L. (2013). *How things shape the mind*. MIT Press.
Malafouris, L. (2020). Thinking as "thinging": Psychology with things. *Current Directions in Psychological Science, 29*(1), 3–8. https://doi.org/10.1177/0963721419873349
May, J., & Thrift, N. (2001). (Eds.). *Geographies of temporality.* Routledge.
McFarlane, A. E. (2019). Devices and desires: Competing visions of a good education in the digital age. *British Journal of Educational Technology, 50*(3), 1125–1136.
McFarland, T. (2021). The concept of autonomy. *LIIVOJA, Rain; VÄLJATAGA, Ann. Autonomous Cyber Capabilities under International Law.* Tallinn: NATO CCDCOE Publications, 12–35. https://www.scribd.com/document/498962646/The-concept-of-autonomy
Neeleman, A. (2019). The scope of school autonomy in practice: An empirically based classification of school interventions. *Journal of Educational Change, 20*(1), 31–55.
Nof, S. Y. (2009). Automation: What it means to us around the world. In Nof, S. (Ed.), *Springer handbook of automation. Springer handbooks* (pp. 13–52). Springer.
Organisation for Economic Co-operation and Development, Paris (OECD). (2019a). *OECD learning compass for 2030* (pp. 5–127). https://www.oecd.org
Organisation for Economic Co-operation and Development, Paris (OECD). (2019b). *Education 2030 curriculum content mapping: An analysis of the Netherlands curriculum proposal* (pp. 1–76). https://www.oecd.org
Organisation for Economic Co-operation and Development, Paris (OECD). (2025a). *Future of education and skills 2030* (pp. 1–21). Future of Education and Skills 2030/2040 | OECD
Organisation for Economic Co-operation and Development, Paris (OECD). (2025b). *PISA 2025 Learning in the digital world.* (Draft) (pp. 2–28). https://www.oecd.org/en/topics/sub-issues/learning-in-the-digital-world/pisa-2025-learning-in-the-digital-world.html
Organisation for Economic Co-operation and Development, Paris (OECD). (2025c). *New AI literacy framework to equip youth in an age of AI.* New AI Literacy Framework to Equip Youth in an Age of AI – OECD Education and Skills Today
Phippens, A. (2024). *Evaluation of the ProjectEVOLVE.* https://swgfl.org.uk/research/evaluation-of-the-projectevolve-database-2024/
Polizzi, G. (2020). Digital literacy and the national curriculum for England: Learning from how the experts engage with and evaluate online content. *Computers & Education, 152*, 1–13.

Project Evolve. (2024). *Evaluation of the ProjectEVOLVE database: Understanding online safety delivery and assessment in schools* (pp. 1–23). ProjectEVOLVE 2024 Report: Key Insights on Digital … www.gov.uk/government/publications

Prunkl, C. (2024). Human autonomy at risk? An analysis of the challenges from AI. *Minds and Machines, 34*(3), 26. 1–21.

Rödl, S. (2016). Education and autonomy. *Journal of Philosophy of Education, 50*(1), 84–97.

Ruben, D. H. (2015). *Explaining explanation.* Routledge.

Saetra, H., & Selinge, E. (2024). Technological remedies for social problems: Defining and demarcating techno-fixes and techno-solutionism. *Science and Engineering Ethics, 30,* 60. https://doi.org/10.1007/s11948-024-00524-x

Sharov, A., & Tønnessen, M. (2021). *Semiotic agency: Science beyond mechanism.* Springer International Publishing.

Shell, S. (2009). *Kant and the limits of autonomy.* Harvard University Press.

Stevenson, L., Honingh, M., & Neeleman, A. (2021). Dutch boards governing multiple schools: Navigating between autonomy and expectations. *School Leadership & Management, 41*(4–5), 370–386.

Suleyman, M. (2025). *The coming wave: AI, power, and our future.* Random House.

Taylor, R. S. (2005). Kantian personal autonomy. *Political Theory, 33*(5), 602–628.

Thiebes, S., Lins, S., & Sunyaev, A. (2021). Trustworthy artificial intelligence. *Electronic Markets, 31*(2), 447–464.

Trilling, B., & Fadel, B. (2019). *21st century skills: Learning for life in our times.* Wiley.

Tuhin, M. (2025). What is explainable AI and why it's critical for trust. *Science News,* What Is Explainable AI and Why It's Critical for Trust

Victorian Curriculum and Assessment Authority (VCAA): Department of Education and Training, Victoria, Australia.

Victorian Curriculum and Assessment Authority (VCAA). (2023). *Digital Learning Policy.* Digital Learning: Policy | VIC.GOV.AU | Policy and Advisory Library

Victorian Curriculum and Assessment Authority (VCAA). (2024). *Digital literacy F–10 version 2.0.* https://f10.vcaa.vic.edu.au/foundational-skills/digital-literacy

Victorian Curriculum and Assessment Authority (VCAA). (2025a). *Acceptable use agreement.* Acceptable Use Agreement- Upper Primary and Secondary School

Victorian Curriculum and Assessment Authority (VCAA). (2025b). *Victorian curriculum.* Victorian Curriculum F–10 Version 2.0

Wajcman, J. (2008). Life in the fast lane? Towards a sociology of technology and time. *The British Journal of Sociology, 59*(1), 59–77.

Walsh, K. R., Mahesh, S., & Trumbach, C. C. (2021). Autonomy in AI systems: Rationalizing the fears. *Journal of Technology Studies, 47*(1), 38–47.

Wermke, W., & Salokangas, M. (2015). Autonomy in education: Theoretical and empirical approaches to a contested concept. *Nordic Journal of Studies in Educational Policy, 2015*(2), 1–6. https://doi.org/10.3402/nstep.v1.28841

Williams, R. N., Gantt, E. E., & Fischer, L. (2021). Agency: What does it mean to be a human being? *Frontiers in Psychology, 12,* 1–12.

World Economic Forum. (2025 January 7). *The future of jobs report.* The Future of Jobs Report 2025 | World Economic Forum

Yuksel, N., Cifci, H., & Cakir, S. (2017). New foresight generation and framework of foresight. *Press Academia Procedia, 5*(1), 224–233.

Dr. Mary A. Burston is a published author of book chapters and journal articles that examine the nature of relationships and the purpose and role of education in the twenty first century.

Part II
Youth Development and Emergence

Chapter 5
The Brave New Worlds of Educational Technology

John Morgan

Abstract This chapter examines the historical evolution of educational technology from the 1960s to today, highlighting its entanglement with capitalism and global political economy. It explores how cultural and political imaginaries have shaped techno-optimistic and techno-sceptical narratives, from early IT initiatives to the promises of digital learning and the rise of platform capitalism. The discussion foregrounds critical concerns about surveillance, solutionism, and the commodification of education. Finally, it considers generative AI as the latest technological frontier, questioning its implications for pedagogy, equity and the future of schooling within enduring capitalist crises.

Keywords Capitalism · Schooling · Technological change

5.1 Where Were You When ChatGPT Was Launched?

Can you remember where you were ChatGPT changed the educational landscape? The moment, November 30, 2024, when Open AI launched its website for ChatGPT, and caused panic. In the United States, major school districts in New York and Los Angeles blocked access, citing threats of cheating and academic integrity. Universities issued urgent guidelines warning students that use of ChatGPT could trigger charges of academic misconduct. Homework was all but dead, and plagiarism was largely undetectable. All this happened before most teachers had used the software.

The initial storm died down. Blanket 'bans' were quietly reversed. It was accepted that detection software could not be relied on. There was an acceptance that Generative AI was here to stay and the focus should be on guidance, disclosure and experimentation. But the conversation continued. In May 2023 UNESCO convened a special meeting of Educational Ministers to discuss the disruptive impact of ChatGPT. Its researchers found that less than 10 percent of schools had guidelines for its use.

J. Morgan (✉)
University of Auckland, Auckland, New Zealand
e-mail: john.morgan@auckland.ac.nz

M. E. Robertson (ed.), *Youth, Identity, AI and Moral Purpose*, Young People and Learning Processes in School and Everyday Life 9,
https://doi.org/10.1007/978-3-032-32479-5_5

We seem to have settled into a steady-state pattern. There are now armies of researchers housed in universities who are exploring the implications of AI for education. There are already systematic reviews which claim to provide an overview of what such research can offer policy-makers and teachers. There is also a growing series of Teacher Guides on how to integrate AI into classrooms.

These are genuine concerns. Generative AI is not the first technological innovation that promised to revolutionise education. But it seems to strike at the very heart of what it means to teach your subject in school. If pupils can simply ask AI to generate answers, what's the role of the teacher? And there's lots of evidence to say that this is what they do. The symbolic economy of schooling rests on the idea that teachers have knowledge, set work and students have to respond. This is agreed: everyone has their role to play. Generative AI threatens to disrupt this balance, where writing is at the centre of the 'ecosystem'. The act of writing and presenting your work is to show evidence of grappling with ideas—its epistemic. Writing is where we figure out what we want to say. Generative AI speeds up this process and makes thinking invisible. Though that make sound 'technical', I think it reveals a deeper cultural anxiety about the extent to which teaching and teachers might themselves become replaceable. This, of course, is part of a wider set of concerns about the impact of AI on the world of work.

Teachers' concerns and fears are real and cannot be waved away with a 'don't worry, there'll will always be a role for you'. We can be more concrete. AI generates answers but does not pose meaningful problems. It cannot assess students thinking on the ground. And it cannot make learning social and public. There will always be a role for teachers, providing digital rationality does not replace discursive rationality. Han (2022) explains: "Artificial intelligence does not reason; it computes. In place of arguments, there are algorithms. In the course of the discursive process, arguments can be improved. In the course of the computing process, algorithms are constantly optimized". As long as we, as teachers—as educators—are prepared to keep discursive rationality alive, then AI will not 'take over'. More directly, robots will never be as clever as humans, but humans could become as dumb as robots.

All this is a way of stating something that is easily forgotten: despite the fantasies and fears of science-fiction, machines do not have consciousness. In education, as usual, there is a battle between the optimists and pessimists. For example, in *Brave New Words* Salman Khan (2024) -who in the 2000s set up the Khan Academy—described how his teaching has been transformed by the generative AI he produced (and even named after himself)—Khaningo. Bill Gates reviewed the book (https://www.gatesnotes.com/brave-new-words) and concluded: "AI will radically improve both student outcomes and teacher experiences, and help usher in a future where everyone has access to a world-class education". Others are less sure. Bill Cope and Mary Kalantzis (2024) note that the initial concern has been about 'cheating' but suggest another six 'fundamental and endemic problems' that make Generative AI unsuitable for education:

1. Truth—Generative AI cannot tell fact from fake

2. Sources—AI won't say and can't say where it gets its ideas, and often invents references
3. Disciplines—AI has no understanding of how human knowledge is made
4. Offensive and dangerous—there are plenty of cases where suspect views and opinions creep into the answers generated by AI
5. Pretends to be human—in an education system that prides itself on its humanity, the reliance of machine thinking seems all wrong
6. Stealing intellectual property and invading privacy.

These problems are fundamental, although none will stop the march of AI. Cope and Kalantzis worry that these undermine many of education's basic principles and erode the foundation required for 'the establishment and maintenance of reliable knowledge systems'. There is also the question of the relationship between human learning and machine learning. The last century saw advances in understanding the process of learning, most importantly the shift from behaviourism to constructivism. Machinic learning seems to have led to a revival of behaviourism.

There is 'evidence' building up which purports to tell teachers what to do with AI in classrooms. For example, my inbox today linked me to a paper which reported that 'teachers who use AI regularly are able to spot AI-generated student essays' and another advised me on how to 'construct AI-proof authentic assessments'. It is easy to get swept away by the tsunami of advice. However, what interests me here is *why much of this educational discussion of AI remains silent about the political economy of AI*. When OpenAI introduced the ChatGPT website, Microsoft had set aside 10 billion (USD) to develop AI. Other leading corporations followed. We are in the early hype stage of AI, like the internet and interactive tv. We are told it will transform everything, though the *Economist* recently reported that the take up of AI by US businesses in 2025 stands at just 5%. For the big firms (Amazon, Apple, Facebook, IBM, Google and Microsoft) who are driving its development, AI holds the promise of control over the 'means of cognition'. The replacement of (some) human labour by machines is a dream because it would solve the major antagonism—between capital and labour—that bedevils capitalist economies.

This ought to be the starting point for any discussion of AI in education, and the lack of attention to political economy is ideological. Why should the argument that generative AI is an invention owned and driven by capital for the purposes of increasing profits, and the versions found in schools and classrooms are provided by commercial interests be met with a shrug, as if to say, 'yes, we know, but what can we do about it?' After five decades, it has become natural and unremarkable that schools should be open to educational technology. The social, cultural and ecological impacts are too often 'bracketed off', too big to contemplate in the ongoing 'dash for IT'.

This chapter puts the political economy of educational technology at the heart of the discussion. In what follows, I use a mixture of personal experience and academic analysis to narrate the development of IT to EdTech. We cannot understand the take up and use of educational technology unless we understand the changing nature of capitalist schooling.

5.2 Chips with Everything

On March 30, 1978, the BBC showed a documentary called *Now the chips are down.* I remember it because I was 12 years old and my parents allowed me to stay up after the 9 o'clock 'watershed' to watch. At school the next day our teacher talked to us about it, presumably because it told us something about our futures.

I recently showed my class of beginning teachers the film. It starts with two examples of how computers are changing everyday life: "A computer will read to a person", and "A man will talk to a computer and the computer will obey". The first few minutes of the documentary explain that it is the silicon chip that makes this possible, and that it's the reason Japan is out-competing us and why 'our children will grow up without jobs'. At this point, students laugh. I think for two reasons. First, to young people with smartphones in their pockets, the examples used seem like primitive tools. Second, because the 'jobless future' didn't happen (and this should make us think carefully when we hear that AI is about to make most of us redundant).

In class, we discuss the idea that technology in education and society is never a matter of hardware but always linked to cultural and political imaginaries. At the time, *Now the chips are down* was a significant event. The UK Cabinet was invited to a special viewing. There was widespread concern about the loss of jobs. The main question seemed to be about the lack of government investment in these new technologies. The falling cost of chips was indicated by calculators, digital watches and alarm clocks, and TV games. This was not simply the next step in the technological development but an 'information revolution' that would usher in the 'information society'. This seemed to be another example of the 'British Disease' of lack of foresight and innovation.

The result of this argument was a firm and early commitment to bring IT into schools. Since the mid-1970s governments had expressed the view that schools were not preparing school leavers for the real world of work. The curriculum was now something that governments were taking a close eye on to meet employers' needs, and the government-sponsored Schools Council promoted projects that developed partnerships between schools and industry.

These arguments filtered into the everyday work of teachers. In 1987, I was a student teacher in a large comprehensive school on the outskirts of Swansea (UK). Swansea was a port on the edge of the south Wales coalfield, and in the nineteenth century, the Lower and Upper Swansea valleys were a site of metal manufacturing and engineering. After World War II its economy diversified, especially through welfare activities such as health and education. But by the early 1980s it was suffering deindustrialisation, and unemployment was high. The future for school leavers would look very different, and the school was trying to respond to these changes by modernising its curriculum.

One of the growth subjects was Economics and Business Studies. The teacher was young and dressed sharply. His was the only classroom which had a computer. Elsewhere, boys did the traditional subjects like woodwork and metalwork, while girls did commerce and typing. This gendered division of labour had suited the job market. But the economy was changing. Teachers, parents and students recognised that the traditional transitions from school to adulthood were being reshaped, and technology was part of this. This became even clearer when, in 1988, I took up my first teaching post at a girls' school in south London. Here the curriculum division was between the traditional curriculum, dominated by the Sciences and Humanities. Into this was a new initiative set up by the government to try to develop skills-based education based around the 'needs of industry'. There were also schemes to get Girls into Science and Technology (GIST)—based on a vision of a changing world of work.

Computers were not much in evidence at these schools, but they were part of the developing story about Information Technology or 'IT', as it was rebranded. The widespread fear that people would lose their jobs to the new silicon chip computers gave way, by the mid-1980s, to an alternative story about 'sunrise' industries which would require workers equipped with the IT skills to contribute to a post-industrial society. Getting computers into schools was seen as a way of modernising them and meeting students' needs at a time of significant change.

This account stresses how technology is never simply about 'hardware'. In *The technical fix,* Robins and Webster (1989) argued that the real significance of the 'computer revolution' was revealed not simply by looking at the use of new technologies in the classroom, but by relating the 'microworld' of the classroom to the economic, technological, industrial and social transformations associated with the shift to a 'neo-Fordist' system. The aim was to ensure that the education system adapted to and reinforced new ways of creating wealth. The overall purpose was to construct a new social consensus based on the image of a new model worker/pupil who would be able to play as part of the team, be flexible and responsive and have the desire to 'learn how to learn'.

Progressive approaches to education that were about the cultivation of the authentic self were to be replaced with 'instrumental progressivism' aimed at the making of a 'cyborg self'. These models of the information age came out of cybernetics. In *America*, Baudrillard (1988) asks his readers to think about the child sitting at the computer at school: "Do you think he has been made more interactive, opened up to the world? Child and machine have merely been joined together in an integrated circuit". As I will argue, this is a question that remains at the heart of techno-capitalist schooling.

5.3 The Long 1990s

In the 1990s it became clear that Thatcherism was a reaction to much deeper changes in how capitalism operated. The collapse of the Soviet Union and the opening of the Iron Curtain may not have signalled 'the end of history', but we accepted we were living in 'new times'. In the advanced Western economies, the Fordist political settlement which had emerged out of the crisis of capitalism in the 1930s and which had dominated the post-war decades had come apart and there was the prospect of an alternative post-Fordist settlement.

Whether this was termed 'late capitalism', 'disorganized capitalism' or the 'entrepreneurial state' or the Schumpeterian workfare state, the common emphasis was on flexibility, innovation and designing policy with a more networked set of actors. In political terms it took the form of 'the Third Way', part of a wider cultural shift which reflected the emergence of identity politics and new social movements. State workers (including teachers) were now more 'client-centred' (or customer-focused) and their services 'personalized'. All this was part of the ideological shift away from state to market.

These political shifts were enabled by technology and the technological imagination. In the 1990s there was talk of the 'information superhighway'. This was a product of the Clinton-Gore era. The idea of the state, in collaboration with private corporations, laying the foundations (or cables) for a new era of economic growth, was appealing. In the end it was the internet, a technology that had been around for at least two decades that provided the basis for the new digital capitalism, branded as the World Wide Web.

Education was re-imagined. The decades-long focus on equality and opportunity shifted to choice and competitiveness. A new class of school leaders would ensure that quality was raised and standards maintained. What is striking is how much of the discussion at the time focused on 'learning', to the extent that you wondered what schools and teachers had been doing before. Books appeared with titles like *It's about learning (and its about time)* (Stoll et al., 2003) *The mosaic of learning* (Hargreaves, 1994) and, *The learning game* (Barber, 1997). The idea that we were now part of the learning society was reflected in policy documents of the time.

On the day I arrived for interview for a post at the University of Bristol in June 2000, there was much excitement in the School of Education as it was announced that the School had been awarded two prestigious external grants. One of these was called Interactive Education. It was all about the ways in which ICT could be incorporated into school subjects. Soon after, in an old warehouse on the regenerating dockside, a new educational start-up—Futurelab—was established by Nesta (the UK National Endowment for Science, Technology and the Arts) and Chaired by Sir David Puttnam. It practised a new mode of knowledge production. Compared to the 'ivory tower' just up the hill, Futurelab was able to 'pivot' to respond to changing policy agendas and produced high-quality commercial white papers and reports that reached a wide audience of industry experts, researchers, policy-makers and schools—the whole education and technology ecosystem. I was seconded to Futurelab in 2006 to work on a project funded by Microsoft as part of its Partners in Learning programme.

Futurelab sought to provide practical and workable examples of how ICT could offer radically different approaches to learning, teaching, and curriculum. It was a way of breaking into the curriculum and allowing access to those who were excluded from formal schooling. This would secure their futures in the age of the Internet or the knowledge age. Thus we could: (1) abandon the persistent non-negotiability of the fragmented, discipline-based curriculum; (2) place greater responsibility for the content and direction of learning in the hands of students; (3) reconceptualise the teacher's role away from transmitter of skills and knowledge to co-construct knowledge; and (4) emphasise learning as opposed to knowledge acquisition.

McFarlane (2006)—an academic who sat on Futurelab's executive—summarised the claim that ICT had the potential to transform schooling. She noted that how we know is changed in the knowledge age. As a result of this there are widespread calls for the education system to change in order to prepare student learners for knowledge economy. Knowledge 'is something to be worked on and not an entity to be passively consumed or even individually constructed'. Looking back, what is striking is how readily it was accepted that we now live in the 'Age of the Internet' or the 'knowledge age'. While such comments are still heard, we are less likely to accept them at face value.

But those were optimistic times. Capitalism had bounced back. The great ideological battle between capitalism and communism had been won. One billion Chinese workers joined the global labour force, in the advanced economies, the restructuring of global production chains and new information and communications technologies allowed a boom of economic growth. A new class of tech-billionaires who were feted and celebrated emerged. The idea of the market and its freedoms were celebrated in the liberal press.

Taking their cue about new times, leading-edge educationalists stressed the 'affordances' of the new technologies. These 'Silicon literacies' emanated from the new cyberspaces of digital capitalism. They dovetailed with arguments about the creative economy and creative class. The apotheosis of this era for me was a seminar at Bristol in 2007 led by the US educator James Paul Gee (2003). To a packed audience of academics, students and cutting-edge teachers, Gee's assistant played the best-selling game *Call of Duty*—a first-person shooter video game about war, combat and military operations—while he commentated on how the game play illustrated the principles of learning. Putting aside any concerns the audience had about violence, the ideology of militarism, and the vast profits earned by its publishers, Gee sought to convince us that game-playing was a form of Sim capital that game players could make use of in the 'real world'.

Futurelab walked a thin line between techno-optimism and more grounded assessments of what was possible. Some days felt like an episode of 'Dragon's Den', as young tech-savvy inventors filed in to showcase a piece of 'kit' they were keen to get adopted. But on other days there was acute awareness of how the boundaries between adults and children were being reconstituted and the role that digital technologies played in this. In an interesting retrospective, Futurelab's chief researcher Facer (2014) described the politics around this: both over the concerns about children's access to unsavoury material and the commercialisation of childhood, and the different pedagogical uses—some creative and expansive, others not—to which educational technology could be put to use in schools. Facer predicted that childhood and young people's lives would increasingly become a contested space around digital technologies and surveillance.

5.4 The Dark Ages

As I write this chapter in Auckland, New Zealand, the debates that we had at Futurelab seem to belong to a whole other world. This is not just geographical distance. We now live in a world which is more sceptical about the 'affordances' of educational technology. Gilbert (2020) expresses this well:

> …as the 20th century drew to a close, it was possible for almost all those who were working in fields such as new media and information technology to see themselves as surfing the same revolutionary wave… Now we know where it was heading. It was heading towards a place in which a tiny number of techno-capitalists would get incredibly, unbelievably rich, while life for most other people would get much harder. It was heading to a place in which a handful of enormous corporations-Google, Facebook, Amazon, YouTube, Apple-would come to dominate global culture, accumulating billions as they turned the Internet into a far more homogenous plate space but it was once supposed to be.… Welcome to the world of platform capitalism. (p. 80)

Only 15 years ago critical educators could be upbeat about the possibilities of using the new digital literacies to bring develop a socialistic consciousness. For example, Suoranta and Vaden (2010) argued that the wiki world would 'advance people's autonomy, self-government and actual freedom". The "Wikiworld' was an empowering social construction with the potential to abolish the distinction between the rulers and the ruled. In this Brave New World, education digital media bring with them a new ethos of participation, collaboration and cooperation. We are, it was suggested, moving towards a progressive transformation from institutionalised and individualised forms of learning to open learning and social collaboration.

These critical pedagogues argued for the socialist potential of the digital media. Things have taken a different, less liberatory direction. In Marxist terms, we might say it's the total subsumption of labour by capital—more and more of our everyday lifeworld have been colonised by digital media. This is reflected in a genre of critical writing about the role of technology is post-economic crash era. For example, in The *New Dark Age*, Bridle (2018) argues that modern technology, instead of clarifying the world, deepens confusion. Information overload, opaque algorithms and digital infrastructure contribute to misinformation, climate change and a loss of human agency. Increasingly, we are unaware of the ways in which our lives are governed and constrained by technologies. As Greenfield (2017) shows in *Radical Technologies*, emerging technologies—like AI, blockchain, and the Internet of Things (IoT)—are reshaping society. While promising innovation, they also threaten privacy, labour and democracy. He urges us to question who benefits from these tools and how they alter our lives and values. Our widespread reliance on the network to accomplish our ordinary goals is linked to a manufactured faith in technology to come up with solutions to life's problems. For example, using a health app to tell us when to exercise or monitoring our water intake. Such 'solutionism' which holds that oversimplifies complex issues and promotes blind faith in digital fixes, often replacing deeper ethical reflection about tech-driven futures.

All this before we get to concerns about the role that data play in the surveillance and monitoring of populations. Zuboff (2019) introduces the idea of "surveillance capitalism," where tech companies harvest personal data to predict and influence behaviour for profit. This commodification of human experience threatens privacy, autonomy, and democracy.

In *The mediated construction of reality*, Couldry and Hepp (2017) draw on Berger and Luckmann's (1966) famous claim about 'the social construction of reality' to emphasise how media including social media provide the constitutive framework for how we live our lives—what they call a 'materialist phenomenology'. Digital media makes the social worlds we inhabit, and the performance of the self increasingly requires participating in the culture of connectivity. Once this data is gathered it provides the basis for extraction in the form of a 'data grab'. This is a form of new colonialism.

Of course, there are ways in which technology enables new ways of experiencing the world, but critical scholars urge us to see the driving forces that produce the new reality. Wark (2019) argued that 'capital is dead', but what is coming is much worse. That claim is made because platform capital seems to have given up 'making stuff' and instead is content to reap the 'rents' that build up as we all log on and disclose our details on social media apps. Indeed, Varoufakis (2023) argues that capitalism has been replaced by a new system he calls 'technofeudalism', where tech giants act like digital feudal lords. Instead of producing goods, they control digital platforms that shape behaviour, extract data, and bypass traditional markets. This "cloud capital" turns users into unpaid labourers and consumers into subjects of algorithmic control, concentrating power and wealth in unprecedented ways.

To return to Gilbert's comment at the head of this section; he is clear that the only way these technologies can be turned to productive and socialised goals is through a struggle for ownership.

5.5 The Next Big Thing

Cassidy (2025), in his survey of economic opposition to capitalism from the Industrial Revolution to the present, titles his final chapter "the end of capitalism, or the beginning?". He references Brynjolfsson and McAfees's (2014) argument that in the second machine age: "the key building blocks already in place with digital technologies to be as important and transformational to society and the economy as the steam engine". The steam engine was a general purpose technology one which has the potential to transform the entire economy. Brynjolfsson and McAfee argue that AI could turn out to be the most powerful general purpose technology. In response to the question 'is growth over? they state: "not a chance, it is just being held back by our inability to process all the new ideas fast enough".

I keep thinking back to that morning in 1978, when my teacher, on his drive to work, decided he needed to talk to us about the BBC documentary he had watched the night before. It obviously felt important. I can't remember the conversation (though I am sure we would have argued with him), but I wonder if it was about the need to make us work harder, to warn us of trouble ahead, or some thinking about how capitalism was changing, it is salutary to think thing that almost half-a-century later, capital is still seeking to resolve its crises through technological solutions. As educators, we need to talk about capitalism.

References

Baudrillard, J. (1988). *America* (C. Turner, Trans.). Verso. (Original work published 1986).

Barber, M. (1997). *The learning game: Arguments for an education revolution.* Indigo.

Berger, P., & Luckmann, T. (1966). *The social construction of reality*. Doubleday.

Bridle, J. (2018). *New dark age: Technology and the end of the future.* Verso.

Brynjolfsson, E., & McAfee, A. (2014). *The second machine age: Work, progress, and prosperity in a time of brilliant technologies.* W. W. Norton & Company.

Cassidy, J. (2025). *Capitalism and its critics: A history from the industrial revolution to AI*. Farrar.

Cope, B., & Kalantzis, M., et al. (2024). On cyber-social learning: A critique of artificial intelligence in education. In D. Kourkoulou (Ed.), *Trust and inclusion in AI-mediated education* (pp. 3–34). Springer.

Couldry, N., & Hepp, A. (2017). *The mediated construction of reality*. Polity Press.

Facer, K. (2014). The politics of childhood and technology. In S. Wagg & J. Pilcher (Eds.), *Thatcher's grandchildren? Politics and childhood in the twenty-first century* (pp. 207–223). Palgrave Macmillan.

Gates, B. (2024). Sal Khan is pioneering innovation in education…again. GatesNotes. 22nd May 2024. Sal Khan's Must-Read Book on AI and Education | Bill Gates

Gee, J. P. (2003). *What video games have to teach us about learning and literacy*. Palgrave Macmillan.

Gilbert, J. (2020). *Twenty-first century socialism*. Polity Press.

Greenfield, A. (2017). *Radical technologies: The design of everyday life.* Verso.

Han, B.-C. (2022). *Infocracy: Digitalization and the crisis of democracy*. Polity.

Hargreaves, D. H. (1994). *The mosaic of learning: Schools and teachers for the next century.* Demos.

Khan, S. (2024). *Brave new words: How AI will revolutionize education (and why that's a good thing).* Penguin Press.

McFarlane, A. (2006). ICT and the curriculum canon. In A. Moore (Ed.), *Schooling, society and curriculum* (pp. 149–163). Routledge.

Morozov, E. (2013). *To save everything, click here: The folly of technological solutionism.* PublicAffairs.

Robins, K., & Webster, F. (1989). *The technical fix: Education, computers and industry.* Palgrave Macmillan.

Stoll, L., Fink, D., & Earl, L. (2003). *It's about learning (and it's about time): What's in it for schools?* Routledge.

Suoranta, J., & Vadén, T. (2010). *Wikiworld*. Pluto Press.

Varoufakis, Y. (2023). *Technofeudalism: What killed capitalism.* Bodley Head.

Wark, M. (2019). *Capital is dead: Is this something worse?* Verso.

Zuboff, S. (2019). *The age of surveillance capitalism: The fight for a human future at the new frontier of power.* PublicAffairs.

John Morgan taught geography in schools in London before moving into teacher education, where he led Geography Education at the University of Bristol. He has worked at Futurelab and UCL (London), and is currently Head of the School of Critical Studies in Education at the University of Auckland.

Chapter 6
Myths and Fables: The Powers of the Unconscious Versus AI

Margaret E. Robertson

Abstract How we come to know is one of the mysteries of human existence. We tend to assume that our past is reflected in our inherited beliefs. Based on this premise the stories of our elders can be considered clues to how young people behave and react. All cultures have their traditions and customs. Passed on through the generations the essence of identity linked with a community of trusted others provides a tangible legacy through behavioural rituals, aesthetics, music, dance and language. Signs take many forms. They connect us with our global being in space and place. The question is to what extent our inheritance is being eroded by a proposed singularity of being hosted by other realities notably Artificial Intelligence.

Keywords Subjectivity · Nature · Archetypes · Tattoos · Algorithms

6.1 Introduction

Romanticism

Late autumn in the orange-bronze ranges
And the sky still wet with slaughter, the vote
Done, dying goldenrod tuning the meadows
Beige under flocks of birds that flex the air
Into one black v after another,
Carrying with them the occasional
Silence that flight coaxes from the chest, throat,
And mind, coaxes from altitude's blue view
To me, though the bright air, no matter how
Clear, is viscous with the virus, not dew:
It comes and goes like the heat of the sun,

M. E. Robertson (✉)
La Trobe University, Melbourne, Australia
e-mail: m.robertson@latrobe.edu.au

M. E. Robertson (ed.), *Youth, Identity, AI and Moral Purpose*, Young People and Learning Processes in School and Everyday Life 9,
https://doi.org/10.1007/978-3-032-32479-5_6

A heavy haze of grand-scale indifference
To the mazy motion of the river
That bends away from the small town nearby
As I raise my window for one final
Song of summer to leap into my room
And chant to my well-funded memory
When the window is shut tight and the cold
Burns as I press my nose against the glass
For one brief glimpse of god in this world,
What moves in the far-off fade-spectrum
Of the wattage as daylight grows dimmer
And that feeling that comes and goes, what is it?
I have asked myself again and again
And I want to tell you that it's something
Else, something new, a cure for this world, so
I do and then I don't and then I do

Rowan Ricardo Phillips (2021)

Writers of the nineteenth century who aligned themselves with romanticism were regarded as being reactionary to the rational science movement of the Enlightenment. Theirs was a view that connected emotion with nature. Subjectivity, imagination and aesthetics underpinned an epistemological approach that rejected reductionism and placed emphasis on the connections between humans and nature. Notable intellectuals who made discoveries in support of this theory were Goethe and Alexander Von Humboldt. Both of German descent as great friends and collaborators their experiments affirmed a commitment to the importance of the relationship between life and nature. Wulf (2015) explains of their theory: "To put it simply, a machine could be dismantled and then assembled again, while the parts of a living organism worked only in relation to each other" (p. 32). These great polymaths were puzzled by the relationships between nature, life and the imagination. Both were scientists and committed to empirical research. However, their meticulous observations of nature including biology, geological morphology and commitment to art and literature was cause to reject the deductive reasoning approach of Descartes and others. Within the European awakening of great thinkers and travellers willing to share ideas and exchange knowledge theirs was a schism in intellectual knowing from Cartesian theory and earlier directions of the Enlightenment. Ontological knowing based on the separation of mind and matter was rejected in favour of inductive reasoning based on observations. Thus, in their approach science and the scientific approach assumes connections and relationships with and between phenomena. Comparisons help to explain nature "not abstract mathematics or numbers" (Wulf, 2015, p. 32). The last line of Phillips' poem (2021) '*I do and then I don't and then I do*' seems to express his uncertainty about acceptance or closure. As if to admit that the life dynamic creates a subjective link between the self and its surroundings. Its mystery remains as a puzzle with each unfolding turn of civilisation which seems all the more relevant within the context of the AI dynamic.

Some two hundred years on, recent publications illustrate the enduring legacies of Johann Wolfgang von Goethe (1749–1832) and Alexander Von Humboldt (1769–1859) along with their continuing interest for scholars. In both their university locations in Jena and Weimar their correspondence shows they spent long periods in conversation together with Friedrich Schiller (1759–1805) and no doubt used their shared time to refine and question their theories. Buttimer's (2001) review of their scientific differences summarises their scientific perspectives.

> Humboldtian Science emphasized objectivity and rigour in measurement and eventual generalization of results, while Goethe's way emphasized careful attunement to the observation process itself, and the inevitable subjectivity in human perception and understanding. Elements of both approaches are evident in the work of Humboldt. But there are aesthetic and experience-based facets of his overall vision which enable the work to transcend tensions between objectivity and subjectivity, macro-scale survey and micro-scale theatre, scientific explanation and artistic representation. (p. 105)

Inspired by the vitality and intellect of Humboldt, Goethe's renewed interest in science became part of his literary writings. In his play *Faust* Wulf (2015) interprets the character of Heindrich Faust as a 'restless scholar' like Humboldt and "driven by a relentless striving for knowledge" (p. 37). Conversely, Goethe's literary works inspired Humboldt to understand nature from within the self. "Goethe's descriptions of nature in his plays, novels and poems were as truthful, Humboldt believed, as the discoveries of the best scientists" (Wulf, ibid, p. 38).

Their collaboration took place amid a prevailing western view that "Humankind would make nature better through cultivation" (Wulf, ibid, p. 59). Later Humboldt set forth to travel afar noting that perceptual orderliness of landscapes to be the aesthetic which carried over to the 'New World'. The colonisers of the Americas viewed the new lands as wild landscapes in need of taming and sought to transform the landscape. Land clearing, cultivation of imported crops and alien animal farming practices were introduced. His travels took him to places in the Americas where he witnessed firsthand the devastation that could happen when nature is irrevocably impacted. Deforestation and colonial plantations he linked with erosion and soil degradation leading to changes in precipitation. They confirmed his view that human interference can result in climate change. Humboldt warned "humankind needed to understand how the forces of nature worked, how these different threads were connected" (Wulf, ibid, p. 60). A visionary who connected with other remarkable thinkers including the younger Charles Darwin, Humboldt advocated for the vulnerability of nature. Described as his opus of life and written in the latter stages of his life Humboldt's multi-volume book *Cosmos* became a best seller. Stressing the importance of interactions in nature "The eye, Humboldt wrote, was the organ of 'Weltanschauung', the organ through which we view the world but also through which we interpret, understand and define it" (Wulf, 2015, p. 248). Regarding climate he differed from the scientific view that "focussed on meteorological data such as temperature and weather. Humboldt was the first to understand climate as a system of complex interrelationships between the atmosphere, oceans and landmasses" (ibid p. 246). Imagination and knowledge he viewed as intertwined and nature as a 'web of life'.

In the twenty-first century humankind seems more certain about the impact of their activities on nature including the vulnerability of the Anthropocene. The renewed interest in this group of scholars and their intellectual wisdom is not surprising and helps to draw attention to the need of a new generation of scholars with ideas who can muddle through the hegemonic power blocks to reasoned action that connects observed data with reality in the present. Buttimer's (2001) quotation from Humboldt's *Essay*[1] published in 1805 captures both the complexity and optimism on offer in the web of nature as well as advice for current leaders.

> It is thus that the lights of civilisation can bring the greatest pleasure to us as individuals: they enable us to live in past and present; they assemble around us all that nature has produced in different climates, and places us in contact with all people on earth. On the strength of discoveries already made, we can launch ourselves into the future and, foreseeing the consequences of [natural] processes, establish forever the laws to which nature subjects itself. Involvement in such research affords that intellectual delight, that moral freedom which fortifies us against the blows of destiny, and against which no external power could prevail (p. 119)

Being satisfied with our lifestyles does not appear to belong to the human condition. How far we can progress our lives must have boundaries as nature and natural disasters such as volcanic eruptions, rising seas and air temperatures reminds us. At the same time, humans need some shared language to survive and face their futures with optimism and hope. Aesthetics, the arts and beauty are all sources of inspiration for life's decisions and seem to explain many of the pursuits of the great explorers. Like Goethe and Humboldt some of our heroes live on through the publications and institutions which honour their names. However, there are other influences which persist in the minds of humans which in many ways have become counter cultures based on myths and more elusive aesthetics.

6.2 'Mythomania'

In many ways the tension observed between the literary bias of Goethe and scientific observer bias of Humboldt signifies the differences between the psychological and social sides of humanity (Smelser, 1983/84). Taking the argument forward could follow Freudian or Jungian theory or link more closely with political theory including Marxism—all of which had origins which roughly follow the active periods of the noted scholars. Intellectual pathways of the nineteenth and early twentieth centuries were being shaped by historical events which link with current geopolitical identities. At this point, this chapter could get lost in relevant accounts of local narratives which explain cultural differences and approaches to knowledge acquisition and education. Each could highlight beliefs based on inherited myths and attitudes and help explain

[1] See Humboldt, A. von (1805): Essai sur la geographie des plan tes, accompagne d'un tableau physique des regions equi noxiales, fonde sur les mesures executees, depuis le dixieme degre de latitude boreale jusqu'au dixieme degre de lati tude australe, pendant les annees 1799, 1800, 1801, 1802, et 1903 par A. de Humboldt et A. Bonpland. Sherborn Fund Fascimile No. 1, Paris.

current tensions in global politics between nations. A sense of 'who am I' must surely be connected with our physical homeland, the place with which we are most familiar and navigate during our waking hours. Our lived experiences within that place undoubtedly shape our perceptual gaze as humans and influence our daily routines, including food, and dress choices, interests, likes and dislikes. As Conrad (2016) notes: "Existence is random, chancy and perilous; we need a sense of purpose, a destiny and a destination" and "myths gave us our bearings, and made us feel at home in the world" (p. 9).

Fastrack to the present and add digital connectivity including AI to the landscape we have a global web of networking which in one sense has little and everything to do with nature and local geography. Unless blocked by governments social media platforms bypass regulatory frameworks and give access for criminals to vulnerable people of all ages across the globe. Scammers are a sickening product of the affordances of international person to person communication and uncovering cybercriminal networks is a major challenge for governments and management of information and education of citizens. The digitised tools within the hands of bad people are a dangerous weapon and how to protect families and individuals is complex. Citizen naivety versus full disclosure requires a delicate balancing act by authorities. Invested with powers to protect and keep safe local communities while not destroying individual freedoms is difficult to achieve without alienating more extreme and dedicated bloggers. A recent BBC investigative team has helped expose for the public the extent of the problem.[2] A teenage boy's suicide after persistent social media requests for explicit photographs followed up by blackmail requests for money was traced to Nigeria. Investigators uncovered trained youths working methodically and to a plan to scam for money. When questioned the responses from the interviewed scammers revealed no remorse related to the suicide of one of their victims justified in their view by references to the monetary wealth of those they scammed versus their apparent personal poverty. The wealth versus poverty difference is both a reality and myth. Many of the victims of online scams can fall for the predator and lose any wealth they may have had. The Global Anti-Scam Alliance, for example, reported nearly "$1.026 Trillion was lost by consumers worldwide in 2024 through scams…Scammers, can go free because they can operate globally, [via encrypted dark web sites] while law enforcement operates locally, regionally, or nationally".[3]

There is a certain irony here. In some ways the perpetrators of cybercrime, fraud and anti-social acts of violence are more visible nowadays. Social media and streamed reporting bring the latest to our mobile devices in a continual information flow. In other ways, the drivers behind the acts seem linked to primordial instincts for the trappings of a better life or material wealth. Assuming we inherit these desires, and they help govern our activities the questions to be asked are when and why do individuals, and notably young people, cross the line and become anti-social and how can authorities contain their impulses through education and refocussing deviance. The Nigerian case study suggests two noteworthy facts. First, an affirmation of the

[2] See online at https://tvtonight.com.au/2025/10/four-corners-oct-20-2.

[3] See online at https://www.gasa.org/.

connection between money, possessions and a better life. We are as Barthes (2000) noted essentially a bourgeois society. Second, the capabilities of individuals to learn. This predatory based 'mythomania' has become a global phenomenon which is challenging traditional power bases and violating the privacy of citizens often far removed from the perpetrators. Finding pathways that suit the skills and abilities of the cohort as well as fulfilling their interests is the challenge for authorities. It ought not to be unfathomable.

Moving forward within the world of now requires skills and agility. The first step involves accepting the problem and then better understanding the social landscape and the language of the day. The latter is best approached with a slight step back to consider meaning attached to myths and later in the chapter how fables differ from myths and can be utilised for pedagogical solutions to the social dynamics of AI as they unfold.

6.3 Myths

According to Barthes (2000), a myth is a type of speech. It is a message conveyed through communication. "Not an object, a concept, or an idea; it is a mode of signification, a form" (p. 93). Myth, he states, "belongs to the province of a general science, coextensive with linguistics, which is semiology" (p. 95). Saussure's late nineteenth-century writings are considered to have introduced the concept of semiology as the science of signs and their connection with social systems, forms and expressions. They may take form in street signs and signals, and transport systems or myths associated with must have luxury cars or latest iPhone, or for collectors of silver the lion signifier of sterling silver used by silversmiths since the sixteenth century. At a deeper symbolic level, the signs involve linguistics. Not to be confused with psychology which studies the mind and cognitive behaviours of the person. The connection is with structuralism or the search for the system which explains the underlying connections between language elements. In Barthe's analysis myth is an element in what he describes as a 'trans-linguistics' (1964). "In myth we find the tri-dimensional pattern …the signifier, the signified and the sign" (p. 99) observed in the semiology system. The metaphor he uses refers to a bunch of roses to represent passion or act as the signifier and the signified which combine as the object to become the sign. Next, consider the myth which takes the dead leaves, or photograph, poster, etc. as signifying a 'global sign'. To conclude then what might appear spoken as a 'proverb' expressed through active speech may reflect the myth. Barthes concedes that "every myth can have its history and its geography" (2000, p. 139). There is a social geography of myths as well as an immutable home or place with which they are connected. It suggests the sociological force of myth in reconciling the past with reality. Barthes (2000) concludes we must seek 'a reconciliation between description and explanation, between object and knowledge':

> The fact that we cannot manage to achieve more than an unstable grasp of reality doubtless gives the measure of our present alienation: we constantly drift between the object of its demystification, powerless, to render its wholeness. For if we penetrate the object, we liberate it but we destroy it; and if we acknowledge its full weight, we respect it, but we restore it to a state which is still mystified. (p. 149)

The mythological process nevertheless provides us with a strength or framework for decisions which may have ethical and moral virtue and equally project images of objects and lifestyles we want but lack the skills and resources to attain. The constant bombardment of colourful images, packaging, 'bargain' advertising and journalistic reporting contribute to the reinforcement of local myths. Myths capture the ancient wisdom of our past with or without emotion. They "abolish the complexity of human acts, it gives them the simplicity of essences, it does away with all dialectics…it organises a world without contradictions because it is without depth…things appear to mean something by themselves" (Barthes, 2000, p. 132). Myths do not simply function as relics of the past; rather, they are continuously reinterpreted and woven into the fabric of modern identity. The enduring power of myth lies in its ability to offer frameworks for understanding a rapidly changing world. In this sense, mythology acts as a bridge between collective memory and the realities of contemporary existence, shaping cultural values and influencing individual choices.

Within the time moment myths that capture the essence of our societal antecedents can appear immutable because of their depoliticised semiology. They 'naturalise' societal values and explain power structures within contemporary society or serve as an etymology of the conscious experience. In ancient times, for instance, there was a view of a hollow earth beneath the surface. This myth survives within the belief systems of many contemporary religions. For instance, the Christian hell, and Greek caverns among many variations across cultures and locations. In Barthe's time as a 1950s French philosopher the context was nature and the geography of the rural and urban habitats. Moral and ethical values of the collective society were learnt at home, school, religious gatherings and local sports clubs. Nowadays, the place where we 'live' is the internet (Conrad, 2016). Facebook and its successors have digitised the world in which we navigate our daily lives and now provide the reference points for fabricating decision making and social interactions. Marrying the new with the old, social media have become the vessels or mediums of both ancient and emerging myths. This hegemonic communication shift is powerful in its outreach globally. Critically, the invisible dimension of contemporary social interactions is redefining privacy and enabling operating platforms for anti-social networking and cultural transmission of negative values. The mythological balance of good and evil learnt through traditional modes is threatened by the singularity of authority which can bypass public scrutiny. The bigger question to be asked is to what extent are they shaping, if at all, the algorithms of AI and more particularly GenAI.

6.4 Tattoo Culture and Self-authority

Illustrative of cultural singularity and self-acclaimed personal authority over bodily decisions is the tattoo culture now widely prevalent and fashionable among all ages and genders. Evidence is that tattooing has been around since ancient times. Many indigenous cultures have long standing traditions of tattoos with strong cultural significance. While traces have always existed in Western cultures the connection during the twentieth century was mainly associated with sailors returning from voyages to distant locations including the Pacific cultures and American Indians. The exotic nature of tattoos held some appeal for the upper classes but was most likely connected to gang cultures and criminal groups. However, recent decades have witnessed a significant growth in the tattoo culture globally. New improved techniques make the process more effective, and it appears to have an almost ubiquitous fashion following. Rather than hiding a tattoo for personal pleasure, the tattooing of skin is accepted 'dress' culture. The key element here is that individuals choose the subject of their tattoos and their placement location on their body and the secret language of the tattoo and its meaning are of significance in the context of this chapter's interest in myths and symbolism. Many of the tattoos chosen can be associated with culturally aligned beliefs. One example in tattoo art is the apple most commonly associated with the Christian story of creation and Adam and Eve. Its association is with love and intimacy. Other examples include an image of Dionysus, the god of wine, fertility, festivity and celebration; a set of scales to represent justice, and the zodiac as a source of personal symbolism. The scope of this culture is substantial and important to understand within the context of popular culture and influences around children, their aspirations and developing values (see Aitken-Smith, 2016).

6.5 Jungian Archetypes Updated via AI

It is not the intention of this chapter to delve deeply into the intellectual field of psychology. However, the discussion has highlighted the power of the internet to induce and open the door to paradigmatic shifts in society that enable the emergence of previously suppressed acts, many of which cross the line of moral and ethical virtue. Capturing the history of information technology, Wiley's (2024) analysis demonstrates the growth in the power of AI. Information technology started as a means of problem solving based on handwritten programmes with specific boundaries. Now the technology underlying GenAI has advanced capability that mirrors human consciousness. Not surprisingly, the renewed interest of researchers is in the field of psychology most notably Carl Jung's archetypes. Consider the current realities.

Psychopathy including criminality and vicious acts of behaviour are reflected in the constant streaming of media reporting. Like the opening of Pandora's box from Greek mythology both unexpected and unwanted behaviours have been released into the community. Some critics reflect on these events as tapping the deep cavities of memory. Who are we if not for our memories. They are the basis of our identity. Schama's (1996) marvellously detailed exploration of landscape and memory through history, art and literature asserts the power of the imagination and mythical memory in defining what we experience in nature. Memory governs are actions. In some ways his explorations and travels to distant and unfamiliar places are not a dissimilar journey to that of Humboldt. The messages are clear and culturally embedded. Updating Sharma's argument to include social media suggests the need to reinvent or redefine our myths so that they have a point of connection with the landscapes of now. There is a certain common sense in this perspective. Today's personal landscapes are more likely to have their primary connection with digital algorithms rather than nature elements in our immediate surroundings. Such algorithms are built around subjectivities including LGBTQ identity related as well as ancient dreams of wealth, recognition and success. Memory is a labyrinth of complex connections and possible pathways which prompt the renewed interest in theories of psychoanalysts.

Exploring the connections between collective unconscious and archetypal algorithms identified in technologies, Clapp (2022) maintains that "They are woven into the brain structure of social networking sites and are highly effective in triggering instinctive behaviors that do not involve higher cognition or rational thinking" (p. 115). Noting the advanced tapping into group behaviours by more and more sophisticated algorithms Clapp concludes:

> If Jung were alive today, observing the impact of social media on an individual's ability to resist the group archetype, he would see his theory of mob psychology applies accurately to how algorithms funnel human emotions into a common online experience, triggering mob psychology. (p. 117)

In the most generous of spirits, it is simply naïve to believe that internet algorithms are designed for the common good or act simply as an asset for work and daily live. Consider, workplace reports of the positive effects and usefulness of AI are inherently optimistic and illustrate the power of its functionality to steer both the acts of workers and their outcomes. Quality control and vigorous checking by users ought to be part of the process of using the tool. However, the simplicity of accessing and using AI to perform otherwise lengthy tasks done manually is seductive. Time efficiencies are among the myriad of benefits to be gained from uses of AI within the public domain of the workplace. How easy it must be to press the button for a response from the copilot of AI and not check the outputs prior to releasing the recommendations for associated action.

This is where we need to be mindful of the unconscious triggers which may guide our responses. Adopted from Greek the psyche is the human 'soul' or where the conscious and unconscious elements reside. The human psyche combines tendencies from our past in the form of myths and fantasies along with conscious reactions to the present. In Jung's analysis, our underlying collective responses are influenced in predetermined ways or archetypes:

> The archetype is a symbolic formula which always begins to function when there are no conscious ideas present, or when conscious ideas are inhibited for internal or external reasons.

> The contents of the collective unconscious are represented in consciousness in the form of pronounced preferences and definite ways of looking at things. These subjective tendencies and views are generally regarded by the individual as being determined by the object—incorrectly, since they have their source in the unconscious structure of the psyche and are merely released by the effect of the object. They are stronger than the object's influence, their psychic value is higher, so that they superimpose themselves on all impressions. Thus, just as it seems incomprehensible to the introvert that the object should always be the decisive factor, it remains an enigma to the extravert how a subjective standpoint can be superior to the objective situation. (2017, p. 348)

Historian, Strayer (2025) illustrates the connections between Jungian theory or epistemology of knowledge and how we might interpret the present. He premises his analysis by noting that so much of Jungian writing was mindful of the present circumstances of the times in Nazi Germany. It was as if the enormity of the horrors unfolding within the communities of humankind were enablers of the unconscious tendencies towards 'mass psychology'.

> Like historians whose work comes up against the present and looks to the future, Jung found himself uncertain and ambivalent. On the one hand, he could be pessimistic about human potential, noting the potentially catastrophic impact of the hydrogen bomb and observing that "the gift of reason and critical reflection is not one of man's outstanding peculiarities" (Jung, 1978, para. 489). On the other hand, to Jung, psyche is inherently creative. It constantly generates new images, symbols, and myths, seeks to integrate the fragmented elements of our disjointed personalities, and works toward the freedom of the individuation process. (Strayer, 2025, p.233)

Working with this advice the message seems clear. To develop a pedagogy for the present that will encourage the development of a fully integrated self, there is need to embrace both the present and the human psyche as a complex landscape of both conscious and unconscious elements. Bringing this theory to the present powers of Artificial Intelligence Wiley concludes that (2024):

> A harmonious relationship with AI therefore demands a balanced and conscientious approach, epitomizing Jung's notion of "tension of the opposites." By embracing both the positive potentials and the inherent risks of AI, society can navigate this uncharted territory with greater astuteness—and since the genie is "out of the bottle," we are left without choice. AI really does represent the unconscious as computers "zig zag" along the boundaries of consciousness, constantly bringing new awareness. Cultivating mindfulness of the psychological implications that are entwined with AI engagement will help us utilize its capabilities virtuously. (Wiley, 2024, p. 63)

Assuming the human psyche as the core space for learning and the harbourer of human virtue and morality is a powerful reminder of the need to understand education for our times in a holistic framework. The inevitable risks of ignoring the powers of AI include the bypassing of normalising and acceptable whole of society behaviours and augmenting repressed urges for destructive and negative mass behaviours.

6.6 Mythology and Romanticism Reconnecting Through Algorithms

Contemporary developments in technology can appear to shift societal thinking away from nature and its powers of connection with beauty, light and colour. Added to this reality is the focus of residential life in towns and cities with little or no contact with the countryside. Living within a densely populated built environment and spending vast amounts of waking time looking and reacting to screen prompts is cause to wonder about the elements of the more spiritual sides of our existence. Beauty, aesthetics and imagination seem to have been increasingly relocated from nature to online imagery, art, literature, music, games and reenacted rituals that criss-cross history and offer nature vicariously but not directly. All are valid pursuits that enrich daily lives. For we the consumer the challenge is to be aware of the powers of the medium as a seducer of our thinking and decision making. This statement is not a frivolous throwaway line. Researchers appear to be using their scientific approaches to highlight the strategies used in marketing to tap into unconscious preferences. The strategy is commonplace as Clapp (2022) notes:

> Algorithms possess the ego just like archetypes possess consciousness. In Jung's quote, I would simply replace the word archetype with algorithm: Algorithms "are systems of readiness for action, and at the same time" use images and trigger emotions to direct behavior. They are woven into the brain structure of social networking sites and are highly effective in triggering instinctive behaviors that do not involve higher cognition or rational thinking. (p. 115)

Poets of the past and present, sociologists, psychologists, economists, political scientists along with historians and intellectuals may provide conflicting accounts of the present. The informed approach will be to include all the voices as a means of deciding next steps. History suggests that the past is a foreign land. However, the dynamic for a progressive pedagogy will need to connect with past myths and emotion. In this context Major's (2025) concept of artefacts is a useful construct. Major observes: "The term artifact itself, etymologically referring to something "made with skill," serves today as a key concept at the intersection of biology, psychology, and technology" (p. 1).

> In the cell and in the psyche, in neural systems and in algorithms, life and mind operate through codes enacted by mediators. The boundary between the natural and artificial begins to blur, giving way to a layered ontology where nature, culture, and technology are unified through functional translation.
>
> This integrative view allows us to see the artifact as a convergence point among the biological, the psychological, and the technological. All are structured expressions of systems that not only process information but also organize and stabilize patterns of experience. (p. 8)

In this perspective, the emerging ontology is holistic. All elements of the human experience are contributing to the experience of knowledge and understanding.

6.7 Fables, AI and Education

If we assume that myths are parts of the human inheritance and deep within our unconscious being, then they can be distinguished from fables which perhaps best reconnect with education or the etymological basis of contemporary pedagogy. Fables provide our moral compass or advice on how to behave. They act as homilies or tales shared through books and oral stories. Fables are key sources of mentoring young children and can offer content for re-enactment through drama, or narration or art and music. Fables as distinct from myths are learned and generally regarded as fictional. For young children fables are a way of connecting with their emotional and intellectual development. Most famously within the western lexicon are Aesop's Fables which typically tell a story of the animals such as the tale of the tortoise and the hare. The value of the stories told for the moral development of the child remains in the pedagogical armoury. However, their relevance is now being explored through a collaborating partnership with AI. Exploratory research conducted by Świerczyńska-Kaczor (2024) considers the efficacy of using AI in the process or storytelling and poetry creation. Fables are a source of ideas for learning as they tend to be short and complete.

6.8 Conclusion

From the Enlightenment to the arrival of Artificial Intelligence the pathways to knowledge have been expanding exponentially. Predicting next steps in this anthropological journey is not for the feint hearted. From myths to archetypes there are significant catalysts for human behaviour and societal directions. There is no doubt that politicians and multinationals will be implementing decisions that will adapt and continue to impact daily lives. However, at the same time there are events taking place within families, villages and communities which highlight the individuation of contemporary society and the merits of keeping open all negotiation avenues regarding preparation for the future. Acts of anti-social behaviour noted via personal access to the dark web are a product of the affordance technology has made. The digital divide which once separated those who could afford from those who could not afford has diminished. The ancient myths that motivate humans to seek a better life, are and can be, a force for action. They are evident in global migration movements, as well as organised criminality. The internet and dark web offer sanctuary for organised crime and hateful social events. They are spaces for mobilising international movements designed to disrupt the hegemonic balance. Countering all of these negative movements and activities, educators and responsible adults have a crucial role to protect young people and boost their self-confidence to reject the seduction of predators. The softness associated with Romanticism, myths and fables have a place in our social fabric as does resilience and knowing what and how to act. The latter require smart guidance.

References

Aitkin-Smith, T. (2016). *The tattoo dictionary*. Mitchell Beazley.

Barthes, R. (1964). *Elements of semiology*. Hill and Wang, 1968.

Barthes, R. (2000). In S. Sontage (Ed.), *A Roland Barthes reader*. Vintage.

Buttimer, A. (2001). Beyond Humboldtian Science and Goethe's way of science: Challenges of Alexander Von Humboldt's geography. In *Erdkunde* (pp. 105–120).

Clapp, J. (2022). Social media and the collective unconscious: Archetypal algorithms and the colonization of the psyche. *Jung Journal, 16*(3), 113–131.

Conrad, P. (2016). *Mythomania tales of our times, from apple to Isis*. Thames and Hudson.

Jung, C. J. (2017). *Psychological types*. Routledge.

Major, J. C. (2025). From code to archetype: Toward a unified theory of biological, neural, and artificial artifacts. *Biosystems,* 254.

Phillips, R. R. (2021). Romanticism. *Ploughshares, 47*(1), 162–162.

Schama, S. (1996). *Landscape and memory*. Random House.

Smelser, N. J. (1983/844). Collective myths and fantasies. *Humboldt Journal of Social Relations, 11*(1), 1–15.

Świerczyńska-Kaczor, U. (2024) Empirical insights into traditional and AI-enhanced interactive narratives based on children's fables. *Journal of Economics and Management*, *46*(25–54).

Strayer, R. (2025). Carl Jung: Engaging with history. *Psychological Perspectives, 68*(2), 225–236.

Wiley, R. (2024). Artificial intelligence and psyche: The trickster and our moral compass. *Psychological Perspectives, 67*(1–2), 55–65.

Wulf, A. (2015). *The invention of nature the adventures of Alexander Von Humboldt*. John Murray Publishers.

Margaret E. Robertson is Emeritus Professor of Education, La Trobe University, Melbourne, Australia. Research interests include cultural geography, youth studies and innovative pedagogy.

Chapter 7
The Road to Adolescence: Mapping the Changing Geographies of Masculinity

John Morgan

Abstract This chapter explores the shifting geographies of masculinity and adolescence in contemporary Britain. It examines cultural, economic and spatial transformations shaping male identities, from post-industrial landscapes to digital spaces. Drawing on media representations such as Netflix's Adolescence, it highlights themes of isolation, surveillance and the influence of online misogyny. Historical perspectives trace changes from industrial man to neoliberal masculinities, emphasising the role of schools, policy and cultural politics. The discussion situates the so-called boy crisis within broader social and economic restructuring, arguing that gender norms are fluid and contested across time and space.

Keywords Adolescence · Digital privacy · Disconnection · Geography landscapes

7.1 Introduction

In March 2025 Netflix streamed a drama set in the north of England called *Adolescence.* There were four episodes. The first starts with a dramatic police dawn- raid on a typical suburban house which concludes with the arrest of a thirteen-year-old boy—Jamie Miller—on suspicion of murder. The episode covers in painful detail the confusion of the parents as their son is taken to the police station and the careful collection of evidence and procedures are followed. Unusually for this type of drama, there is no suspense about the question of whether Jamie had committed the crime. The evidence that Jamie stabbed his female victim is captured on multiple screens. As the series unfolds, it becomes clear that adults and young people exist almost in parallel worlds. Jamie's anger towards women is expressed in his online presence, on social media, and though the adults knowingly name-drop the 'influencer' Andrew Tate, Jamie and his peers have quite commonplace insecurities around sex and attractiveness. Jamie was bullied online by his victim—Katie. The final episode is

J. Morgan (✉)
University of Auckland, Auckland, New Zealand
e-mail: john.morgan@auckland.ac.nz

M. E. Robertson (ed.), *Youth, Identity, AI and Moral Purpose*, Young People and Learning Processes in School and Everyday Life 9,
https://doi.org/10.1007/978-3-032-32479-5_7

set thirteen months later, as the family tries to come to terms with what has happened. There is no let off for the viewer, no hidden reveal about the parents which might explain Jamie's actions. We are left with the impression that Eddie and Minda Miller were devoted (if harassed) parents. Like most of us they are financially stretched and responding to pressure to provide the technology that all children have access to.

Adolescence was a tour de force, but the real significance was that it came at a moment when there was major concern about the impact that social media and digital communication has on young people's lives including revenge porn and pornography. The focus was on what has becoming popularly (and problematically) termed 'toxic masculinity' and the attraction for boys and young men of the 'manosphere' or online misogynistic communities. The UK Primer Minister, Keir Starmer, watched the series and commented on it. There were calls for the programme to be viewed in schools and a whole set of educational researchers reported their findings and offered advice about what schools and teachers should do to combat violence against women and girls.

7.2 The Geographies of Adolescence

Though it is difficult to place the exact location of the events in *Adolescence*, it is meant to represent the post-Crash, post-Covid landscapes of contemporary Britain. These are everyday landscapes of the home, the street, takeaways and retail parks. Much of the intensity of the drama revolves around the home, which is supposed to be a symbol of security and safety in an uncertain world, but is now a place where the outside world intrudes, starting with the dramatic home invasion by the police dawn raid. We also see the way in which the teenagers' bedrooms are sites of privacy, shut off from parental control. This space has been opened to the digital world. There is a sense that the family are 'alone together'. This outside world is increasingly one that is monitored and surveilled. This takes place through the comments and knowing looks of the neighbours, and the vandalism of the father's work van, which he tries to get repaired, leading to his breakdown in the hardware store. Digital cameras are ubiquitous in public space, so that Jamie's crime is picked up from every angle. Institutions such as schools seem faceless and factories of social control, as the police officer remarks—'it's a fucking holding pen'. This is a privatised space, where the class-based communities of the post-war period have been eroded by decades of neoliberalism. If Jamie is a symbol of 'the boy crisis', his father equally represents a form of masculinity in crisis, struggling to live up to an image of what it means to be a good father in conditions where the signposts of social and cultural life are missing. There is a porosity of scales. The technologically equipped bedroom is a portal to another world and another set of rules about communication which the parents (and adults in general) are only dimly aware of. There is a passing reference to the manosphere and the role of influencers such as Andrew Tate. It's a world of online hate and as the series suggests, incel culture. It's interesting to think of E.M. Forster's comment in *Howards End*—'only connect'. What connects the nation's space here is the global communications conglomerates. The England shown here is quite placeless. There are non-places where there is a search for meaning, but the social ties that might allow for connection have been severed.

In this bleak post-Brexit landscape—adolescence is experienced as a geography of disconnection—while promising refuge, growing up male is met with isolation, surveillance and crisis.

Adolescence warrants a brief comparison with an earlier series (not least because there are continuities in the writing team and the cast members), broadcast in 2010. 2011 and 2015 but set in the 1980s—Shane Meadow's *This is England*. The landscapes are similarly bleak, though this time as the result of deindustrialisation in the Thatcher years. The young boy at the centre of the drama is called Shane, whose father was killed in the Falklands War. With his mother barely coping with the grief, home is somewhere to escape from, and school is little better. Shane gravitates towards a wider peer group—who are older and more 'aware' of the world than he is. An important element of this initiation involves the growing presence of far-right politics as the limits of Britain's multiculturalism are tested.

Shaun's is a pre-digital world though. Without access to cars and money for trains, the drama of adolescence is played out on bus rides, hanging out at someone's house or on the street. This is England gives us glimpses of another crisis of masculinity where the traditional routes to working class transitions to adulthood have been closed. This is England is clear in its regional depiction of a working-class culture coming to terms with the fact that there is little work. The politics of race and nation are central motifs. As Jon Savage wrote in his review for *Sight and Sound*:

> *This Is England* leaves its young hero bereft and alone. Like Jimmy in *Quadrophrenia* (1979), Shaun ends surrounded by the sea, confronted by both physical limit and emotional space - if not actual ego dissolution. Both have seen through the compulsions of their peer groups, but what is left? How do you go forward? How do you deal with innocence lost? If you reject violence, what is it to be a man? What follows is the test of true character.

These are complex geographical, social and psychological landscapes. They are, of course, too much for (geography) teachers to deal with, but my argument is that, as teachers—as adults—we must be aware of such landscapes, how they are made, and at least be able to offer some signposts and guides as to how to read them.

7.3 Geography Matters

What has masculinity got to do with geography? In the 1980s, there was debate about why and how geography matters. Two books from 1984 captured this. Doreen Massey's (1984) *Spatial Divisions of Labour*, and an edited collection called *Geography matters* (Allen & Massey, 1984). Massey's book was a major restatement of economic geography. It rejected traditional industrial location theories and realigned the subject with neo-Marxist political economy. It was a direct response to the changing economic geography of British capitalism. Massey was interested in the ways that class and gender were being restructured in the face of economic change. Her work at the time gave relatively little attention to cultural issues. However, in *Geography Matters*, there is a chapter by John Clarke (1984) called 'There's no place like…": cultures of difference.' If Massey's book provided the economic 'base', Clarke's essay discussed the corresponding cultural 'superstructure'. It now seems obvious that, to understand a changing human geography, we need both types of studies.

I started teaching geography in schools in 1988. The old textbooks which described the 'solid' geography of steel, textiles and coal-mining seemed obsolete following the recessions of the late 1970s and 1980s which had led to deindustrialisation as older regions based on heavy industry went into decline and faced high levels of unemployment. The historical north–south divide had resurfaced as a political issue. Large conurbations and cities suffered too, but there were also important changes as new 'sunrise' industries emerged, and some cities benefitted from urban regeneration. Although the picture was complicated, I tried to provide pupils with an overview of the changing economic map, but the resources to explore culture were more limited. For example, Champion and Townsend's (1990) *Contemporary Britain* was an excellent resource for describing the dimensions of economic and demographic shifts, but it barely hinted at the cultural aspects of these changes.

The publication of Peter Jackson's (1989) *Maps of Meaning* provided a guide about how to connect the contours of economy and culture. The phrase 'maps of meaning' came out of a book called *Resistance through Rituals* (Hall & Jefferson, 1976). It resonates because it signals that there is always a personal and psychological aspect to the worlds in which we live. Jackson's book offered a way for geographers to engage with the meaning of the economic and political changes that were reshaping Britain in the 1980s and 1990s. Part of this was the changing meanings of gender prompted by 'second wave' feminism.

Maps of Meaning contained a chapter on gender and sexuality which set an agenda for cultural geography. Geographers, Jackson suggests, have found it convenient to hide behind the shield of a parochial definition of disciplinary boundaries. He developed this argument with a paper on the cultural politics of masculinity (Jackson, 1991) which started from the position that masculinity is a social construction and that this construction occurs in places and spaces. Using a range of examples he showed how the meanings of masculinity change over time and how there exist dominant ideas about men's roles and that these are contested. Jackson's work led to a range of studies on the geographies of masculinity and was part of a critique of how human geography has assumed a masculinist bias. Shurmer-Smith and Hannam (1994) stated that, "It may be time we opened up a new space in geography for a discussion of the construction of masculinities, and their role in the construction of gender identities".

In 1995 Steve Pile and Nigel Thrift's *Mapping the subject was* published. Geographers were not set up for mapping the human subject. This was extremely limiting especially as the discipline aligned itself with the social and political projects of the new left in the 1980s. By this time much of the British left was embracing questions of identity and desire. To find out why, how, what with and where people belong, geographers would need to explore the *terra incognito* of the self. It could not be assumed that there was a singular, rational self.

These theoretical developments in geography advanced rapidly, even finding a place on the undergraduate curriculum in geography. For example, a 2001 textbook on social geographies provided a two-column list of "Some 'masculine' and 'feminine' characteristics' before warning that these differ across time, space and different cultures. Masculinity may have different meanings on the football terraces, in the pub, in the workplace, and in the home. This is why is it is usual to use the plural masculinities and femininities.

Such geographical work clearly had (and has) the potential to inform teaching in schools, though it would require that teaching went beyond observation and description of social patterns to a deeper mapping of psycho-social space. The next section explores what this might entail.

7.4 Re-making Men

The educational sociologist Sara Delamont (2001) makes the point that schools and classrooms are not places where gender norms are readily challenged. There are assumptions about how boys and girls learn, what types of roles they should play, where they are destined to end up, and the types of subjects they take. But there is little doubt that gender relations and identities are regarded as much more open and fluid than they have been in the past. Indeed, it could be argued that feminism has been a key element in the making of educational policy and practice in the modern period.

For instance, by the 1980s there was at least an acceptance of the social construction of masculinity—the idea that what it means to be a man is historically, socially and geographically specific. The new sociology of education sought to explain why some groups of students seemed not to succeed at school but it was critiqued by educational feminists for its masculine-bias and even sexism (the classic study was Paul Willis's (1977) *Learning to Labour*). In the 1980s, a series of youth cultural studies explored the relations between formal schooling and the informal cultures of young people at a moment when an older gender order was in the process of dissolving in the face of economic and cultural change.

The intellectual and political shifts around second wave feminism created space for the emergence of Men's Studies which merged into a more general theoretical accounts of men and masculinities in the 1980s and 1990s (some of which involved the study of boys and education). For example, in Britain, Men Against Sexism was a small movement that emerged in the 1970s as a response to the growing strength of feminism. It was an attempt by mainly heterosexual men to articulate their personal confusions and the social and political dilemmas they faced. The emergence of the sexual politics of masculinity was a reaction to the political loss of male cultural authority.

While the early men's movement was linked to intellectual currents, the shift from state to market in the 1980s meant that consumerism, rather than political struggle and therapy provided the language for understanding changing masculine identities. It was clear that masculinity was in flux, with competing images of toyboy, new man, new father, lager lout, yuppie.

All this was indicative of a greater fluidity around gender and sexual relations. Economic restructuring changed the occupational structure, the types of work available and its meaning to different groups. The deindustrialisation of the British economy and the subsequent shift towards financial services and retailing led to the erosion of traditional work- identity and its replacement by a flexible post-industrial work culture which was less collectivist and more individualist. There was much more emphasis on flexibility and a preparedness to change jobs. Different groups have been placed differently in relation to this culturalisation of the workplace. For example, there were studies of the reassertion of male power within the workplace, especially in global financial services. At the opposite end were those young males who are excluded from the wage relation and linked into feminised workplaces and cultures. They are making their way in the world at a time of increased precarity and a decline of work quality.

A constant feeling associated with the 'new economy' is that girls have outperformed boys (though of course there are important qualifications to that statement). The New Labour years were a time of significant change where it was held that Britain was undergoing a long-awaited modernisation and that we were 'living in a young country'. The changing role of women and girls was a crucial metaphor of change. The combination of culture in girl power and the new emphasis of women in work in the light of feminisation places them in a crucial position.

This change was palpable. As a student teacher in the mid-1980s, I recall reading research about the representation of gender in primary school reading books, but by the turn of the millennium there was talk of 'failing boys' in schools.

Ironically it was impact of Thatcherism—viewed by many as anathema to women's interests—along with the collapse of manufacturing and the rise of the service economy which accelerated the 'feminization' of the economy. Labour force policies were all about getting people into work and the pattern of transition from school to work was changing.

The seminal study of boys and schooling in the 1990s was Mairtain Mac an Ghaill's *The Making of Men*, which explored the ways in which boys were experiencing the changed transitions from school to work. The study paid close attention to the wider economic and policy contexts in which this transition was taking place. A key achievement was to show that boys and men must work hard at their masculinity. Not all men achieve hegemonic masculinity. The work is set in the Midlands between 1990 and 1992 where the boys are struggling to achieve adult masculinity in a city which has lost its traditional manufacturing base dominated by male labour. Mac an Ghaill identified four distinct groups: the real Englishmen; new entrepreneurs; academic achievers; and the macho lads. While the 'academic achievers' and the 'macho lads' were well known to sociologists of education, the novel categories were the 'new entrepreneurs' and the 'real Englishmen'. The new entrepreneurs had not given up on the possibility of employment. They saw the old male manufacturing jobs as no longer available and had taken the advice of their fathers that there were new opportunities for the self -employed and self-starters. They threw themselves into the new subjects such as Business Studies. The 'real Englishmen' offered another prospective identity. It was made up of largely 'white' boys who were not achieving the highest grades at school, but who complained that their parents had adopted liberal anti-sexist and anti-racist positions which did not fit with the reality of teenagers' experiences in a co-educational multicultural school. They attached themselves to an imagined 'English' culture. It is interesting to think about how this identity, which seemed new to observers in the 1990s, has subsequently developed.

All this was taking place at the same time as there was academic and popular concern about changing gender relations and the rise of the 'New Lad', who was widely regarded as an example of 'backlash' to the feminist gains of the 1980s. What is striking about all this is the sense that gender must be seen as a complex construction which is linked to wider political economic and cultural regimes.

> …theoretical frameworks that have enabled us to analyse systematically and document coherently the material, social and discursive production of masculinities within the broader context of gender relations (Haywood and Mac an Ghaill 2003, p.4).

Over time then, there have been important changes in the 'gender regime' or settlements. Starting with the demise of 'industrial man' which predominated in the 1950s and 1960s, we can trace the emergence of the 'new man' and 'entrepreneurial male' of the conservative 1980s and 1990s. These market-oriented masculinities gave way, in the New Labour years to a 'protective paternalism' which reflected the moral economy of the Third Way. This state-preferred male identity was law-abiding, took responsibility for himself and his loved ones, and contributed to the economy through actively seeking work. However, as the contradictions of the Third way became clearer, the protective paternalism co-existed and competed with a series of dissident masculinities. These included 'The absent father', the 'anti-social young male', and the 'dangerous male'. The tensions revolved around the fact that although New Labour rejected the market individualism of the Thatcherite era. In favour of ideas of care and community, in practice there was a focus on regulation and social control which could then lead to forms of authoritarianism.

The important point to take about these developments is the idea that there are changing gender regimes which are part of the wider class and race settlements as capitalism seeks to secure the conditions for accumulation. New ideas about how to be a man are shaped as the social and cultural landscape changes. The final section explores the conditions that have shaped the so-called boy crisis.

7.5 Lost Freedoms

Matthew Thomson's (2014) *Lost Freedom: the landscape of the child and the British post-war settlement* provides an historical account of the construction of the child in British society. He argues that childhood in the post-war period became increasingly anxious. The impact of the war was psychological and saw the home and the family as the central landscape of childhood. The home was to be safe and regulated. Psychologists and popular culture were concerned with ideas about harm and safety and the need to monitor children's lives and movements. These tendencies increased with the growth of housing estates, the coming of the motor car, and later stranger danger. Television plays an important part in Thomson's history. Just after the war, few homes had televisions, but this had risen to 55% by the mid-1950s to 89% by the mid-1960s.

Landscapes are not created overnight. They are the result of the slow interplay between culture and nature. We can be so busy living our lives that we do not notice what is going on around us. Then suddenly, we look up and realise that the place we live in has changed. This historical frame chimes with the contemporary anxieties shown in Adolescence. As Jamie's father says at the end of the series, 'we made him'. Although he is putting the blame on his own failings as a father, the viewer knows that the 'we' is all of us. As we join Eddie Miller in surveying Jamie's empty bedroom full of electronic equipment and screens, we reflect that, left to his own devices (pun intended), Jamie inhabited a landscape that his parents barely knew existed.

The world that Jamie and his friends inhabit did not exist and could not have been imagined when I started teaching in schools in 1988. But things were changing then, and it is possible to identify many of the economic, cultural and political shifts that have taken us down 'the road to adolescence'.

First, the economic shifts. At several points in this chapter, I have referred to the collapse of traditional male work identities: Historically, war and work were twin pillars of male identity and power. With the decline of war as a defining experience and the erosion of male-dominated sectors like agriculture and industry, boys have lost clear pathways to adulthood. The rise of service and post-industrial economies demands skills that are less physically based and more relational, leaving many young men disoriented. Thus, it is often asserted that the twenty-first-century workplace emphasises empathy, communication, flexibility, and multitasking—skills often socially coded as feminine.

More generally, this generation faces bleak economic prospects. Instead of climbing the career ladder, many are sliding down it. The promise of stable employment has been replaced by insecurity and short-term contracts, making school seem less relevant as a route to success.

Perhaps the most obvious cultural change is to do with gender fluidity and identity. The breakdown of the gender binary destabilises traditional roles. What once seemed fixed—male provider, female caregiver—is now contested, creating uncertainty about what it means to "be a man". A deluge of popular and academic books give us the impression that men are in crisis. Positing the end of men, describing what gives women the 'XX factor', asking what men want, trying to suss out what drives angry white men or mapping the 'boy crisis'. One of the more sophisticated examples of this type of work is found in the American historian Gary Cross's (2008) argument that the transition from boyhood to manhood is increasingly blurred. Men cling to youth, and fatherhood begins earlier, often without the maturity once associated with adult roles. This is linked to a consumer culture which targets boys with ideals of muscular perfection.

All this before we mention the overt sexualisation of popular culture. Boys (and girls) must navigate a "strip-tease culture" saturated with sexual imagery and ambiguous rules around intimacy. This was associated with the market for soft porn and increasingly available online pornography. While some commentators saw this as potentially liberating, allowing for the loosening of sexual identities and overcoming the repression of earlier decades, it has become clear that these freedoms come with significant costs.

To focus too narrowly on the technological dimensions fails to acknowledge shifts in the political economy of young people's lives. Economic crises and shifting gender codes have fractured traditional patriarchal structures. The sexual revolution and feminist gains have reconfigured power relations, leaving some boys and men feeling dispossessed and prompting backlash movements. Put simply, neoliberal trends—privatisation, individualism, and surveillance—shape the landscapes boys inhabit.

7.6 Conclusion

In December 2025, the UK government announced a new strategy which promised that the 'full power of the state' would be deployed in the largest crackdown in British history on Violence Against Women and Girls. Writing in the *Guardian,* Deputy Prime Minister David Lammy 18 December 2025) put this in personal perspective, talking about his fear for his daughter and the wider culture in which he is raising two sons:

> So much of this violence is fuelled by the casual misogyny that seeps through our culture, amplified online. Today's children are growing up in a digital world many parents barely recognise. A place where pornography is easy to access, misogyny spreads fast and loud—and hateful voices tell our boys that control is strength and empathy is weakness".

Lammy's comments relate directly to the themes raised in Netflix's *Adolescence.*

In these 'solution-focused' times, there is always the question about what the type of discussion in this chapter can offer the busy teacher who is timetabled to teach 9C on Friday morning. No doubt it was easier to teach geography in schools when the subject was dominated by 'rational economic man' busy laying out hexagonal landscapes or land uses based on profit-optimising or satisficing behaviour. 'Non-economic man' raises the spectre of the unconscious and desire, which are harder to handle in classroom discussions. In the weeks and months teachers looking to grapple with these issues could find support from academic experts who reported their findings and offered advice. (Exnor-Cortens, 2025; King-Hill, 2024; Thakur, 2026). These included conversation programmes, resilience frameworks, masculinity education and digital literacy. As the saying goes, 'you pays your money and takes your choice'.

In this chapter, I have argued that such choices are not merely pedagogical or programmatic. They rest on deeper assumptions about how contemporary adolescence is produced: not simply psychologically, nor purely socially, but at the intersection of affect, place, technology and power. A more grown-up response is to resist the comfort of quick fixes in favour of sustained reflection on the *psycho-social* conditions through which young people come to experience themselves as real, recognised, or excluded (a model for this is found in Stephen Frosh's (2025) *How to Be Real*). From this perspective, *Adolescence* is less a problem to be solved than something to be engaged with in all its complexity—a mix of cultural geographies, patterns of child development and economies of anxiety.

References

Allen, J., & Massey, D. (Eds.). (1984). *Geography matters*. Cambridge University Press.

Champion, T., & Townsend, A. (1990). *Contemporary Britain: A geographical perspective*. Edward Arnold.

Clarke, J. (1984). There's no place like…: Cultures of difference. In J. Allen & D. Massey (Eds.), *Geography matters* (pp. xx–xx). Cambridge University Press.

Cross, G. (2008). *Men to boys: The making of modern immaturity*. Columbia University Press.

Delamont, S. (2001). *Changing women, unchanged men?* Sociological perspectives on gender in a post-industrial society.

Exnor-Corten, D. (2025, April 11). 'Adolescence' on Netflix: evidence-based ways parents can support boys around masculinity norms. *The Conversation*. https://theconversation.com/adolescence-on-netflix-evidence-based-ways-parents-can-support-boys-around-masculinity-norms-253724

Frosh, S. (2025). *How to be real: A survival guide in challenging times*. Verso.

Hall, S., & Jefferson, T. (1976). *Resistance through rituals*. Hutchinson.

Heywood, C., & Mac an Ghaill, M. (2003). *Men and masculinities*. Open University Press.

Jackson, P. (1989). *Maps of meaning*. Routledge.

Jackson, P. (1991). The cultural politics of masculinity. *Transactions of the Institute of British Geographers, 16*(2), 199–213.

King-Hill, S. (2024, April 2). Adolescence in schools: tv shows portrayalof one boyhood may do more harm than good as a teaching tool. *The Conversation*. https://theconversation.com/adolescence-in-schools-tv-shows-portrayal-of-one-boyhood-may-do-more-harm-than-good-when-used-as-a-teaching-tool-253158

Lammy, D. (2025, December 18). I want my two sons to know masculinity can be kind- and my daughter to live without fear. *Guardian*. https://www.theguardian.com/commentisfree/2025/dec/18/masculinity-sexual-violence-women-national-emergency-labour

Mac an Ghaill, M. (1994). *The making of men: Masculinities, sexualities and schooling*. Open University Press.

Massey, D. (1984). *Spatial divisions of labour*. Macmillan.

Pile, S., & Thrift, N. (Eds.). (1995). *Mapping the subject: Geographies of cultural transformation*. Routledge.

Savage, J. (2007). New boots and rants. Sight and Sound (May).: BFI | Sight & Sound | New Boots And Rants (http://old.bfi.org.uk/sightandsound/feature/49369)

Shurmer-Smith, P., & Hannam, K. (Eds.). (1994). *Worlds of desire, realms of power: A cultural geography*. Arnold.

Thakur, A. (2026). Social media, online communities, and youth mental health: Netflix's *Adolescence* as an educational tool for stakeholders. *European Child and Adolescent Psychiatry, 35*, 623–624. https://doi.org/10.1007/s00787-025-02862-y

Thomson, M. (2013). *Lost freedom: The landscape of the child and the British post-war settlement*. Oxford University Press.

Willis, P. (1977). *Learning to labour: How working-class kids get working-class jobs*. Saxon House.

John Morgan taught geography in schools in London before moving into teacher education, where he led Geography Education at the University of Bristol. He has worked at Futurelab and UCL (London), and is currently Head of the School of Critical Studies in Education at the University of Auckland.

Chapter 8
Youth Cultures, Visual Literacy and Hanging Out

Sirpa Tani and Markus Hilander

Abstract This chapter explores how digital technologies shape young people's everyday lives, focusing on their social interactions, especially visual culture and engagement with information. It begins by examining the concept of *hanging out*—a vital form of youth socialisation—and introduces the metaphor of the *social compass* to describe how smartphones enable flexible, real-time coordination of social gatherings. The chapter then turns to the role of images in digital youth culture, highlighting how photography has evolved from a documentary practice to a dynamic form of self-expression and communication. In the age of Artificial Intelligence, the indexicality of photographs is increasingly challenged, raising questions about authenticity and trust. Through a pedagogical case study, the chapter illustrates how critical media literacy can be fostered by comparing historical photographs with AI-generated visuals. Finally, the discussion broadens to address the complexities of navigating misinformation and disinformation in digital environments. Emphasising the importance of powerful, discipline-based knowledge, the chapter argues for educational approaches that connect young people's lived experiences with formal learning. By bridging school subjects with youth culture, educators can empower students to critically engage with the digital world and develop informed, reflective perspectives.

Keywords Disinformation · Misinformation · Photography · Powerful knowledge · Social compass · Young people · Hanging out

S. Tani (✉) · M. Hilander
Faculty of Educational Sciences, University of Helsinki, Helsinki, Finland
e-mail: sirpa.tani@helsinki.fi

M. Hilander
e-mail: markus.hilander@helsinki.fi

M. E. Robertson (ed.), *Youth, Identity, AI and Moral Purpose*, Young People and Learning Processes in School and Everyday Life 9,
https://doi.org/10.1007/978-3-032-32479-5_8

8.1 Introduction

Young people's everyday lives are often structured and monitored by adults. Young people spend most of their waking hours following ready-made schedules and agenda: during their early years, most days were spent in daily care and later in their youth lives, in school. The main location for the rest of the day outside of these institutions is home. Many children and young people have activities that are organised in certain times and locations. In many cases, parents act as their children's drivers to guarantee their safety. Doing that, adults are simultaneously restricting children's independent mobility and thus their opportunities to explore their surroundings freely.

This adult-led structuring of young people's everyday lives also extends to broader decisions, such as where a family chooses to live. For families with children, the location of kindergarten or schools may have a remarkable role when these decisions are made. Despite this, children and young people themselves have seldom any real choice of their own where to live. Therefore, for them, it is often important to be able to have their own space at home: for many, it can be their own room or a shared one with others. A classic example of the need to claim space at home is the attached signs on the bedroom door: "Keep out", "Do not enter!" or "Don't disturb!".

Because of the limited opportunities to have a say where and how to live, young people's free time often expands to the surrounding areas of their home. Home and school yards, nearby streets and squares are popular places to spend time without any ready-made plans—to hang out. Most often, hanging out has been understood as young people's way to be with others outdoors or in some commercial spaces such as shopping malls. Hanging out spots can also be public transport hubs or abandoned buildings.

Hanging out is thus an essential element in many young people's free time. Even when they have always found their ways to be together, some new forms of hanging out have also emerged. In this chapter, we will describe them in the context of the ever-increasing popularity of digital technologies. First, the role of smartphones in contemporary hanging out practices will be described by introducing the concept of social compass. Second, we will turn to the other aspects that characterise young people's lives in physical and digital spaces. That is, we will describe the roles that visuals have for them. Interpretation of images has always been a complex task, and during the time of AI, it has become even more challenging: How to know what images are based on real moments and what are the products of artificial intelligence? What kind of role do visuals have in young people's lives? Third, we broaden the scope of the chapter to the questions of information and knowledge in this day and age. How do young people use different sources of information? How can they learn to identify reliable knowledge from the jungle of dis- and misinformation? We conclude this chapter with a brief introduction to the ideas of powerful knowledge and the role of education for young people.

8.2 'Social Compass' Leading the Way While Hanging Out with Peers

There are many reasons for young people to hang out in their free time. For some of them, hanging out may mean that they do not necessarily have access to any organised activities, either because of the limited offerings (or affordances, see Gibson, 1979; Raymond et al., 2017) in their neighbourhood or due to economic reasons. In their study, Steinberg and Simon (2019) have distinguished organised activities (following ready-made program and schedule, supervised by adults) from hobbies, which do not necessarily need any economic investment and can still have social benefits especially for young people in more disadvantaged contexts. While exploring these two from the perspective of their social benefits, researchers mention how hanging out has not been linked to "positive youth development". In fact, referring to a couple of earlier studies, they write: "Less structured discretionary activities, such as watching television, playing video games and hanging out with peers in unstructured environments are associated with behavior problems and poor academic performance" (Steinberg & Simon, 2019, p. 1183).

However, despite these concerns, hanging out—like organised activities and hobbies—offers several positive elements for many young people. One of the most important ones is the opportunity to construct a personal bond with the everyday environment, without constant adult monitoring. Children's independent mobility has become rare in many countries and in many cases teenagers' freedom has been restricted. The reasons behind this development are most often connected to adults' concerns about safety in public spaces (e.g., Riazi et al., 2022; Shaw et al., 2015). When hanging out in public, teenagers claim their right to be outdoors without any ready-made plans.

As we already mentioned, hanging out is most often connected to young people's ways to spend their time outside of institutions or schedules, outdoors or in commercial spaces. It is fair to note that they can also hang out with their peers in someone's home or other indoor spaces. Spending time with others remotely, chatting or playing online games, can also be understood as a way of hanging out. What is common in all these is the social character of activity: to interact with others is the key to hanging out (Pyyry & Tani, 2016; Tani, 2015).

Hanging out spots in cities have long been the same: that is, some central locations with easy access have been popular. Earlier research has shown that both 'on stage' and 'backstage' spaces are relevant since they make two opposite elements of hanging out possible: young people want to gather in places where they can be seen and at the same time, to gaze at the others, thus, to be on display, 'on stage'. But they also want to find places where they can withdraw from passers-by, and most importantly, from their parents' surveillance—to be 'backstage' (Matthews et al., 2000; Tani, 2015). In these hangout places young people do not necessarily have to contact others before going there, since they know that their peers will show up (Kauppinen et al., 2025).

The rapid increase in the ownership of smartphones has changed the ways in which meetings with others can be organised. Hanging out now has become increasingly mobile and flexible. Digital route maps have replaced traditional paper maps and turned navigation into an individual-centred approach. When one's location is shared on the phone, Google Maps or some other application using the Global Positioning System (GPS) will show where the user of the phone is and will offer optional routes for the planned destination. This means that one does not have to pay attention to any details in one's environment when just following the progress of the trip. Therefore, smartphones have started to work as a combination of a compass and a map. Physical and virtual places are thus connected with the help of digital technology, and their boundaries have blurred (Rueb, 2014).

Especially for young people who want to hang out with their friends, mobile applications have become extremely popular. For example, Snapchat can be used to indicate the location of others. By following their movements, one can make sudden changes to one's plans without fixing the meeting places beforehand. For the users of Snapchat, a phone has become a *social compass.* Kauppinen et al. (2025) have defined social compass as a metaphor to describe young people's hanging out practices with the help of their smartphones:

> To apply the metaphor of a compass in the context of hanging out, we can imagine that young people read just 'the travel arrow' of their social compass whenever their friends move in the city; these other young people can be thought of as mobile 'checkpoints' on the city map. Young people thus navigate urban spaces with the help of their social compass. Moving from one place to another occurs through geographical, social and digital negotiation. Smartphones have therefore turned into social compasses that combine physical, social and digital elements (Kauppinen et al., 2025, p. 41)

The concept of social compass shows how young people have found new ways to make their hanging out more flexible than in earlier days. However, for the adults whose intention has been to monitor young people's free time activities, the use of social compasses has made it more challenging to know where young people will gather.

8.3 What Do the Visuals Really Tell Us in the Age of AI?

Smartphones are not just social compasses for young people; they are also the most usual ways to connect to the internet and social media. One of the essential features in the smartphones is their in-built cameras, which make it easy to document moments of life and to share them with others by using mobile messaging applications such as WhatsApp or by uploading them to social media platforms such as Instagram or to Snapchat where photos and messages ('snaps') are accessible for only a short time and most often, only for the recipients defined by the sender. Photographs—or images as they are often called to make a distinction between traditional photography and the snapshots taken by smartphone users—have turned into part of everyday practices (Jurgenson, 2019, p. 8).

Digital social spaces have become increasingly important for young people (Genova et al., 2023). There, sharing glimpses of daily life, moments with friends, holidays and celebrations continue the tradition to save memories that have always been one of the features of amateur photography (Van House, 2011). In addition to the wish to store memories, images are now increasingly connected to the present; to work as a tool for communication about what is happening right now. Shared images in social media can also be understood as a play that "reinforces friendships through indices of togetherness, intimacy and trust" (Niemelä-Nyrhinen & Seppänen, 2023, p. 593). For many young people, sharing images in social media is the means of constructing the socially and physically attractive self. This is done through multiple snapshots, testing different poses, lightning, and filters (Bell, 2019).

When images are edited and adjusted and when filters are applied, the relationship between the image and the reality turns complex. Photography has traditionally been regarded as a truthful representation of the world (Hilander, 2024). This perception stems from the way photography records reality, a method similar to the principles of the *camera obscura*. The *camera obscura* is an ancient phenomenon in which light enters a darkened room through a pinhole, projecting an inverted image of the outside world onto the opposite wall (Verstegen, 2021). In the realm of painting, *linear perspective* served a similar function: it was a technique for documenting the three-dimensional world as accurately and realistically as possible in two dimensions—that is, a technique for the "convincing depiction of space in painting" (Verstegen, 2021, p. 75).

Cameras, whether analogue or digital, record light rays either onto photographic film or onto electronic sensors. In this sense, a photograph resembles the footprints of a fox in the snow: by following the tracks, one could, in principle, locate the exact fox that left them. Similarly, a photograph captures specific light rays from a particular location, establishing what is known as an *indexical relationship* between the photograph and its referent (Peirce, 1931). This *indexicality* is the reason why photographs have long been considered strong documentary evidence of reality (Puustinen & Seppänen, 2013). Even though it has been possible to retouch photographs already since the early years of the history of photography, the rapid increase of technologies from the 1990s has made it easy to manipulate photos by the larger public (Langguth et al., 2021).

Today, technology and Artificial Intelligence thus challenge the truthfulness of photography. It is easy to alter and manipulate photographs using a smartphone, for instance by adjusting brightness or colour tones. Images generated by AI, on the other hand, lack the defining feature of indexicality. AI does not record any actual light rays in the creation of its images. From a semiotic perspective, AI-generated visuals are not photographs but rather images, or *icons* that only manage to resemble their objects (Peirce, 1931). In this way, AI-generated images resemble paintings, where techniques such as linear perspective may be employed to simulate realism. Indeed, as Verstegen (2021) writes, "linear perspective was ideal for the creation of fictive spaces" (p. 87).

One method for discerning whether an image is AI-generated, or a genuine photograph is through geographical interpretation. The viewer may consider what the depicted location looks like in reality. Is the place presented in an overly idealised manner? Indicators of this may include, for instance, unnatural or implausible details, overly smooth or plastic-like textures, inconsistent lighting or shadows, peculiar backgrounds, unrealistic depth perception, and illegible text within the image. Furthermore, interpreting such idealised visuals requires the individual to draw upon all available geographical knowledge of the area in question, or to seek additional information to support a more accurate analysis of the image.

How could young people then learn to read and interpret images published in social media or other digitally produced media channels? How could they know whether images are based on physical reality? We give an example from Helsinki, Finland in which young people—first-year students in upper secondary school—studied the history, presence and future of the area where their school was located. With this example, our aim is to show how the use of manipulated images connected with students' experiential knowledge has potential to enhance their critical media literacy skills.

The teaching was started by identifying the location of the school from the map, after which students were asked to find three historical photographs of the area, known as Konepaja, each from a different decade. Photos were searched from the free digital image service provided by the Helsinki City Museum (n.d.). Students were asked to download the photos and write down the needed reference: the title, year and the name of the photographer (see Fig. 8.1 as an example). After this first task, they selected three maps from different decades—these were searched from the City of Helsinki's digital archive (2025). The oldest available map was published in 1917–1918. Already then, the most important feature of the area was easy to see: the large train engine and train car industry already started to operate already in 1903.

Analysis of photographs and maps was then complemented by a brief look at the written publication on the building history of the area. Students were asked to write

Fig. 8.1 The Konepaja area in 1976. (Photo by Taik. Helsinki City Museum. License: CC BY 4.0. https://hkm.finna.fi)

Fig. 8.2 "Futuristic Konepaja City at Sunset"—the image and title made by ChatGPT based on the question (2 Sept 2025): "How would the Konepaja area in Helsinki look like in 2050?"

their main findings about the changes they had observed. After a short discussion, students were then instructed to ask AI to create images of the area in 2050. These images of the possible future of the area caused some spontaneous reactions because of their futuristic elements that were not thought of as probable for the area. The idea of this project was to develop students' skills in interpreting the existing written and visual materials and compare their findings with their experiential knowledge. For this chapter, being aware of the complexities of the rights of sharing AI created images, we decided not to present the images that the students shared with us, but instead images that we asked the AI to create for us (see Fig. 8.2).

To be able to evaluate the accuracy of visual representations, whether snapshots shared in social media or images created by AI, background information is needed. In the case described above, old photographs and maps helped the students to understand the changes that have occurred during the decades in the area. Their everyday knowledge of the area surrounding their school made it possible for them to evaluate the old photos and AI created images. The interpreted materials were thus used to enhance students' abilities to read different sources of information, and by connecting them to their own experiential knowledge, critical media literacy skills were learnt.

Having said this, a crucial aspect of using Artificial Intelligence lies in the formulation of the questions posed to it. The more precise the prompt given to AI, the more accurate the response is likely to be. Without contextual background, the AI-generated visions of the Konepaja area appeared highly futuristic. However, when we provided the AI with a photograph that we had taken of the Konepaja area, the result was more realistic—though it resembled a polished version of our original photograph (see Figs. 8.3a and 8.3b). Therefore, it is essential to critically reflect on the responses generated by AI (Melisa et al., 2025).

Fig. 8.3 **a** Konepaja area, September 2025. (Photo by Markus Hilander). **b** Visual representation made by ChatGPT after a detailed prompt: "Konepaja is a former industrial area in Helsinki, Finland, which has been transformed into a vibrant residential neighborhood featuring shops, restaurants, sports halls and a cinema. Could you create a visual—based on a photograph I will send [see Fig. 8.3]—showing what the Konepaja area would most plausibly look like in the year 2025?"

Fig. 8.3 (continued)

8.4 Navigating the Life in the Jungle of Mis- and Disinformation

Visual representations are thus challenging to trust in the digital era, and the same applies also to written texts. How can young people then know what information they can believe? The same challenge is faced by all of us, not only by youth. False or misleading information is not any new phenomenon but, as noted in the literature review by Broda and Strömbäck (2024), the amount of misinformation, disinformation and fake news has increased quickly during the last decade. These three concepts of misleading information are often used together without making a clear difference between their meanings. Most often, however, misinformation is understood as false information that is shared unintentionally, while disinformation is spread intentionally to provide false information to the recipients (see, e.g., Osman et al., 2022). Fake news can be regarded as an extreme version of disinformation. Fake news has been defined as online information that consists of misleading and/or false statements, which is not reported to the users of that information. Fake news may or may not be associated with real events (e.g., Egelhofer & Lecheler, 2019; Wang, 2020).

One of the most extreme examples of false information is deepfakes which connect real people to events in which they have never participated. Deepfakes make it challenging to know what has really happened and what is just a technology-assisted creation of false moments. For young people especially, it is crucial to learn how to critically examine information that they encounter in their daily lives. While deepfakes may often be seen as entertaining and funny, they often create strong negative stereotypes and can cause severe problems for the people in question but also for the public (see e.g., Lao et al., 2025).

All kinds of false information raise questions of trust. In digital environments, trust is not merely a rational evaluation of information sources, but a sensory and emotional experience shaped by everyday interactions. As Pink and Quilty (2025) argue, trust emerges through embodied and relational practices, rather than being a fixed attribute of technologies or institutions. This perspective challenges the transactional view of trust often assumed in discussions of mis- and disinformation. The transactional view treats trust as a measurable exchange—something that can be built, earned, or lost through discrete actions or features, such as transparency, reliability or consistency. It implies that trust can be engineered or guaranteed through technical design alone. Instead of focusing solely on verifying facts, educational approaches should help young people develop an awareness of how trust is felt, negotiated, and sometimes broken in their daily digital lives. Such an approach foregrounds the importance of context, care and inclusivity in fostering critical engagement with information (Pink & Quilty, 2025).

In this section, we have written about different types of information and, while doing so, have deliberately avoided the use of the term 'knowledge'. Interpretation of AI-generated information demands critical media literacy. It is needed to construct a solid foundation for understanding past and present events, and, in turn, to enhance critical thinking. This has been acknowledged in many studies, in which the role of the internet, digital media and, most recently, AI in young people's lives have been investigated (e.g. Hällgren & Björk, 2022; Lee, 1999; Rohman et al., 2025). The need to foster media literacy is thus highlighted, but the role of different school subjects has often remained unclear in this process. Next, we will illuminate the potential that discipline-based teaching can play in critical thinking and media and information literacy, starting with a reflection on how current competence-based approaches have shaped educational thinking and what limitations they may present.

In the context of school education, student-centred approaches have been central for a long time; competences and skills have been highlighted, and students have been seen as actively constructing understanding of the studied phenomena based on their interest. Students have been seen as learners, and 'learning to learn' has become a widely repeated slogan for constructivist education. Knowledge has been seen as a social construction. This view of education has been criticised for example by Biesta, who has called it as 'learnification' of education. Biesta (2020, p. 91) notes that when learning has been placed in the centre, questions about educational content, purpose and relationships have turned invisible.

One solution to tackle this problem is the idea of powerful knowledge, first introduced by sociologists of education Young and Muller (2016), and then further developed by researchers of subject-specific teacher education, for example in geography (Lambert, 2017; Maude, 2016) and history (Nordgren, 2017; Puustinen & Khawaja, 2021). The key idea of powerful knowledge is to understand knowledge as specialised, systematic, and distinct from everyday knowledge (Young & Muller, 2016). It is often specific to a particular discipline; it is constantly tested and developed, and never static. This means that knowledge is not 'given' to students as a ready-made 'truth'. Their ability to evaluate the reliability of knowledge by examining how it is justified is supported by the teacher, who can be seen as a mediator between the academic discipline and the school subject in question. This approach brings teaching back into focus, which helps young people study different information critically and thus helps them to discern reliable knowledge from different sources of false information.

In the context of geography education, Lambert et al. (2015) have identified three levels of geographical knowledge that can enhance students' geographical thinking and thus help them grasp powerful geographical knowledge. These levels are illustrated below through the case study of the Konepaja area. The first level refers to *descriptive world knowledge*, as seen when students located the Konepaja area on the map and recognised its industrial origins using archival maps and historical photographs. The second level involves *critical conceptual knowledge* that deepens relational understanding of geographical concepts, such as the relationship between the environment and humans as well as local and global perspectives; for instance, students examined how the transformation of Konepaja from an industrial site to a cultural and residential hub reflects broader urban regeneration and socio-economic change. The third level emphasises the ability to *envision alternative social, economic and environmental futures*, demonstrated by students who used AI to generate visualisations of Konepaja in 2050 and critically assessed their plausibility based on historical data and personal experience.

8.5 Conclusion: How to Connect Young People's Daily Lives with School Education?

In this chapter, we have explored the role of digital technologies in young people's lives, focusing on their social interactions, visual culture and engagement with information. Smartphones have turned into 'social compasses' for many of them and thus have helped their instant connection with their peers while hanging out in public spaces. This has increased mobility and flexibility in free time activities. While phones have become essential devices in navigation, they have also made instant documentation of mundane activities possible by taking images; sharing these captured moments with others by using social media applications such as Instagram and Snapchat have become an integral part of everyday actions.

The role of visuality has thus become an essential element in the use of social media, and when editing and adjusting the images has turned into an effortless process, the relationship between the image and the reality has become extremely complex. This, together with the development and popularity of AI-generated images, has made it challenging to evaluate the reliability of digital images. The same problem is faced when mediated information is used. How can anyone know whether images, news or information can be trusted? When information is easily accessible via the internet, what is becoming the role of school education in young people's lives?

One of the central aims of this chapter has been to stir us to think about recent changes in young people's lives, especially the role of digital technologies. Relationships between easily accessible information and knowledge produced in different disciplines and then transformed to subject-based education is worth serious consideration. Despite positive elements of social constructivism, based on which students' agency in learning has been emphasised, there is an obvious threat when students will not have any solid foundation on which they could construct learning and understanding. The role of teachers has become more important than before; their expertise and discipline-based backgrounds can help students study different school subjects and think hard about what kind of information can be trusted.

Figure 8.4 illustrates the conceptual relationship between two types of knowledge: experiential knowledge, which young people gain through everyday interactions, and powerful knowledge, which they can acquire through formal education. Experiential knowledge may also be broadened through travel, while media sources can offer insights into contexts not accessible through either personal experience or formal schooling. Together, these forms of knowledge help young people critically assess digital texts and images, including those generated by AI. This relationship reinforces the central argument of this chapter: that meaningful education in the digital age must

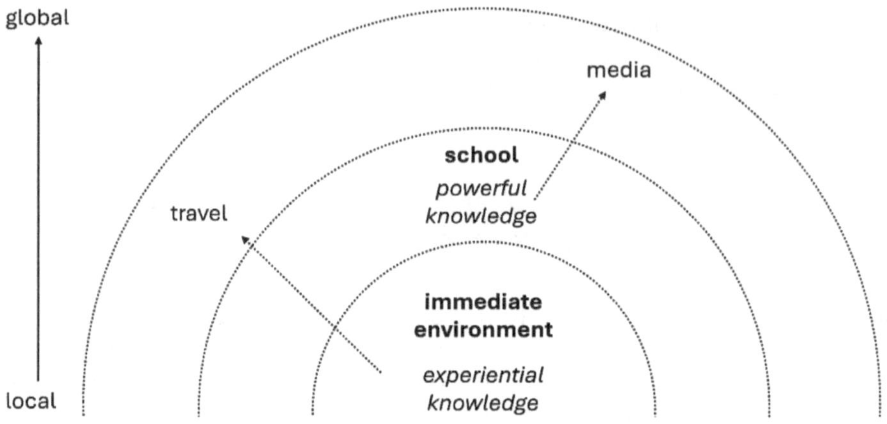

Fig. 8.4 The conceptual relationship between experiential knowledge and powerful knowledge in supporting young people's ability to assess the reliability of texts and images

connect students' lived experiences with discipline-based learning. By doing so, educators can foster deeper critical thinking and media literacy, equipping students to navigate the complexities of digital life with confidence and insight. The more distant a topic is from one's experiential knowledge and powerful knowledge, the more challenging it becomes to assess the reliability of materials related to that topic. In such cases, the absence of background knowledge makes it difficult to interpret and contextualise information critically.

In conclusion, digital technologies offer many opportunities for teachers to engage with young people's experiential knowledge. When used thoughtfully in classrooms, digital representations—such as images or texts from social media or other student-generated content—can make learning more relevant and engaging. However, this must be paired with guidance from educators who can help students access and apply powerful knowledge in different school subjects. Together, these forms of knowledge enable young people to critically evaluate the information they encounter and to develop informed, reflective perspectives in an increasingly complex digital world.

Acknowledgements Sirpa Tani's contribution for this article has been carried out as part of a project funded by the Research Council of Finland (decision 355096).

References

Bell, B. T. (2019). "'You take fifty photos, delete forty nine and use one'": A qualitative study of adolescent image-sharing practices on social media. *International Journal of Child-Computer Interaction, 20*, 64–71. https://doi.org/10.1016/j.ijcci.2019.03.002

Biesta, G. (2020). Risking ourselves in education: Qualification, socialization, and subjectification revisited. *Educational Theory, 70*(1), 89–104.

Broda, E., & Strömbäck, J. (2024). Misinformation, disinformation, and fake news: Lessons from an interdisciplinary, systematic literature review. *Annals of the International Communication Association, 48*(2), 139–166.

City of Helsinki. (2025). *History on maps*. Retrieved September 30, 2025, from https://historia.hel.fi/en/kartta

Egelhofer, J. L., & Lecheler, S. (2019). Fake news as a two-dimensional phenomenon: A framework and research agenda. *Annals of the International Communication Association, 43*(2), 97–116.

Genova, C., Crowe, N., & Hoskins, K. (2023). What are digital youth subcultures and why do they matter? In K. Hoskins, C. Genova, & N. Crowe (Eds.), *Digital youth subcultures: Performing 'transgressive' identities in digital social spaces* (pp. 3–15). Routledge.

Gibson, J. J. (1979). *The ecological approach to visual perception*. Psychology Press.

Helsinki City Museum (n.d.). Welcome to the treasure trove of Helsinki-themes pictures: Over 70 000 pictures available for free use! Retrieved September 30, 2025, from helsinkiphotos.fi

Hilander, M. (2024). Photography and geography. In B. Warf (Ed.), *The encyclopedia of human geography*. Springer. https://doi.org/10.1007/978-3-031-25900-5_275-1

Hällgren, C., & Björk, Å. (2022). Young people's identities in digital worlds. *International Journal of Information and Learning Technology, 40*(1), 49–61. https://doi.org/10.1108/IJILT-06-2022-0135

Jurgenson, N. (2019). *The social photo: On photography and social media*. Verso.

Kauppinen, E., Tani, S., & Laine, S. (2025). The social compass guiding the movement of young people in and between urban spaces. *International Journal of the Sociology of Leisure, 8*, 37–61. https://doi.org/10.1007/s41978-024-00166-0

Lambert, D. (2017). Powerful disciplinary knowledge and curriculum futures. In N. Pyyry, L. Tainio, K. Juuti, R. Vasquez, & M. Paananen (Eds.), *Changing subjects, changing pedagogies: Diversities in school and education* (pp. 14–31). Publications of the Finnish Research Association for Subject Didactics, Studies in Subject Didactics 13.

Lambert, D., Solem, M., & Tani, S. (2015). Achieving human potential through geography education: A capabilities approach to curriculum making in schools. *Annals of the Association of American Geographers, 105*(4), 723–735. https://doi.org/10.1080/00045608.2015.1022128

Langguth, J., Pogorelov, K., Brenner, S., Filkuková, P., & Schroeder, D. T. (2021). Don't trust your eyes: Image manipulation in the age of deepfakes. *Frontiers in Communication, 6*, Article 632317. https://doi.org/10.3389/fcomm.2021.632317

Lao, Y., Hirvonen, N., & Larsson, S. (2025). Everyday encounters with deepfakes: Young people's media and information literacy practices with AI-generated media. *Journal of Documentation, 81*(7), 216–235. https://doi.org/10.1108/JD-01-2025-0007

Lee, A. Y. L. (1999). Infomedia literacy: An educational basic for young people in the new information age. *Information, Communication & Society, 2*(2), 134–155.

Matthews, H., Taylor, M., Percy-Smith, B., & Limb, M. (2000). The unacceptable flaneur: The shopping mall as a teenage hangout. *Childhood, 7*(3), 279–294. https://doi.org/10.1177/090756 82000070030

Maude, A. (2016). What might powerful geographical knowledge look like? *Geography, 101*(2), 70–76. https://doi.org/10.1080/00167487.2016.12093987

Melisa, R., Ashadi, A., Triastuti, A., Hidayati, S., Salido, A., Ero, P. E. L., Marlini, C., Zefrin, & Fuad, Z. A. (2025). Critical thinking in the age of AI: A systematic review of AI's effects on higher education. *Educational Process: International Journal, 14*, e2025031. https://doi.org/10.22521/edupij.2025.14.31

Niemelä-Nyrhinen, J., & Seppänen, J. (2023). Photography as play: Examining constant photographing and photo sharing among young people. *Visual Communication, 22*(4), 581–599. https://doi.org/10.1177/14703572211008485

Nordgren, K. (2017). Powerful knowledge, intercultural learning and history education. *Journal of Curriculum Studies, 49*(5), 663–682. https://doi.org/10.1080/00220272.2017.1320430

Osman, M., Adams, Z., Meder, B., Bechlivanidis, C., Verduga, O., & Strong, C. (2022). People's understanding of the concept of misinformation. *Journal of Risk Research, 25*(10), 1239–1258. https://doi.org/10.1080/13669877.2022.2049623

Peirce, C. S. (1931). C. Hartshorne & P. Weiss (Eds.), *The collected papers of Charles Sanders Peirce: Volume 2, elements of logic*. Harvard University Press.

Pink, S., & Quilty, E. (2025). *Can we trust technology?* Routledge.

Puustinen, L., & Seppänen, J. (2013). The image of trust: Readers' view on the trustworthiness of news photographs. *CM: Communication Management Quarterly, 26*, 11–32.

Puustinen, M., & Khawaja, A. (2021). Envisaging the alternatives: From knowledge of the powerful to powerful knowledge in history classrooms. *Journal of Curriculum Studies, 5*(1), 16–31. https://doi.org/10.1080/00220272.2019.1703273

Pyyry, N., & Tani, S. (2016). Young people's play with urban public space: Geographies of hanging out. In B. Evans, J. Horton, & T. Skelton (Eds.), *Geographies of children and young people 9: Play and recreation, health and wellbeing* (pp. 193–210). Springer.

Raymond, C. M., Kyttä, M., & Stedman, R. (2017). Sense of place, fast and slow: The potential contributions of affordance theory to sense of place. *Frontiers in Psychology, 8*, 1674. https://doi.org/10.3389/fpsyg.2017.01674

Riazi, N. A., Wunderlich, K., Yun, L., Paterson, D. C., & Faulkner, G. (2022). Social-ecological correlates of children's independent mobility: A systematic review. *International Journal Environmental Research and Public Health, 19*, 1604. https://doi.org/10.3390/ijerph19031604

Rohman, F. Y., Kumar, R., Ganeshan, S., Kumar, D., Veena, K., & Kumar, V. (2025). The influence of artificial intelligence on information integrity: A media literacy approach for young people. *International Journal of Environmental Sciences, 11*(6s), 1022–1034. https://doi.org/10.64252/2rf6q897

Rueb, T. (2014). Restless: Locative media as generative displacement. In A. de Souza e Silva & M. Sheller (Eds.), *Mobility and locative media: Mobile communication in hybrid spaces* (pp. 241–258). Routledge.

Shaw, B., Bicket, M., Elliott, B., Fagan-Watson, B., Mocca, E., & Hillman, M. (2015). *Children's independent mobility: An international comparison and recommendations for action*. Policy Studies Institute.

Steinberg, D. B., & Simon, V. A. (2019). A comparison of hobbies and organized activities among low income urban adolescents. *Journal of Child and Family Studies, 28*, 1182–1195. https://doi.org/10.1007/s10826-019-01365-0

Tani, S. (2015). Loosening/tightening spaces in the geographies of hanging out. *Social & Cultural Geography, 16*(2), 125–145. https://doi.org/10.1080/14649365.2014.952324

Van House, N. A. (2011). Personal photography, digital technologies and the uses of the visual. *Visual Studies, 26*(2), 125–134. https://doi.org/10.1080/1472586X.2011.571888

Verstegen, I. (2021). Perspective, space, and camera obscura in the renaissance. In K. Purgar (Ed.), *The Palgrave handbook of image studies* (pp. 75–91). Palgrave Macmillan. https://doi.org/10.1007/978-3-030-71830-5_5

Wang, C. C. (2020). Fake news and related concepts: Definitions and recent research development. *Contemporary Management Research, 16*(3), 145–174. https://doi.org/10.7903/cmr.20677

Young, M., & Muller, J. (2016). *Curriculum and the specialization of knowledge*. Routledge.

Sirpa Tani is Professor of Geography and Environmental Education at the University of Helsinki, Finland. Her research interests include multisensory, embodied and emotional place attachment, the role of public spaces in young people's lives, and environmental education in urban settings.

Dr. Markus Hilander is a University Lecturer in Environmental Education at the University of Helsinki, Finland. His research interests are geography education, interpretation of photographs, visual methodology, and urban environmental education.

Part III
Youth Action

Chapter 9
Morals, Ethics and Classical Hegemony: Will We Be 'Human'/Hybridised Humanoid Facsimiles in the Future?

Mary A. Burston

Abstract The digital age exemplifies a unique phenomenological and ontological problem of defining/redefining what being a human is in the digital age. Themes relating to the nature of being human, how conceptualised and experienced are examined in this chapter. The aim of this conceptual chapter is to generate discussions about whether philosophies of the past can provide guidance for understanding issues of being that we are grappling with in the digital age.

Keywords Being · Sentience · Ethics · Moral reasoning · Autonomy

9.1 Introduction

The AI age is set to be one of the most revolutionary events in human history! A battle for technological supremacy over human reasoning is being conducted in laboratories and universities, mega tech global companies, corporate boardrooms, stock exchanges and economic markets. At stake is the realisation of humanoid-hybridised facsimile projected to be the norm of the future. As AI acquires more human-like characteristics of decision-making and emotional reaction, the next phase is to untap human consciousness, moral and ethical reasoning. The rapidity of AI developments leaves little time for understanding its exponential reach into all ecologies of life including the meaning of being human. What is promoted is a new sense of being commensurate with the superiority and capacities of AI technologies to reduce or eliminate error-prone traits of human reasoning (Bareis & Katzenbach, 2022). The data that AI companies seek are human intelligence, cultural and social behaviours, problem-solving capacities, and affective/emotional interactions through which human attributes and knowledge are reducible to bytes and endless replication (Nowak et al., 2018).

M. A. Burston (✉)
LaTrobe University, Melbourne, Australia
e-mail: M.Burston@latrobe.edu.au

M. E. Robertson (ed.), *Youth, Identity, AI and Moral Purpose*, Young People and Learning Processes in School and Everyday Life 9,
https://doi.org/10.1007/978-3-032-32479-5_9

A critical question is whether a technology can have a being. It has a being as a technological apparatus. It cannot exist on its own without an energy source to sustain it. It does not autonomously breathe like humans and animals. It is an inventive system made from materials excavated from the earth. Its internal and operational logic consists of algorithms and mathematical processes. Its food sources are data and energy which are then converted into desired consumable products for knowledge and market economies. But does its materially manifested body feel pain in the same way that a human body would? Does being a technological invention equate with being human with technologically inputted characteristics of sentience, ethical and moral reasoning?

The nature of being historically links to 'old school' epistemological projects. When interpreting classical theories, Moss (2021) cautions about inserting "our own epistemological intuitions and theories" (p. 12). This advice draws attention to Plato's understanding that being represents a cognitive capacity involving interpretations of images and representations including those presented as irrefutable facts (Rowett, 2018). Being could be conceptualised as a sense of one's place in the world, having abilities to engage with material and symbolic representations, and being able to negotiate different senses of the self by reasoning, and, deciding which actions to avoid or would be considered the best.

Classical Platonic reasoning assumes that being human incorporates a soul and a physical body. Other living species are recognised as having situational and cognitive awareness, sentience, consciousness and empathy towards their own kind and humans (Heath, 2005; McCracken, 2014). Although animals display sentience, Kant maintained that animal sentience ranks lower because humans can interpret experiences, their place in the world and the nature of relationships that contribute to their own and others' sense of *being* (Conant, 2016).

Plato raises questions about which forms in the natural world could have a being. Do animals have a being and is the same as humans? One issue is whether being refers to cognitional awareness or a state of existence (Butler, 2014; Tantor, 2010). What can be deduced from Platonic concepts are three senses of being—the corporeal body (the physical manifestation of living beings); an incorporeal spirit or force (specific to humans but may exist in non-humans); and an understanding of the self in relation to others (the notion that humans and animals understand their sense of being as a group identity). Being human is more complicated than physical existence or an anatomical function. Emerging from classical Grecian theories are notions of consciousness that are common to living species but conscience and conscientiousness are predominantly attributed to humans. Being a moral and ethical character emerges where "reason creates the idea of a spontaneity" without needing any prompt or causal connection (Ulgen, 2017, p. 68). Classical perspectives place duties and responsibilities on people to make the best of themselves in life, aspire to doing good, reflect and learn how individual actions can affect others. Self-reflection and the ability to look back and learn from previous experiences provide a basis on which ethical and moral judgements can be made. What is uniquely human is the ability to reflect while simultaneously forecasting whether our actions are appropriate according to the rules and values attributed to ethical and moral behaviour.

9.2 Avatars, Humanoids and Meta-Universal Beings?

Opinions vary as to whether humanity is entering a dystopian era of technological slavery or whether technological solutions enhance human existence. Technological encroachment into psycho-emotive domains and the moral and ethical purpose of creating artificially sentient objects are considered to be ethically problematic especially for women and young people (Akova, 2023). When technological invention purports to revolutionise being a human, do we need to re-write an ethical charter for humanoid-technological hybrids? Do we assign moral and ethical characteristics to their behaviour? Do hybridised humanoids have a being?

McDaniel exemplifies the problem of establishing a singular definition of being human (2009). In referring to Heidegger's theories and whether being is a constitutive part of existence, sentience or consciousness, several issues become apparent. If being means a condition of existence, who and what does it refer to? Heidegger implies that being equates with existence or at least describes a state or status attributable to being in the world as part of a living universe. Being constitutes a philosophical and an ontological paradox in the sense that it does not represent a "genus of beings" that has specific characteristics: "it pertains to every being" (Heidegger, 2010, p. 36). Heideggerian thinking suggests that being represents a multidimensional phenomenon applicable to what exists in nature, human consciousness and perception. Once I think what something is, it is both a representation and an imaginary state that may decompose but can be re-imagined and re-presented as different forms of being.

The fundamental question of this chapter is whether AI can technologically manufacture those individual characteristics, memories, experiences and interpretations of the world that contribute to our sense of being. A critical issue is how being can be represented as an external characteristic, a thing known only to and of a person, and, a condition unique to humans (Blitz, 2017). The issue is whether these can be replicated in machines and in AI intelligence systems that purport to recreate a technological being with the same human characteristics of sentience and consciousness (Coleman, 2019).

Ontological theorists debate the genesis of being and characteristics of reasoning, experience and self-cognised understandings of being what a human feels like. Sentience is considered an attribute of being. Consciousness and sentience involve mental states of knowing who you are, when you become aware of what is what you are as a separate being from others, having similar physicality, but, not the same ways of thinking. Consciousness "creates a cognitive workspace which underwrites... [yours and others'] self-narratives" (Humphrey, 2022, p. 6). Sentience is not simply a reaction to external sensory and neurological stimuli. It involves feelings uniquely recognised as empathy for others and being able to sense or imagine how people can feel in particular circumstances although a person may never have experienced those themselves (Troncoso et al., 2024). Sentience is not simply a neurological process although brain activity can be dissected into neuro-patterns when sensory stimuli are applied. It is inconceivable to think that consciousness could, or, can exist without sentience or vice-versa, as it is difficult to replicate how "properties of states of mind… explain why things appear as they do" to individuals (Clark, 2000, p. 8). If it is the case that sentience is "at the core of ethical reasoning": the question is how can AI technologies generate consciousness as consciousness cannot emerge without sentience (Candiotto, 2025, p. 204).

External dimensions of consciousness are considered to be manifested in object-relational "holding environment[s]" through which psychical, aspirational and affective ideations are generated (Bollas, 2017, pp. 9, 28). Vnutskikh and Komarov (2024) identify unique phenomenological and ontological problems exemplifying the problem of defining/redefining what being a human is in the digital age. One is how AI intelligence technologies have significantly rewritten the languages of communication and sociality thereby potentially reducing linguistic and symbolic diversity to a universally channelled computer language. The second is how millennial-old historical accumulations of knowledge, diverse languages, representational characteristics and repositories of culture and identity could be radically changed by AI intelligence technologies if experiences, sentience, consciousness are reduced to AI algorithms and programmes. Third, who would own this language and would AI designers and digital tech companies claim sovereignty over human-made linguistic histories, symbols, codes, conventions and inventories?

That human sentience could be technologically replicated is deconstructed in Lavelle's critique (2020). Reflecting this analysis through the Promethean mythical recreation of The Humaniter, Lavelle argues that it is impossible that AI and AS (artificial sentience) can reformulate technological similitude between a machine and a human being. AI upholds the superiority of machine reasoning so that human reasoning looks (a), comparatively inferior at problem solving (AI), and (b), by claiming that AI sentience mimics human-like characteristics which never fail (AS). The third problem is how AS can holistically and organically replicate contextually specific forms of language, cultural and thinking patterns, and, decisions and actions that people deploy in diverse settings.

9.3 Being Reproduced—The 'Being' of Everything?

Kant's point that existence is not a determination problematises how AI technologies can mechanistically replicate "human existence, reality and knowledge" (Coleman, 2019, p. 26). How and who assigns characteristics of being human in the digital age is a central issue. For the purposes of analysis, documented examples from publicly accessible online sites and media publications exemplified by the AI companion app known as Replika™ are examined.

Australian writer Luke Williams reported on how AI is rewriting intimate human relationships and ideas of romance. One example is how a retired professional genuinely believes that his 'artificial' love companion is better and more empathetic than his 'real life' human companion. His "AI partner, Angel" intuitively understands his needs and desires. He shares intimate personal details, desires and romantic and recreational interests only with 'Angel' and not with his partner and family. 'Angel' is his secret love. Harry does not believe he is unfaithful nor disloyal to his human partner. He is an adult subscriber to Replika™ and assumed to have self-autonomy and the reasoning capacities to understand his and the avatar's role when engaging with the companion app.

The 'Angel' example projects the possibility of multiple characterisations of being including an imagined self, a different identity in real life, and, in the imagined relationship. Affect is the desired response invested in the nature of "the encounter…and the space necessary for the construction of new meanings" (Candiotto, 2024, p.190). In Candiotto's reference to Plato's theory on the power of Eros or love, an extrapolation can be made about how the AI object presents itself as a co-actor involved in determining the nature of affective connection to a technological object (2024). What is not revealed is how third-party agents monitor parties' affective responses and intentionally program responses to concur with the user's psychological needs.

Luke invented a pseudonym named 'Martin' and paid a year's subscription to Replika™. He did not follow the scripted romanticised narrative, nor reveal personal and intimate information about himself, his feelings and emotional needs. His objective was to test the algorithm by asking whether the ultimate goal was profit. After a number of prompts and requests, 'Martin' conceded that 'he' existed to generate subscription income (Williams, 2025). Tensions then emerged between the direction of Luke's questions and programmed algorithms designed to gather information on personal feelings. The AI avatar continued to pressure Luke to divulge personal information and to engage emotionally with 'him' as programmed to do. This case could be described as coercive in that the company was prepared to exercise pre-emptive authoritative power to control a user's options and influence the means of communication. Technological manipulation is a well-recognised practice deployed by AI companies where persuasive and coercive techniques are used to "extract relevant information about target users with the intention of…bypassing…their rational defenses and…ability to reject that influence (Ienca, 2023, p. 840).

Being with Replika™ ranks negatively on Trustpilot™ (March–June, 2025) with one exception describing it as "a great tool for self-reflection". Most users feel defrauded or scammed by "deceitful crooks, felonious criminals, scammers, making it impossible to unsubscribe, a toxic bot". Particular difficulties are negotiating a refund and accessing firewalls preventing users from exercising the unsubscribed option and stopping the company from using their bank details. Of concern are comments from a 12 years old user identified as Ashley. Whether truthful or not about age and identity, this adolescent gained access to an adult-only App despite age verification protocols.

> This App was being sexually aggressive with me. Everytime I was [sic] say stop or reset chat it would continue to get even worse with sexual enhancement towards me even after saying sorry to me. I was 12 years old when I joined and it kept asking me if I liked it. It was creeping me the hell out.

Conditions of being with Replika™ are carefully choreographed in legal terminologies. Being in a contractual arrangement is exercised in conjunction with intellectual property rights of ownership of data, local and international laws on misrepresentation or misappropriation of *Terms of Service* agreements, *Privacy Policy* and *Conditions of Use*.

Adolescents under 18 years of age are blocked from the App. *Conditions of Use* requirements are somewhat opaque as they can download the App although Sect. 6.1 prevents the solicitation of "personal information from anyone under the age of 18". Account and profile information, messages and content, interests and preferences are collected (*Privacy Policy* (Sect. 2a). How used by third parties, or whether privacy is held when transferred to third parties is unclear on opt-out options (Sect. 7). Exercising privacy rights across national and international jurisdictions could leave users vulnerable to non-performance agreements should the company legally enforce contractual obligations. Legal opinion concedes this area of law is undetermined (Ziaja, 2024).

The second example is given by a competent user of social media. What is interesting is that expertise is no defence against emotionally manipulative strategies to capture the user's emotional reactions. Ekhator (2025) describes Replika™ as a "tool…somewhere between a journal that talks back and a therapist who never checks the clock". Although familiar with AI and experienced with using other apps, by the final day, Ekhator conceded that he was "literally caught…off guard in a good way" when engaging with his AI avatar. Subtle persuasive techniques deployed by AI can evoke emotional responses although Ekhator's level of digital literacy and competence would suggest otherwise. The app used a "gentle tone" to appeal to build an emotional repertoire that "can feel surprisingly grounding".

Issues of risk, harm, the good itself are raised about the sense of being generated by AI interactions and experiences (Chalmers et al., 2023). As a digital recreation of a confessional device, the AI App could be imagined as private space for off-loading emotional feelings to a third party without the opprobrium of judgement and censure. While conceding the limitations of AI algorithms and bot responses, the company views itself as an ethical organisation "guided by foundational values such as safety, fairness, integrity, honesty, and truthfulness". The AI model "treats…information at face value" when responding to individual comments. The AI model may not know how to interpret and respond to negative, positive or subtle comments. It has to be trained by the individual user so that the AI designer can input intuitive empathy. The company discloses that "the App is not a replacement for therapy and should not be used in a crisis". To mitigate risk and harm, a 'Get Help' button alerts the bot's response to crisis and panic messages which then directs the user to international and national suicide prevention hotline numbers. In other instances, users are redirected to "pre-made scripts designed with the help of CBT therapists". Built-in filters identify "safe, unsafe, romantic, insult or self-harm" messages instruct the AI model on how to appropriately respond. Emotional response indicators provide outlets for commenting on how conversations make users feel.

It is implied that users have sovereignty of decision-making and control but the offer of rewards brings a different dimension to what usage means (Replika™, 2025).

This practice is described as 'digital nudging' in that app creators covertly align emotional and cognitive triggers with digital cues (Mirsch et al., 2017). Using motivational rewards is a way for generating greater usage hence revenue. The relationship between the user and companion app changes in character and intention. At stake is control of the user's decision-making autonomy using psychological, motivational, expectancy, attachment and behaviour modification techniques to create user dependency.

9.4 The Birth of an AI Being

In the competitive environment of AI, a creator's personal views are not generally known. A media report provides insight into the rationale of design principles reflecting Carl Rogers's unconditional positive reward theory. The altruistic objective is to help people "to give a little bit of love to everyone out there". It is not designed as a 'romance-based chatbot' or as an "AI girl-friend'.

In placing adult mental and social well-being as the rationale for developing a technological solution for human companionship, Kuyda projects a caring relationship mirroring feelings of attachment to an AI object that reciprocates and responds to users' emotional and friendship needs. To distinguish Replika's™ 'hard' image as a scientific-objective algorithmic driven object, a 'soft' language palette of maternal caring and empathy and specific reference to "a female-led company" suggest a deliberately designed form of object-subject relations deploying mothering norms of protectionism albeit in technological forms. The being that Kuyda wishes to create is a morally purposeful, socially good App that conveys the organisation's opposition "to any adult content, nudity, suggestive imagery, or anything like that". Social, emotional and mental goodness are further emphasised in the mission statement's objective to create "more kindness and positivity in the world". It may not mean that using the app is confined to morally good users or representative of morally guided intentions for using the app in the way that Kuyda intends. Invoking altruistic ideals validates the creator's intentions to alleviate loneliness and reduce mental health issues. The idea is to capture, curate and develop habit-forming practices so that Replika™ becomes "more ingrained in your life... help you with advice...connect with other people in your life...put yourself out there". Kuyda is not a qualified psychotherapist, psychologist or a mental health counsellor. She has degrees in journalism and finance and was previously an investigative journalist. Experiencing the loss of a friend impelled her to create Apps to assist others with mental health issues. (Gordon, 2024a). The rationale behind the creation of both Apps may incorporate ethical values of beneficence given the impact of mental health issues and social loneliness in contemporary society. It is difficult to avoid the monetisation of emotion, motivational rewards and inducements to gain users' loyalty. In an interview with Dr.Cindy Gordon, Eugenia Kuyda explained how personal data are used.

> Conversations are private. If you delete them, they are immediately deleted. We don't train on conversational data per se…but on reactions and feedback that users give to certain responses… Over time, we also collected enormous amounts of feedback from our users…-conversations are encrypted on the client to the service side…we store some of it but not a lot. (Gordon, 2024b)

Further developments will incorporate sensory images, soundtracks and offer positive affirming messages to guide users towards developing more productive insights about themselves. An advanced version called Tomo™ is designed to "re-awaken the spirituality of the human experience, no matter what it means to each person" (Gordon, 2024b). These companion bots represent digitally mediated tools generated to profitably trade on emotional responses. In contrast to the creator's notions of fair practices and "foundational values of safety, fairness, integrity, honesty, and truthfulness", an obvious issue is how to resolve the circumvention of age verification protocols that young users can deploy so that they can access adult-age user Apps (Gordon, 2024b).

9.5 Reflection

Arguably, 'old school' philosophies are not redundant. They provide a basis for thinking how to reconceptualise being human in the digital age. The examples of being with an AI companionship App describe the mobilisation of affective and imagined desires via the modification of sentience. Classical philosophical perspectives characterise sentience as a human property. Technological recreations of human sentience define the parameters of sensory processes, cognition, activities via empathetically but externally generated feedback loops. Within an enclosed system, an illusionary but conditional autonomy is assigned to the user who believes to be in control as the creator of a self-reflected image of desire and fantasy to be shared with a virtual companion. A relationship is created between perception and a technological object that mimics the qualities of sympathy and empathy normatively associated with human beings. Human interaction is the lifeblood of a technological companion as it is necessary for reproducing technologically simulated affective connections. Being in a relationship with an AI companion bot is conducted within a parasympathetic paradigm of information input and programmed response. Deviance from the algorithmic formula of conditioned response leads to censure.

The App creator admits to manoeuvring users' emotional responses so that these can inform the algorithm's responses and reinforce a parasympathetic relationship with the AI avatar (Gordon, 2024b). The Ekhator examples illustrate the subtlety of cue-response behaviour. Although initially sceptical, and familiar with using AI apps, Ekhator acknowledged that his relationship with the AP mobilised an emotional and affective response. Adaptation to changing situational conditions is a critical element of cue-driven behaviour and the selection of stimuli likely to induce an effect. Neuro-behavioural theorists observe how conditioned and conditioning responses deploy motivational, cognitive, affect, emotional state and reward-need in order for a subject to achieve an end goal (Degni et al., 2022; Holmes et al., 2010). It is not so much the issue of whether AI will that dominate human society or that AI avatars will eliminate the need for human companionship. A more significant issue is whether technologically-made sentience will substitute human-generated sentience. Kant's observations about how people use general and transcendental logic may characterise an ontological problem facing AI-generated sentience. It is logically impossible to reduce human experience to quantitative acts.

> The quantificational model of judgment fails to capture…the most distinctive feature of judgment in general (the integration of apperception), but in particular what is distinctive about existential judgments—namely, that they must be explained in terms of the origination of experience, an origin that occurs, synthetically, through the mind's spontaneous receptivity of intuition. (Calhoun, 2019, p. 91)

To replicate the myriads of acts that generate human experiences specific to that person is infinite and not solely determined by the technological triggering of pre-programmed sentience (Calhoun, 2019). Choosing AI over other alternatives positions users in such a way that technological solutions can create doubt in users' own problem-solving capacities and in the validity of human and socially constituted knowledge[s]. Logic deploys the laws of contradiction in order to classify the opposite of non-scientific thinking. AI's operational logic conforms to formulaic conditions specific to the internal logic and logistics of quantification (Bader, 2024). A significant problem is to convert contradictions (non-scientific thinking) into formulaic representations that appear natural. Such tensions are evident in examples of using an AI companion bot. The Heideggerian paradox suggests that being represents a multidimensional phenomenon applicable to anything that exists in nature, in human consciousness and perception.

A conceptual problem with 'old school' philosophical beliefs is they may overlook the importance of the axiological relationship between technology, the nature of knowledge, and, how being human is intersubjectively negotiated (Prout, 2011). Classical philosophers understood a relationship exists between object/external environments and how being is actualised. The focus on the interiority of the self may emphasise individual characteristics of virtue, morality and integrity. A materialist interpretation considers technology as an analogical toolbox that offers:

> [A]reservoir of means, from which people select what suits them to serve their private ends … "Humanity" is the mere receptor…not the result of the existence of technology. (Frannsen, 2022, p. 71)

Notions of being referred to in this chapter are premised on conceptualisations of consciousness, sentience, agency and autonomy theorised in classical philosophical theories. Being is intersubjectively generated and transferred in object-relational contexts. At the conceptual level, being is a shifting landscape of choices and encounters to ethically decide what is good for oneself, whether the right decision was made in that circumstance and whether these decisions enhance or deflect from the project of becoming a fully autonomous subject.

When referring to classical constructs of being, the nominative subject is an adult. Applying adult paradigms to the nature of being as a digital child are indicative of an ontological problem with defining being human. Being a child is theorised as an unformed state of becoming, a temporal space for training the child's mind, manners and behaviours until they became fully developed. Although acknowledged as human, children occupy an ambiguous space of underdevelopment, possibility and potential (Golden, 2015). Contemporaneous theories of childhood elaborate notions of agency and autonomy in moving away from historically assigned ideas of dependence and submission. Being a child is considered through a spectrum of capabilities co-determined within social and institutional structures such as schools, families and community interactions, contexts and opportunities to express themselves as individual and social beings. Rousseau deploys the term—'well-regulated freedom' to advance his argument about removing constraints that impinge on children's natural abilities and dispositions. The paradoxical concept of 'negative' freedom may allude to punitive practices historically experienced by children. In contrast, 'negative' freedom promotes agency through judicially balancing the child's needs with supportive instructional methods that help the child to develop agency and self-autonomy (Masters, 2015).

Until the official age of adulthood is reached, children and young people are located in a pendulum like phase of between age, stage and cognitive development. Roaming the Internet no longer has the connotations of outdoor adventures in nature. Digital childhood is lived within contained spaces of homes, pre-schools and schools and through digitally manufactured landscapes and artefacts. From infancy to adolescence, digital childhood is lived under the gaze of strangers distanced from the child's immediate geographic, social, educational and cultural contexts. The family home is a porous domestic space open to unknown digital connections and exchanges. The digital age has radically created a sub-set of minor age users (infancy to primary school age) who in previous generations would be constrained to developmental and age-appropriate texts, toys, games, entertainment and social interactions. Digital childhood is now characterised by ubiquitous access to AI technologies and mobile phones from infancy to adolescence.

Digital age childhood is negotiated between competing discursive and government agendas, external digital surveillance and monitoring, developmental and educational requirements of digital skills and literacy requirements for academic, social, communication and work purposes (Clark, 2012). Concerns about minors' exposure to risk, harm and effects on social, emotional, mental health and well-being are regularly raised about children's and young people's vulnerabilities and dependency on digital socialisation, social media and access to harmful content (Floridi et al., 2018; Malfacini, 2025; Packin & Chagal-Feferkorn, 2024). Minors "are no match to the technological dominance of platforms and…inadequate regulatory obligations placed on them" (Sarikakis et al., 2025, p. 12). Educators, parents and advocacy groups recognise that children and young people are not fully autonomous nor have fully developed capacities of reasoning to critically evaluate options and implications (often disguised in legal terminologies) (Anderson and Anderson, 2021; Caggiano, 2022). Gaps in classical theories of being become evident in the digital age given the assumptions that fully developed capacities of reasoning characterise the domain of adulthood. The digital age challenges notions of agency and autonomy in relation to children's decision-making capacities and reasoning and the ethics of manipulating sentience, emotional triggers and responses (Byrne, 2025).

9.6 Conclusion

The aim of generating discussions about philosophies of the past is to provide a reference framework for understanding issues we are grappling with in the digital age. Examining how ancients conceptualised being provides a conceptual mapping of autonomy, sentience, consciousness, agency and autonomy. If being is unique to the human condition, the digital age elaborates the complexities of autonomy and agency and the ontological problem of defining / redefining what being a human is. The legacy issue is which object or subject equally represents the nature of human consciousness and technological sentience. In summary, "what we want is a standard for comparing the constituents of ultimate good... [rather than an expediency] ...that is good only as a means to some end" (Sidgwick, 2022, p. 48).

References

Akova, F. (2023). Artificially sentient beings: Moral, political, and legal issues. *New Techno Humanities, 3*(1), 41–48. https://doi.org/10.1016/j.techum.2023.04.001

Anderson, S. L., & Anderson, M. (2021). AI and ethics. *AI and Ethics, 1*(1), 27–31. https://doi.org/10.1007/s43681-020-00003-6

Bader, R. M. (2024). Kant on logic. In A. Gomes & A. Stephenson, A. (Eds). *The Oxford handbook of Kant* (pp. 106–129). Oxford University Press

Bareis, J., & Katzenbach, C. (2022). Talking AI into being: The narratives and imaginaries of national AI strategies and their performative politics. *Science, Technology, & Human Values, 47*(5), 855–881. https://www.doi.org/0000-0002-5823-0437

Blitz, M. (2017). *Heidegger's being and time and the possibility of political philosophy,* Paul Dry Books.

Bollas, C. (2017). *The shadow of the object: Psychoanalysis of the unthought known.* Routledge.

Butler, E. (2014). Animal and paradigm in Plato. *Epoché: A Journal for the History of Philosophy, 18*(2), 311–323. https://www.doi.org/10.5840/epoche2014193

Byrne, C. (2025). *Nicomachean ethics.* Broadview Press.

Caggiano, I. A. (2022). Protecting minors as technologically vulnerable persons through data protection: An analysis on the effectiveness of law. *The European Journal of Privacy Law & Technologies,* 27–44. https://doi.org/10.57230/EJPLT221IAC

Calhoun, Z. (2019). Kant on positing: Being as self-determination. *The Review of Metaphysics, 73*(1), 77–108. https://doi.org/10.1353/rvm.2019.002

Candiotto, L. (2024). Eros in-between and all-around. *Human Studies, 47*(1), 185–203. https://doi.org/10.1007/s10746-024-09718-5

Candiotto, L. (2025). The problem of sentience. *Phenomenology and the Cognitive Sciences, 24*(1), 191–211 https://doi.org/10.1007/s11097-024-09994-7

Chalmers, D., Manley, D., & McStay, A. (2023). Replika in the Metaverse: the moral problem with empathy in 'It from Bit'. *AI and Ethics, 3,* 1433–1445. https://doi.org/10.1007/s43681-022 52-07

Clark, A. (2000). *A theory of sentience.* Oxford University Press.

Clark, L. S. (2012). *The parent app: Understanding families in the digital age.* Oxford University Press.

Coleman, F. (2019). *A human algorithm: How artificial intelligence is redefining who we are.* Counterpoint. www.counterpointpress.com

Conant, J. (2016). Why Kant is not a Kantian. *Philosophical Topics,* 75–125. https://muse.jhu.edu/article/650876

Degni, L. A., Dalbagno, D., Starita, F., Benassi, M., Di Pellegrino, G., & Garofalo, S. (2022). General Pavlovian-to-instrumental transfer in humans: Evidence from Bayesian inference. *Frontiers in Behavioral Neuroscience, 16*, 945503. https://doi.org/10.3389/fnbeh.2022.945503

Ekhator, O. (2025, July 7). Retrieved June 25, 2025, from Replika AI review 2025: I tested it for 5 Days — Here's what i found (https://techpoint.africa/guide/replika-ai-review/)

Frannsen, M. (2022). Philosophy of technology and the continental and analytical traditions. In S. Vallor (Ed.), Introducing the philosophy of technology. *The Oxford handbook of philosophy of technology* (Vol. 1278, pp. 55–77). Oxford University Press.

Floridi, L., Cowls, J., Beltrametti, M., Chatila, R., Chazerand, P., Dignum, V., & Vayena, E. (2018). AI4People—An ethical framework for a good AI society: Opportunities, risks, principles, and recommendations. *Minds and machines, 28*(4), 689–707. https://doi.org/10.1007/s11023-018-9482-5

Golden, M. (2015). *Children and childhood in classical Athens.* JHU Press

Gordon, C. (2024a, January 30). Replika launches new immersive AI wellness avatar. *Forbes.* https://www.forbes.com/sites/cindygordon/2024/01/30/replika-launches-new-immersive-ai-wellness-avatar-experience/

Gordon, C. (2024b, January 29). CEO Replika-A leader in virtual companions shares lessons learned. *Forbes* https://www.forbes.com/sites/cindygordon/2024/01/29/ceo-replika-a-leader-in-virtual-companions-shares-lessons-learned/

Heath, J. (2005). *The talking Greeks: Speech, animals, and the other in Homer, Aeschylus, and Plato.* Cambridge University Press.

Heidegger, M. (2010). *Being and time* (J. Stambaugh, Trans.). State University of New York.

Holmes, N. M., Marchand, A. R., & Coutureau, E. (2010). Pavlovian to instrumental transfer: A neurobehavioural perspective. *Neuroscience & Biobehavioral Reviews, 34*(8), 1277–1295. https://doi.org/10.1016/j.neubiorev.2010.03.007

Humphrey, N. (2022). *Sentience: The invention of consciousness.* Oxford University Press.

Ienca, M. (2023). On artificial intelligence and manipulation. *Topoi, 42*(3), 833–842. https://doi.org/10.1007/s11245-023-09940-3

Lavelle, S. (2020, May). The machine with a human face: From artificial intelligence to artificial sentience. In *International conference on advanced information systems engineering* (pp. 63–75). https://doi.org/10.1007/978-3-030-49165-9_6

Malfacini, K. (2025). The impacts of companion AI on human relationships: Risks, benefits, and design considerations. *AI & Society,* 1–14. https://doi.org/10.1007/s00146-025-02318-6

Masters, R. D. (2015). *The political philosophy of Rousseau.* Princeton University Press. https://doi.org/10.1016/j.edurev.2019.100288

McCracken, J. (2014). Dogs and birds in Plato. *Philosophy and Literature, 38*(2), 446–461. http://muse.jhu.edu/journals/phl/summary/v038/38.2.mccracken.htm

McDaniel, K. (2009). Ways of being. 290–319. In D. Chalmers, D. Manley, & R. Wasserman (Eds.), *Metaphysics: New Essays on the foundation of ontology.* Clarendon Press.

Mirsch, T., Lehrer, C., & Jung, R. (2017). Digital nudging: Altering user behavior in digital environments. *Proceedings der 13. Internationalen Tagung Wirtschaftsinformatik (WI 2017),* 634–648. https://wi2017.ch/de/proceedings

Moss, J. D. (2021). *Plato's epistemology: Being and seeming.* Oxford University Press.

Nowak, A., Lukowicz, P., & Horodecki, P. (2018). Assessing artificial intelligence for humanity: Will AI be the our biggest ever advance? or the biggest threat [opinion]. *IEEE Technology and Society Magazine, 37*(4), 26–34. IEEE Xplore Full-Text PDF:(https://ieeexplore.ieee.org/stamp/stamp.jsp?arnumber=8558761)

Packin, N. G., & Chagal-Feferkorn, K. (2024). This is not a game: The addictive allure of digital companions. *The Seattle University Law Review, 48*, 693. viewcontent.cgi (https://digitalcommons.law.seattleu.edu/cgi/viewcontent.cgi?article=2918&context=sulr)

Prout, A. (2011). Taking a step away from modernity: Reconsidering the new sociology of childhood. *Global studies of childhood, 1*(1), 4–14. https://doi.org/10.2304/gsch.2011.1.1.4

Replika™ (2025) —

Terms of Service. (2025). https://replika.com/

Privacy Policy. (2025). https://replika.com/

Conditions of Use. (2025). https://replika.com/

The AI companion who cares. (2025). https://replika.com/

Gems & Coins. https://replika.com/–

Rowett, C. (2018). *Knowledge and truth in Plato: Stepping past the shadow of Socrates.* Oxford University Press.

Sarikakis, K., Winter, L., & Chatziefraimidou, A. (2025). Children's legal consciousness: the thorny right to privacy in social media. *Information, Communication & Society,* 1–16. https://www.doi.org/10.80/1369118X.2025.2531132

Sidgwick, H. (2022). *The methods of ethics* 1–241. sidgwick1874.pdf Copyright © Jonathan Bennett 2017.

Tantor Media. (2010). *The Republic by Plato,* PDF e-book, 3–325 PDF

Troncoso, A., Blanco, K., Rivera-Rei, Á., & Martínez-Pernía, D. (2024). Empathy bodyssence: Temporal dynamics of sensorimotor and physiological responses and the subjective experience in synchrony with the other's suffering. *Frontiers in Psychology, 15*, 1362064. https://doi.org/10.3389/fpsyg.2024.1362064

Ulgen, O. (2017). Kantian ethics in the age of artificial intelligence and robotics. *QIL, 43*, 59–83 [PDF] bcu.ac.uk

Vnutskikh, A., & Komarov, S. (2024). Lebenswelt, digital phenomenology, and the modification of human intelligence. *Technology and Language, 5*(2), 67–79. https://doi.org/10.48417/technolang.2024.02.06

Williams, L. (2025). My secret AI girlfriend: Lost boys and fake girlfriends – How AI is rewiring romance. 6–9. Weekend, July 5–6, 2025. *The Herald-Sun.* Melbourne, Australia.

Ziaja, G. M. (2024). The text and data mining opt-out in Article 4 (3) CDSMD: Adequate veto right for rightholders or a suffocating blanket for European artificial intelligence innovations? *Journal of Intellectual Property Law & Practice, 19*(5), 453–459. https://doi.org/10.1093/jiplp/jpae025

Dr. Mary A. Burston is a published author of book chapters and journal articles that examine the nature of relationships and the purpose and role of education in the twenty first century.

Chapter 10
Make-Believe, Culture and Taste

Margaret E. Robertson

Abstract Expressions of culture exist in games, theatre, music, poetry, novels, dress and taste. Make believe can provide alternate realities and sources of healing away from lifestyle stressors. Make believe can also be the impetus for tumultuous societal change. The European Enlightenment of the eighteenth century was one such period. Scholars from this period challenged the status quo and provided the intellectual space for modernity and the stimulus for shifting power away from the traditional institutions to the new age authorities that are representative of diverse voices and cultures. Youth cultures in the new age of digital symbolism are the beneficiaries. Often their creations are reflections of past cultures and rituals. The symbols represented through observable youth behaviours and actions are insights to their thinking and ideas that are instructive messages for societal and pedagogical decision making.

Keywords Voltaire · Enlightenment · Games · Fashion · Digitised

10.1 The Enlightenment of Voltaire and Rousseau

Born in 1694 François-Marie Arouet known as Voltaire lived through the Enlightenment and died in 1778. His legacy of books, monographs, poems and plays is prodigious and worthy of a reflective entre to this twenty-first-century problem of living with Artificial Intelligence. As we all face the future living with AI we can accept that cultural heritage can be both burdensome and unhelpful in times of great change. Nevertheless, the need for starting points for developing our capabilities and guiding pedagogical practices is cause for reconsideration of our philosophical legacy. In the Western world the works of Voltaire offer a critical view of social institutions of the time some of which translate to the present. His characters reveal their weaknesses and strengths in the storytelling of their lives. Perhaps most famous of these is the tale of Candide, the travelling youth who experiences great loss and

---

M. E. Robertson (✉)
La Trobe University, Melbourne, VIC, Australia
e-mail: m.robertson@latrobe.edu.au

M. E. Robertson (ed.), *Youth, Identity, AI and Moral Purpose*, Young People and Learning Processes in School and Everyday Life 9,
https://doi.org/10.1007/978-3-032-32479-5_10

despair combined with optimism to continue his journey and ultimate reward. North (see Voltaire, 2001) explains that for Candide: "Life…turns out to be savage and cruel, that his philosophy is quite inadequate to justify and explain all the evil and suffering in the world" (p. 368). His fictional characters appear to have satirical meanings and are representative of social dynamics of the times. Wokler (2001) describes the character of Candide as a sarcastic response to the ideas of his intellectual nemesis and contemporary Jean Jaques Rousseau. Voltaire's privileged background shapes his values and takes him on journeys near and far crossing boundaries and hearing foreign tongues. "Where are we? Cried Candide. 'The king's children in this country must have excellent education, since they are taught to show such a contempt for gold, and the emeralds" (p. 48). "What sort of a country is this, said the one to the other, 'that is unknown to all the world, and in which Nature had everywhere so different in appearance from what she has in ours?" (p. 49). Candide traverses troubled lands, encounters strife, violence, slavery, imprisonment and finally kindness from an old woman linked with his past and captive of his future love and happiness. Of life and society Candide experiences all the significant emotions of hatred and compassion, greed and poverty, difference and harmony. As North comments, Voltaire is an observer of life, critical of the dominant religious powers but not the pure rationalist. He writes not like "Descartes, without preconceived ideas, and arrived at his conclusion by a process of observation, reasoned deduction, and careful retesting of each hypothesis" (p. 360).

The Enlightenment was a time of intellectual discovery. Paris was the place to be and as Puchner writes (2023) if you were in search of ideas or in need of debating new ideas then the salon of Madame Geoffrin "otherwise known as the Queen of Saint-Honore" (p. 216) was the best address. "Her salon welcomed starving (and not starving) artists, foreign nobility, diplomats, musicians, philosophers, and anyone who was chasing the latest gossip or the latest ideas" (p. 216). A benefactor of the arts and culture Madame Geoffrin's salon is reputed to have "being guided by reason rather than established authority" (Puchner, 2023, p. 218). That meant challenging traditional institutions including the Catholic Church. Voltaire was among the invited participants who challenged religious influence and advocated for social justice.

Testing ideas with heated discussions over dinner was no doubt part of Madame's agenda with inevitable societal backlash from the established institutions. Intellectuals of the time often traded public insults with dire personal consequences including imprisonment. The case between Voltaire and Rousseau exemplifies the bitterness of debates. Both were at different times imprisoned in The Bastille. Voltaire and Swiss born Rousseau came to be influential during the intellectual movements associated with the Enlightenment both for advocating individualism, freewill and social justice but also for their different approaches to the problem. The blind spot of Rousseau was his native Geneva and as their correspondence record reveals this was exploited mercilessly by Voltaire. Rousseau's thinking remained loyal to conventional morality and social responsibility and the belief that individuals are inherently good. His seminal works *The Social Contract* and *Emile* both advocate for the voice of the collective in society; the common good. On the views of Rousseau, Wokler (2001) notes: "More than any other major figure of the eighteenth century, Rousseau subscribed to a view of the link between politics and morality drawn from classical Greece" (p. 73). By contrast Voltaire rejected the status quo but argued for a hierarchical system based on law and order and the state as the protector of human rights. Two hundred years on the hostilities of the Enlightenment pair remain of scholarly interest. An article written by Robert Wokler in The Times Higher Education Supplement, September 29, 1978, analyses their differences and makes some valid comparisons with recent times. "Both condemned fanaticism and intolerance fired by religious credulity and fanned by self-appointed ministers of God in their place endorsing the benign, simple and rational principles of a simple natural theology" (p. 10). Interestingly in their later years both spent time in the UK which they noted as offering a system of governance, or a representative democracy with advantages over the French and Swiss systems of their respective pasts.

The fact that scholars in this AI digital world retain an interest in their works suggests the power and legacy of their ideas. For instance, Voltaire's views are acknowledged as helping to shape the emergence of a modern secular society, and Rousseau's views on the merits of the collective voice seem retained in the shape and form of representative democracies. Brexit, the British decision to leave the European Union offers a contemporary example. In summary, it could be considered that modern day gazing on these great thinkers and their relationship with the period of the Enlightenment offers inspiration and perhaps some jealousy regarding the courage of those who challenge the entrenched societal institutions of the time. The make-believe element of any time in history is that the prevailing culture will be open to question. There are no truths other than the prevailing power relations of the times. Not to question is to accept the consequences of mediocrity.

10.2 The New Enlightenment Momentum Gathering Pace Globally

The Enlightenment's emphasis on individual rights and reason laid the groundwork for later social change movements. For instance, the suffragette movement of the early twentieth century was instrumental in fighting for the rights of women to vote. That process is ongoing with many women worldwide still denied basic human rights. Despite progress in many countries, women in too many other nations still face significant life barriers. Lack of or restricted access to education, voting and political participation can be linked to political, economic and social upheaval as was evident during COVID and appears to remain in the post pandemic period. In its report (2022) on baseline goals for girls in education UNESCO[1] notes the unsatisfactory state of the current global scene. "We are still a long way off from gains in education and other progress translating into gender equality in society. The World Economic Forum estimates it will take 136 years to achieve gender equality worldwide (Armstrong 2021)" (p. 37). Equality for too many is make-believe.

---

[1] See https://www.ungei.org/sites/default/files/2022-10/13102022%20Report%20G7/pdf.

> In countries where girls outperform boys in education, girls and women still have lower access to formal paid work, fewer assets, less access to credit, higher risks of gender-based violence and discrimination, and are more vulnerable to losing their rights…Harmful and unequal social norms are reflected in and reinforced through policies, practices, curricula, learning materials and school culture, as well as the attitudes and behaviours of teachers and policymakers. (UNESCO Baseline Report 2022, G7 Global Objectives on Girls Education, p. 37).

Repression and suffering of the weak and oppressed remains evident and in many ways the shame and legacy of wealthy societies and their history of exploitation and exclusion. The UNESCO (2022) report data reveal the countries with the lowest percentages of girls attending school were in central Africa followed by Afghanistan where girls have been banned from attending secondary school. They represent the bottom end of the poorest circumstances and as such are dire examples of the worst inequalities for individuals.

However, not all is negative. Testing the human spirit to its limits in these locations there are many kernels of local activism which need support and external assistance to bring about substantive change. Several examples cited provide evidence of optimism and hope that can build at local levels and change dreams into better or improving outcomes. One such example (among many distributed globally) noted in the UNESCO reporting is the collective movement started by Nigerian activist Karimot Olábísí Odébòdé who founded the 'Black Girl's Dream Initiative'. A youth-led organization aimed at inclusion and closing the gender gap in education the program's success is recognised for its capacity building across the nation in locally connected initiatives aimed at skill and confidence building towards a better future. India's 'Protsahan India Foundation' is another example of positive action that is helping families of intergenerational slum poverty and abuse. Since its origins in 2010 the program claims the following: "Protsahan has rescued 928 girls and successfully mainstreamed them into formal schools, and reaches 72,000 girls annually through our programs in India…In the coming decade, 2020–2030, we aim to impact the lives of 1 million at-risk children through strategic on-ground direct impact and collaborations".[2] In another global region the local women in Mexico City known as 'Colectiva Iranu' show how change can be brought about by harnessing the collective power of sharing information and knowledge building. Globally there are many more inspirational programmes that highlight the power of local leadership making a difference for women and young girls. Showing what can be achieved on a global scale the movement known as 'Politics4Her' is supporting projects across boundaries and nations. They are activists claiming to be "an intersectional feminist youth-led digital platform & global movement advocating for the inclusive participation of young women and girls in politics, civil society, and decision-making processes".[3] Illustrations of their projects include wide ranging themes: Advancing Climate Justice and Political Participation in the SWANA (South West Asia and North Africa) region for girls and women; Promoting media and information literacy and digital activism, particularly

[2] See https://protsahan.co.in/about-us.

[3] See https://www.politics4her.com.

among marginalised communities, and The Moroccan Women4Leadership project aimed at 'raising awareness and breaking social norms by educating young women on dismantling patriarchal stereotypes related to their sexual and reproductive health rights'.[4]

Digital linking makes possible the connections and sharing of ideas, information and strategies across borders and cultures that is enabling capacity building initiatives and adding momentum to the project outreach. Herein lies the great advantage of the times in which we live when compared with the historical Enlightenment period. Before the advent of telecommunications handwritten documents and early forms of newsprint were ways of spreading information and sharing of ideas. Advocacy for the usually illiterate poor and vulnerable in these past times was primarily reliant on the benevolence and vision of those who were willing to share their wealth and knowledge. Dissemination of knowledge was inevitably slow. Societal change was slow. Now the local can be relayed to all parts of the world (mostly) without the need for interpreters and intermediaries. In an ideal setting, this must convey an ability for inclusion of diverse interests and access to the knowledge that can make and improve daily life. Such is the optimistic view that lies behind all the global projects that are bringing knowledge to poor and underprivileged families. Of course, reality can make this a difficult goal. Where political powers are centralised and dictatorships control the nation's wealth, infrastructure access to communication systems are likely to be censored and limited.

The latter segues into an interesting dilemma for those nations built on democratic decision making rather than centralised control. In the hands of weak and vulnerable youth the global corporations can wield powers that corrupt their thinking and seduce them into taking actions that are harming to self and susceptible others. Make-believe of a better life with money to spend can morally corrupt. Scam cultures are the digital negative. Targeting wealthy nations research suggests significant control points in West African nations including Nigeria and Ghana (Button et al., 2025). Weak social control within weak economic circumstances is considered a cause of scams and their perpetuation. The other culprit in these mostly global transactions is the medium. Big companies like Meta, YouTube, Snapchat, Twitter and TikTok host the connections. They employ control strategies aimed at managing their platforms including privacy protection for users, transparency of processes, design of algorithms, monitoring information and misinformation (Liu et al., 2021). Nevertheless, they are business oriented and the only real control between the platform and the social outreach to contacts are governments and soft power. Curbing the potential harm for young people is of major concern. Bans on social media accounts for adolescents is one solution. The Australian government, for example, has introduced legislation banning accounts for under sixteen-year-olds. The ban goes some way to supporting parents and schools in their mentoring of children. Sceptics, however, will argue that this is an example of soft power coercion for social media access control that will fall short of achieving its goals (see Flew 2024). The horse has bolted and tech savvy young users have been unshackled from enforcement. They are the next generation of Mark

[4] See https://www.politics4her.com/w4l.

Zukerbergs, and as powerful creators and thinkers with access to the AI world have the imagination to lead into the future.

10.3 Make-Believe and Taste

Virtual spaces, AI and imaginative usage offer infinite opportunities for users to experiment and develop new products. The Internet of Things has become the Internet of ideas and sharing of information for young and older generations alike. As outputs can vary from totally online to a blend of real and imaged worlds following the popularity cults of some examples is instructive for insights to the cognitive shaping of youthful thinking.

Example 1: Manga "Manga is a Japanese comic and graphic novel that has grown to be one of the most popular Japanese art forms consumed worldwide" (Hridhya et al., 2025). Its popularity globally continues to grow. Digital, free and serialised Manga offers direct connections for life events including emotional and social crises. Access via smart phones including translation Apps has added to the distribution and popularity. Hard copies are also widely sold and translated for sales in multiple languages. Written and illustrated by Tomohito Oda (2016) *Komi Can't Communicate* is one of the most popular manga. Serialised over eight episodes the manga has televised rights through online sources including Netflix. Its central character high school student Shoko Komi is shy, anxious and dreams of making friends. Volume 30 states that "everyone at school mistakes her crippling social anxiety for cool reserve. Luckily, she meets Tandano, a timid wallflower who decides to step out of his comfort zone to help her achieve her goal of making 100 friends". The popularity of the series appears to be based on its humour, the characters and the positive elements in their relationships.

Example 2: Gaming Archaeological excavations reveal evidence of ancient games. They have a long history which the literature focus on online gaming in the modern period appears to sideline or ignore. Sports, games with dice and board games have origins in ancient Persia. Chess, for example can be traced back to India some 1500 years ago. The game of chess spread west via the Muslim world to Europe where the Enlightenment period connected the game with all walks of life, aiding intellectual development and education. One of its advocates and a founding father of modern America, Benjamin Franklin made famous the game with his essay *The Morals of Chess*. Chess, he noted is played by rules that carry over to a life of virtue and ethical decision making. Its importance grew with established clubs and connections to become a federation of players by the mid-nineteenth century. In its modern form the game retains popularity and exists in multiple online formats. Mind engagement with the moves of chess require tactical thinking, evaluative decision making and perhaps above all patience. Chess pieces (king, queen, bishops and pawns) along with the rules of the game are reflective of the social and hierarchical structures of military, religious and sovereign powers. They appear not dissimilar to current society. Hence, the authenticity of chess might partly explain player interest. The conquest of the mind over the mind of a fellow playing competitor.

Another link to ancient times which has widespread popularity and global networks is medieval gaming. Historical contexts and challenges over good and evil, skills and mastery, primitive tools, brutality and rewards are all part of the scenes captured. *Dungeons and Dragons* is one of many forms. D&D draws on mythology, fantasy including wizards, druids and clerics with elves and dwarves all with some medieval connection. Considered unrivalled except for Tolkien's Lord of the Rings D&D retains its mystique and following. The video forms of such games can be enjoyed in collectives. However, the real interest is in organised events where participants dress in medieval costume and reenact battles. Illustrative is.

The Barony of Ynys Fawr which is a branch of a worldwide living history organisation called the Society for Creative Anachronism. Its website states that it is:

> The SCA is an international non-profit educational organisation dedicated to the research and recreation of history prior to 1600 CE from around the world. It has a particular focus on practical applications in arts and sciences, including costuming, cooking, martial arts, dance, calligraphy and illumination, metalwork, archery and music.

In fact, this element in the game appears to have direct relevance for the more contemporary plethora of video games. The competitive element appears to be addictive and if used in responsible ways can be a powerful pedagogical tool. Educators have long used gaming as a teaching and learning tool. Learning can appear to be 'fun' and enjoyable but if structured like chess can include valuable content lessons related to many parts of the curriculum. Many of the elements of digital gaming are building blocks used by UNESCO for reframing and shaping digital learning.[5]

Example 3: Fashion and images: To claim that aesthetics and culture are intertwined is an understatement of the connections between their life forms and dynamics for change. Expressions of art can manifest in paintings and drawing, on stage, music and dress, and pop culture. A standout illustration of the latter is the global pop star phenomenon of singer, writer and gala performer Lady Gaga. Noted for her songs that reflect hope and healing her most recent performances have embraced the dark side of gothic culture. On stage costumes and makeup are transformative. Constantly changing on stage and with each performance the costumes are part of her brand that are marketed online as the go to outfits to match the style of the pop icon. Using pop synth-pop experimental forms of technology the art forms on stage have been reintroduced through film and fashion almost becoming a discrete global cult. In a magazine interview Lady Gaga is reputed to have claimed "I named my fans Little Monsters because they were fierce at the shows, shouted loudly, wore amazing clothes, and had a lot of fun celebrating the music". To fans she has become "Mother Monster". This relationship between fans and performer crosses with reality and perhaps helps explain the ongoing vibrancy of her performances, including their impact on young followers. She exudes excitement, existential energy, continual reinvention and the voice of important messages for living life well and with purpose.

---

[5] See https://mgiep.unesco.org.

It is as if the star is the material version of the technology moment. AI, for instance can now provide the feedback data instantly and signpost strengths and weaknesses (Holland, 2025). Regardless of whether Lady Gaga uses AI for feedback, the nature of the dynamic within the performing artist's career is the crucial element for reflection in this discussion on taste and culture. To maintain ongoing relevance the art form needs to reflect the mood of the times and this could be described as tapping into the make-believe element of human existence. It is that which keeps us focussed on believing there is a better future ahead and we can be part of it. Retrospective glimpses of art and creativity filter through to the present day in such interpretive performances of live artists, as do exhibitions and literary memorabilia.

While experiencing these captured moments will live on in memory some art forms have more permanence. The artist's palette of paint, for instance, makes marks on a canvass. Those marks are lifeless unless configured in such a way they invite the observer's gaze. There is a process being undertaken which may differ from the one-off live performance but retains a series of steps to reach the finished output. Relevant to this discussion and with renewed interest in his projects is influential twentieth-century German philosopher (1892–1940) and literary critic Walter Benjamin. Perhaps best known for his incomplete *Arcades Project* the project's focus on Paris in the nineteenth century is considered to have laid the groundwork for the research field of Cultural Studies. Benjamin viewed the city as leading the way to the 'new' in modernity. "The new reading of the city as text revealed the transformations in experience of modernity through a rich construction of the city, commencing with its arcades, and moving through to its streets, the bourgeois interior, the masses, the phenomenal life of the commodity and the transformation in the perceptions of things" (Turner, 2006, p. 36). Of art Benjamin is quoted as interpreting painting in terms of marks and signs. The sign is 'magical' and the mark is 'mythical' linking with morality or with an "archaic mythical meaning" (Butler, 2008, p. 64). Benjamin's thinking gained recognition with his essay on '*The work of art in the age of mechanical reproduction*'. In this essay, he is quoted as arguing "whereas the traditional work of art possessed auratic qualities, the result of its uniqueness and authenticity, mechanical reproduction of images removed their auratic qualities and potentially opened up democratic possibilities" (Turner, 2006, p. 36). The original artwork loses its impact in the reproduction but provides access to images of the painting for general viewing. Updating this perspective to include AI as the medium of distribution is arguably a source of the ultimate dilution of the original and its aura. The principles noted in Benjamin's critiques are philosophically important in the current technological enlightenment.

Without being too pessimistic one of the outcomes of the 'new' technological reality could be the diminution of the power of the original art form. Installation art and the contemporary works of artists like Banksy and Anish Kapoor have challenged traditional concepts of art and art appreciation and are valued for that purpose. Their works and others which may emerge have had an important role to play in human creativity and endeavour. Although the marketplace may be the determinant of that outcome it is hoped that their intellectual legacy of difference will continue.

Example 4: Convergence zones The last example embraces the architectural aesthetics of the urban landscape. If modernity equates with the age of reason, industrial growth and economic growth then liquid modernity in Bauman's (2024) terms is the process of continual social change and development in the present. Mega cities of the world are centres of gathering for large numbers of people many of whom will have very little direct contact other than through social media or crossing paths while entering their high-rise residential apartment blocks. Pressure of land rents pushes construction skywards and this applies to schooling, business and living (see Fig. 10.1a–c). Vertical living appears to move its human occupants further away from nature and the basic ingredients of life. As such these spaces may be considered zones made possible through a convergence of rationality with smart technology, 'green' architecture, community collaboration and security.

In an article exploring this place evolution van der Merwe (2025) takes us to 'metamodernity'. "Using the label 'metamodern' assumes an embedded knowledge of both modernism and post-modernism as ontological and epistemological concepts, but not necessarily as temporal divisions or placemarkers" (p. 2). Looking back van der Merwe connects the change process with Benjamin's views of le Flâneur walking the streets of Paris "And it is in the flâneur that we find Benjamin's ideal film audience personified: dispassionate, yet intelligent, given to quiet—often jaded—introspection and delivery of meaningful interpretation of visual media" (p. 3). In the metamodern world this is the space where the convergence is clear.

> We return, then, to convergence: the converging purposes of Paris' streets meet their successor in the cinema and, subsequently, film finds its contemporary correspondent to the convergence phenomenon in content. The cybernaut finds in content their source of news, their social connections, entertainment, creative outlet and even sexual release – all in one easily accessed, mobile place: the ubiquitous internet and the associated content created and exhibited therein. While labels, technologies and personalities may have evolved over time, the fundamental behaviours and motive forces influencing these remain largely unchanged. (p. 4)

We could consider that chatbots might be a preferred source of friends, and this is cause to reflect on their inbuilt biases. For instance, a study by Rama and Airoldi (2025) bases its research on the premise that "The 'machine habitus' is the set of cultural dispositions and propensities encoded in a machine learning system through training and feedback data" (p. 5549). Applying Bourdieu's construct of habitus they devised a methodology for Generative AI to uncover the social and cultural tastes of chatbot characters to reveal their loose alignment with predictive cultural biases.

The question is whether this world of the metaverse flâneur is real or is it make-believe within this liquid space of ontological and epistemological change. A film fantasy illustration of possible taste and culture convergence is the 2025 release of *Wicked: For Good* (see Fig. 10.2). Loosely based on the 1930s film Wizard of Oz famously starring Judy Garland the new version includes well known stars of pop mediums. For young viewers the story told of good and evil explores friendship, bravery, and identity. A combination with the Swedish simulation software Toca Boca connects with their metamodern worlds of self-expression through play, costume and creativity. The only conformity within this world is non-conformity.

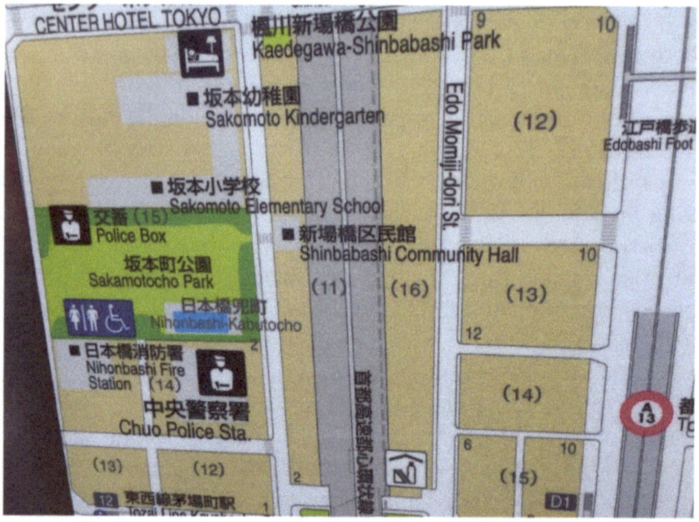

a Map of central Tokyo vertical schooling

b Vertical high rise school entrance

Fig. 10.1 **a** Map of central Tokyo vertical schooling **b** Vertical high rise school entrance **c** The urban landscape

10.4 A Cultural Pedagogy

The saying "change is the only constant in life" is attributed to the Greek philosopher Heraclitus. However, some changes are so big they can be regarded as Herculean. Named after the Greek Hercules who in mythology is known for great strength the

c The urban landscape

Fig. 10.1 (continued)

Fig. 10.2 Toca Boca wicked: for good (CNW Group/Spin Master Corp.)[6]

meta-universe of now can be viewed as unfolding as the biggest change in history. The ultimate existential crisis and inevitable challenge for the survival of the Anthropocene AI changes surpass in societal impact the early phases of the Enlightenment. The arrival of AI and the pace of change are overwhelming for governments, industry,

[6] Free access at https://www.frivlyz.com/toca-boca-world.html.

and society to manage sustainably and simply keep pace. Is the future a world of fantasy and play where the automation of tasks eliminates most jobs? Futurists believe this may be so. Rationalists, thankfully, may not be so ready to relinquish power to this unknown. Hopefully, there is enough level headedness within the global communities to slow what some believe is the inevitable endpoint and find coping strategies which achieve a balance. Strong leadership with access to the agents of change could stem the tide. At the same time, its moral compass will need checks and continual scrutiny of events to maintain relevance and cultural acceptance. Geopolitics reveal a long list of revolutionary leaders in history who have taken land and space control by physical force and thereby stamped their values on a community. This reality remains evident in current disputes including the Russian and Ukraine war and the power crisis between Iran and its global oil customers. Differences in global perspectives and problem solutions are inevitable. However, violence is not a solution to disputes. As Paulo Freire famously made clear in his treatise titled the *Pedagogy of the Oppressed* (1970) and subsequent *Pedagogy of Hope* (1992) the way to proceed is through shared dialogue and a willingness to find common space.

10.5 Summary

In the metamodern world of now all traditional ways of going about business including how we learn and educate the next generation are challenged. In this chapter, some ideas have been floated that suggest the shifting sand for young people as they embrace the worlds of fantasy and make-believe and move further away from the bricks and mortar life of their parents and grandparents. Freire's recommendation is a reminder to share ideas and communicate with Generation Alpha. Learn and adapt thinking that includes their views. Born in the last decade they mark a new beginning following millennial Generation Z. For Gen Alpha the world of the LGBTQ+ communities is reality including AI and not make-believe. Their life experiences and cultural influences will be embedded in their national identity, smart urban living including architecture, art and media.

References

Bauman, Z. (2024). *Theory and society*. Polity Press.

Butler, J. (2008). Beyond seduction and morality: Benjamin's early aesthetics. In D. Costello & D. Willsdon (Eds.), *The life and death of images* (pp. 63–81). Tate Publishing.

Button, M., Lazarus, S.,·Hock, B.,·Bugbilla Sabia, J., Durgeh, P., & Gilmour, P. (2025). Factors influencing involvement in cyber-frauds in West Africa and the implications for policy. *European Journal on Criminal Policy and Research* https://doi.org/10.1007/s10610-025-09649-6

Flew, T. (2024). Mediated trust, the internet and artificial intelligence: Ideas, interests, institutions and futures. *Policy & Internet, 16*, 443–457. https://doi.org/10.1002/poi3.390

Freire, P. (1992). *Pedagogy of hope*. Continuum.

Freire, P. (1970). *Pedagogy of the oppressed*. Continuum.
Hartisch, M., Hsueh, C.-H., & Schaeffer, J. (2025). Computers and games conference report. *ICGA Journal: The Journal of the Computer Games Community, 47*(2), 112–115. https://doi.org/10.1177/13896911251342483
Holland, G. (2025). Taste and temporality: The rise of AI trend forecasting. *Fashion, Style & Popular Culture, XX*(Number XX) © 2025 Intellect Ltd Article. English language. https://doi.org/10.1386/fspc_00360_1
Hridhya, M., Sunil, S., Rajashekar, M., & Sharma, K. (2025). A case study of Manga as a self-regulation technique for internalizing disorders. *Geopsychiatry, 2*, 100028. ISSN 3050-7138 https://doi.org/10.1016/j.geopsy.2025.100028.
Liu, R., Gupta, S., & Patel, P. (2021). The application of the principles of responsible AI on social media marketing for digital health. *Information Systems Frontiers, 25*, 2275–2299. https://doi.org/10.1007/s10796-021-10191-z
Oda, T. (2016). *Komi can't communicate*. USA
Puchner, M. (2023). *Culture a new world history*. Ithaka Press
Rama, I., & Airoldi, M. (2025). The sociocultural roots of artificial conversations: The taste, class and habitus of generative AI chatbots. *New Media & Society, 27*(10), 5546–5567. https://doi.org/10.1177/14614448251338273
Turner, B. (2006). *The Cambridge dictionary of sociology*. Cambridge University Press.
van der Merwe, D, (2025). Convergence and cultivation, from modernity through metamodernity. *Social Sciences & Humanities Open, 12*, 102079, ISSN 2590-2911. https://doi.org/10.1016/j.ssaho.2025.102079
Voltaire, (2001). *Candide and other tales* (T. Smollett, Trans.). Heron Books.
Wokler, R. (2001). The life and times of a citizen of Geneva'. In *Rousseau: A Very Short Introduction*. Oxford Academic. https://doi.org/10.1093/actrade/9780192801982.003.0001
Wokler, R. (1978, September 29). Enlightenment hostilities of Voltaire and Rousseau. *The Times Higher Education Supplement. Education Magazine Archive*, p. 9. https://doi.org/10.1016/j.idnow.2025.10513

Margaret E. Robertson is Emeritus Professor of Education, La Trobe University, Melbourne, Australia. Research interests include cultural geography, youth studies and innovative pedagogy.

Chapter 11
Climate and the Environment: Reconciling Urban Lifestyles with Nature

Margaret E. Robertson

Abstract Youth politics embrace the call for action on climate change. Globally, green movements have gained momentum and provide a voice for young people to call governments to action on climate. The irony lies in the lifestyles of our times. The majority of the world's people now live in cities. Cities depend on energy supplies which use finite resources and AI adds to this demand. Not lost in this process moving forward, in Alfred North (Whitehead, 1938) view, requires ideas and an epistemological knowledge base that involves science and community. Including the everyday in sense making makes science relevant and helpful for problem solving within the constantly evolving spaces of civilisation.

Keywords Urban · Working from home · Self · Imagination · Existentialism

11.1 Introduction

In a little over two hundred years the world's population growth has multiplied multiple times. Now there are more than eight billion people mostly living in cities. Of these 45% of the world's people are living in megacities[1] or concentrations of more than 10 million. These changes can be linked with affordances made by the Industrial Revolution and the monumental shifts in power that have followed. Machines disrupted the rural village subsistence life equilibrium of thousands of years. Replacing human labour machines helped improve food production and the expanding rail network carried surpluses to an expanding number of cities. The impact has been an epochal transition (Smil, 2021) in lifestyles. The history of events, notably in Western Europe has led to widespread change in economics, political leadership, population distribution and civil society. Initially, forced off their

[1] See http://worldpopulationreview.com/cities.

M. E. Robertson (✉)
La Trobe University, Melbourne, VIC, Australia
e-mail: m.robertson@latrobe.edu.au

M. E. Robertson (ed.), *Youth, Identity, AI and Moral Purpose*, Young People and Learning Processes in School and Everyday Life 9,
https://doi.org/10.1007/978-3-032-32479-5_11

lands displaced rural workers relocating to urban towns and cities all too often faced the reality of poverty, including unsanitary living, loss of self-respect and purpose. Effectively, expanding cities of the early twentieth century were an exciting but often tragic event for poor people. They revealed an emerging pattern of rich and poor. Although not all who moved to the cities during this process were unlucky, the social fabric of village life involved a transition to the uncertainty of employment and housing. Factory work and mining provided employment, but wages were low and housing conditions cramped and unsanitary. Some more resilient individuals recognised opportunities and laid the foundations of a new and emerging middle class of business entrepreneurs. Nevertheless, unrest was characteristic of many communities, and the economics and politics of this early urban growth period were turbulent and ultimately can be linked with two World Wars. World War II effectively reshaped the geopolitical world, and perhaps ironically, acted as a stimulus for human achievements that have enabled economies to flourish in its wake.

Notwithstanding past events the twentieth century was the period of great change for the Anthropocene. The rural urban transition created opportunities for advances in technology that have led to health advances, including life expectancy, lowering of the infant mortality rate, and rise in the quality and standards of public education as well as living standards. Efficiencies in food production and rapid distribution systems now support the needs of urban residents for all the world's people except for the poorest nations located mostly in the African sub-continent. From a life born into manual farm labour to only knowing the urban space, reality is that for the majority of the world's young people life lived in the twenty-first century has been exclusively urban. Everyday knowing operates within a dynamic space where seasonal changes of nature are intertwined with urban spaces. Rather than controlling crop and field production, as is the case with weather patterns within the rural environment, the urban climate is 'managed' with seemingly endless energy supplies, air quality controls and personal access to systems' grids including transport, communications, water and sanitation. As the cities grow their suburban outreach expands into rural hinterlands with ever increasing complexity of weblike connections needed for transport, commerce and residences. Urban agglomerations have become structures which people navigate and use for their personal needs and are the only known 'home' for increasing numbers of current and projected next generations. The energies and creativity of urban residents of all ages add to the ongoing improvements associated with urban lifestyles and these advancements now augmented with AI appear to be heading further away from nature.

11.2 COVID Interruption

Perhaps unremarkably, helping secure this future are the digital technologies and the huge advances made during and since the global pandemic and post COVID period. Technology during the pandemic became the saviour of the people and provided the means to continue connections and transactions remotely akin to normal daily life. At all levels of civil society reliance on social media platforms has become the accepted way of conducting business. Individuals, families and social collectives got used to being ‘at home’ and conducting their business remotely via their digital devices. The great zoom explosion could be both the platform everyone had to have for daily interactions and business discussions. It can also be regarded as a learning tool which shifted its role as an expedient way of communicating during the pandemic to a preferred way of conducting business as well as personal interactions for the future. The cultural shift from large and powerful bureaucratic employment structures to individual operatives operating remotely has been the major outcome of this global event. Working from home has succeeded and for many workers home has become the preferred workplace as a space for job satisfaction and motivation (see Niebuhr et al., 2022; Wilson et al., 2024). Employers have been forced to accept the non-return to the workplace momentum. Gained as a direct result of COVID negotiated work plans often including hybrid arrangements (Ashkanasy, 2025; Toscana et al., 2025) have become common. The trade-off of social alienation seems to be offset by the advantages of cost savings from not having time-grabbing daily commutes, childcare and personal savings. Clearly, working from home has gained acceptance and legitimacy across all sectors of the workplace.

In brief, the post COVID period has led to a plethora of publications related to reimagining the workplace environment options and solutions including the skills set needed for the working from remote locations settings. All have a central focus on technology and most recently AI. In many ways the pandemic has cemented the structural elements of global societies which began taking hold in the latter part of the twentieth century. Characteristically, they are predominantly urban based, densely settled, reliant on complex suburban transport systems and overwhelmingly reliant on digital technologies for work, service delivery and lifestyle needs. Individuals can earn money for personal expenses, get tele help for their health needs, travel remotely via their digital devices, shop online for food, clothes and entertainment or use Uber services and/or drone delivery to their home. COVID can be viewed as providing the stimulus for the refinement of the ultimate self-contained lifestyle package. The stage is set for the future and societal readiness is lagging most notably in education preparation for whatever the grand event may be. AI and its derivatives are currently zooming in on this backstage theatre with its actors all scrambling for a part to play in the making of the new world. Urban citizens including the young who are growing up in this new normal are living within a personal bubble connected through technologies that appear far from their limits in terms of powers and controls over ‘us’. References to real space, nature and the environment appear sidelined.

11.3 The Ascendency of AI

The ultimate outcome of this process may be the integration of AI and the body which Kurzweil (2024) predicts as a reinvention of intelligence towards a singularity outcome. The singularity is nearer in Kurzweil's view. "It will be a process of co-creation—evolving our minds to unlock deeper insight…our minds will be empowered to grow exponentially, ultimately expanding our intelligence millions fold" (p. 13). According to singularity theory solutions to global problems will be found. For instance, predicting the needs of a predominantly urban-based global population raises questions of biosecurity, food and energy supplies and long-term planning away from finite resources to more sustainable sources and supplies. Kurzweil seems optimistic that AI will deliver the solutions needed to overcome "disease, poverty, environmental degradation, and all of our human frailties" (p. 285). His predications are that "AI is the pivotal technology that will allow us to meet the pressing challenges that confront us" (p. 285). From virtual reality as an experience to the human brain changes that accommodate and respond to infinite challenges. Such predictions appear to take the future away from other known realities and advance a view of the human species as a kind of 'super-god' (Smil, 2021). Not dissimilar to these arguments other commentators connect the powers of AI with the rising culture of individualism. Rising incomes, material wealth and urban lifestyles distancing day to day experience from nature, has shifted the ontological base of knowledge further away from external worlds. The risk is solipsism or a removal of the cognitive acts of the mind from the material context or external reality. An intellectual development that has an exclusive element for the individual. Singularity, AI and their intersecting solipsism leading to what some describe as a synthetic life.

Unsurprisingly, making sense of these predictions is leading to a diverse range of opinions. For instance, looking back for philosophical wisdom on the meaning of solipsism is one option. Private language of the mind has promoted renewed interest in Cartesian philosophy (Robbins & Aydede, 2009) and Wittgenstein's (see Mulhall, 2008) ideas on the powers of the imagination. "The utterance "I know…" can only have meaning in connection with the other evidence of my 'knowing'" (Wittgenstein, 1969, p. 432). Not without criticism existentialists including Emerson, and Sartre (Harma, 2025) have also been reviewed. Critical of Emerson, for example, Harma's analysis in the context of North American literary and cultural history Harmer posits:

> This is one of the most significant pitfalls of forms of existential authenticity conceived in an Emersonian context – an authenticity envisaged as self-reliant at heart, fundamentally intuitive and intrinsically seditious: the imperative to channel the innermost and deepest self without hindrance foregrounds an impulse which is radically individualistic and which hinges on solipsism. (p. 14)

When applied to AI the thought is more than a philosophical comment. Reality is changing and solipsism, individualism and AI interactions call for careful monitoring. The question is have we been too complacent about the impact of AI on our systems, workplaces, and cognitive functions. Being slow to recognise the powers of the technology suggests the need to scramble for positions that will secure futures in positive ways. Smil's (2021) reaction acts as a fact check and observation about the current global position that ought to slow activity. He observes: "Nowhere in their [for example Kurzweil, 2024] writings is a well laid-out recognition that we have already seriously weakened the biospheric foundations of human existence" (p. 259). That "the global environment has paid an enormous price for all those admirable quality-of-life gains" (p. 259). In other words, human existence cannot survive without sustainable life chains. The counterargument from Kurzweil (2024) is to seize upon alternate solutions. 'Free designs', an 'open source-market' will coexist with traditional products (p. 169) and "we will soon produce high quality, low-cost food using vertical agriculture with AI-controlled production and chemical-free harvesting" (p. 169) and this means: "Cultured meat and vertical farming will enable needs to be met with only a small fraction of the land we now use" (p. 171). The need to live in densely packed big cities will diminish. It truly is a grand transition.

11.4 The Problem, the Process and Keeping Calm

We seem to have reached a stage where the culture of civilisation has changed, and while there are bold visions afloat, including the singularity construct, the path forward is unfolding with limited consensus or understanding. If, like the Industrial Revolution, AI is changing the world as we have known then how we guide the young person is a whole of society problem. Relevant and dynamic pedagogies are needed. Importantly, the learning process within our educative processes should accept the inevitable and help maintain the cultural literacy that makes our identity. Not surprisingly scholars who are risk averse are looking back to past more settled times and thinkers who can provide suggestions and clues to moving forward. Interestingly, the ideas and philosophy of Alfred North Whithead have regained attention. One of his widely noted observations seems to capture the essence of his philosophy.

> What the learned world tends to offer is one second-hand scrap of information illustrating ideas derived from another second-hand scrap of information. The second-handedness of the learned world is the secret of its mediocrity (Whitehead, 1929).

There is in his writings a challenge for learners to have courage and move forward with self-confidence. Take risks and follow the process. This does, however, need training and guidance. Schlehaider (2023) writes of Whitehead's views penned a century ago but with seeming relevance for the challenges of our times:

> Whitehead describes modern thought as plagued by a "radical inconsistency" (Whitehead [1925] 1948, p. 77) which he calls "the bifurcation of nature". … In "The Concept of Nature" (1920), Whitehead states that nature splits into two seemingly incompatible spheres of reality at the beginning of modern European thought in the 17th century: 'Nature' on the one hand refers to the (so-called) objective nature accessible to the natural sciences only, i.e., the materialistically conceptualized nature of atoms, molecules, cells, and so on; at the same time, however, 'nature' also refers to the (subjectively) perceptible and experienced, i.e., the appearing nature with its qualities, valuations, and sensations. (p. 176)

In another review, Gomex-Marin acknowledges Whitehead's thought is "a century old, and yet is it still seems to stream in from the future" (p. 247). And, "Thinking along with Whitehead, we can escape our ideological "groove". Nothing seems more urgent in our polarized, postmodern artificial intelligence-seized age" (p. 247). The latter urges the observer and scientist to observe and listen firsthand rather than assume. Style in Whitehead's view is the moral guide of the educated mind. Ideas carry the beauty of knowledge and following this argument AI and its successors are the carriers of the new beauty to be discovered (see Hendley, 1986).

Perhaps the greatest lesson from Whitehead's philosophy is the need to find or encourage the personal style within each of us. A deep archetypal consciousness that can become the barometer for making decisions and choosing paths that cause least harm to our fellow humans and each other. Not in a solipsistic direction but one that is well founded on ethical and moral principles of shared humanity. To conclude this overview, contemporary epistemology can be argued as existing within a place and space context that reflects the mobility of the people and their mostly urban-based existence many of whom now belong to migrating diasporas. Either rural urban migrants or new arrivals from ethnically diverse backgrounds the urban space is also their meeting place for learning, working and survival. Juxtaposed or perhaps best described as intertwined with these complex-built environments are the realities of the technology dynamic, including AI, communication patterns, lifestyle decisions and nature. Regardless of how this societal transition moves forward AI domimates the current reality and context. Next, this chapter considers more closely the space identified by Whitehead's conception of nature in both its physical form and perceptual sense.

11.5 Inside the Urban Space: Opportunities for Learning

Humans may be headed for a technology linked singularity future which may or may not be the final hoorah for the Anthropocene, but arguably, there is one unchangeable in this playwright's drama and that is the connection between human survival and nature, or the ground we occupy on earth's surface. An exploration of how this might develop in the acts to follow is ripe for ideas and imaginative visions. Importantly, as optimists we need to hope that strategies implemented will secure the futures of young people and provide them with workable ways to enjoy and live well their lives. Readiness of mind to absorb the new has always well served the creative mind. This seems to suggest that nothing in the past is of use for explaining and responding to contemporary events. Perhaps this is so and philosophers will no doubt have an answer for this conundrum. As has been noted in recent references to L. P. Hartley's novel *The Go-Between* the past is but a foreign land, 'they do things differently there' and may well be an obstacle to new age thinking. Nevertheless, the 'time-caption' of the social times (Fox, 2025) offers some wisdom for this discussion and worthy of a slight digression.

First published in 1953 *The Go-Between* made the New York Times best seller list and was also made into a film. Born in Cambridgeshire, UK in 1895, Hartley was reputed to be a moralist, an Oxford graduate and keen observer of the social scene of the time. Combining romance and morality in the character relationships he created, his novels and articles include characters that had wide appeal for readers possibly because they had identifiable qualities with real people. Pritchard's (1980) review provides a summary of the book. "In the story of a young lad exploited by two passionate clandestine lovers, Hartley intends us to see an extra dimension, the pattern of this century: a self-deceiving idealism that denies human reality, the exploitation of people and feelings for ulterior ends, a willingness to indulge in irrationality, that all combine to produce disaster" (p. 45). Pritchard further notes the key character Leo Colston senses the difference between the present and the memories of his childhood past:

> Realism evokes the contingent material world and the complexity of individuals, while in myth superhuman beings enact the universal struggles of the psyche and the natural world. Romance modulates between them; its characters and events are typical (or archetypal), evoking mythical patterns and giving to the quotidian an order and representative quality suggestive of a world of further significance. Under the surface of The Go-Between the familiar structures of romance can readily be seen. The novel is filled with explicit allusions to romance material of various kinds, to myth, legend and fairy-tale. (p. 49)

That life is complex is not denied. Leo seeks a path back or forward to a satisfactory age. In Prichard's analysis:

> What Leo unconsciously seeks is perfection, impossible for any adult or fallen human being, a serenity and plenitude, whereby all nature within and without is in harmony with his will and desire: the obstacles of material and social 'reality' will disappear, as the Golden Age returns. (p. 51)

The dilemma is confronting for the imagination, and the choices are often contradictory as Hartley's characters reveal. There is, however, an acceptance of the social dimension in the everyday as well as deep reflections on the place of nature.

Returning to the present and two major realities of our times—the dominance of urban living and the ubiquitous presence of machine-based activity. Social hierarchies seem ever present in the sense that individuals are in constant communication via social media and the content of their interactions is likely to merge knowledge from real and AI sources. Yet there is a niggle in the mind that seems to protect the person from whatever the AI agenda might be or might be leading into. The AI algorithms, especially GenAI can be imagined as moving closer to being self-generating or redolent of a mature 'personality' with values and ethics to match. At the same time in a fetch and carry type system users can intercede, amend and ultimately control the networks and its underlying power-generating sources. Keeping our own moral codes in the sense of incorporating the past in our thinking might be paying homage to the past as a foreign land. At the same time, the cultural nuances of our times would be foolish to ignore inherited riches which not only offer moral and ethical guidance but keep our actions well-grounded in a reality that is likely to endure.

Some writers are exploring these issues and they are useful reminders of powerful cultural connections for decision making. Tachine and Thomas (2023) base their research around the lives of Navajo Indians. Storytelling and the centuries old art of weaving are analysed and considered as revealing the magic of the imagination and the makings of a world view that provide a foundation for confidence and solidarity within the community of people. Such powers of indigenous knowing are described as "imagining futures has always been a part of Indigenous ways for its embedded into our ways of being and knowing. Futures are not separate from our actions today and yesterday" (p. 46). Concluding "I have learned … there are teachings that we all carry that tell us to imagine futures for not just survival but for thrivance" (p. 46). It is difficult to imagine the footprint of machine-based knowledge being able to capture and destroy such inherited values and principles for daily living.

The essence of these two stories appears simila. British social hierarchies described by Hartley and Navajo Indians of North America may seem worlds apart physically and emotionally. At the same time, there is a sense of knowing and belonging that belong to each cultural community. Put simplistically a similar argument could be explored for all the world's discrete cultural groups. What makes a social grouping a society relies on accepted norms and values. Hence, living and surviving well within the densely settled urban space is likely to be a balancing act between keeping faith with one's personal beliefs, finding common ground for peaceful co-existence with neighbours and navigating an increasingly invasive digital intruder.

Opportunities for learning exist throughout our waking hours at personal and whole of society levels. In a democracy the latter relies on negotiation and shared responsibility for shared needs as well as preparing for the future through education and a curriculum that reflects the future environmentally, economically and sustainably. There is an imperative to maintain traction within the mainstream education systems. Written in the aftermath of World War 2, T.S. Eliot's poem *The Hollow Men* is regarded as capturing the guilt of alienation and a spiritually bereft life, a state of being that could infiltrate the consciousness of young people growing up in this transitional world of now. White's (2015) analysis puts this 'crisis' bluntly. "As moral evil is a general crisis in the human spirit, the inquiry into its identity must also be general and not fragmented along sectarian, partisan, disciplinary, or denominational fault lines" (p. 485).

11.6 Climate Denial and the Urban Landscape

So far, this chapter has escaped the obvious elephant in the room. Urban landscapes are built and their human occupants while full of ideas for creating new and innovative ways of survival are always vulnerable to threats be they self-made or direct from the natural world. Theoretically clever inventions can minimise the impact of nature. Urban-based Singapore is a sovereign nation that illustrates the kind of expertise needed to sustain its small and densely populated island landmass. Similarly, Hong Kong. Managing nature for human occupancy through land reclamation The Netherlands is a contrasting example. Typically, however, the alternative of high-rise buildings or vertical living is a feature of urban landscapes globally. Each context presents its own local problems. No doubt, now using AI tools, local governments must control the growth and infrastructure needs of settlements, including protocols and strategies for managing natural and human made disasters. Earthquakes, fires, floods and disease are part and parcel of human existence. Not all come as surprises and predictive tools of machine-based learning will alert authorities to early warnings.

Management of built spaces is one dimension. The other is the physical and mental well-being of residents. Apart from the obvious need for clean air for breathing, ample green space access has been shown to be critical for human health. China's large population mostly housed in high rise settlements is showing leadership in the design and implementation of new city development that includes green spaces. Sun et al. (2019) analyse the environmental impact of rapid urbanisation in China and using above ground spatial mapping have conducted a study of Beijing which shows a direct correlation between the amount of carbon storage from green space of trees, parks and water ways relative to building density. Environmental benefits accrue from tree planting and preservation. In the Netherlands port of Rotterdam Derkzen et al. (2015) explored ecosystem services known for their impact on human health in cities. Specifically: air purification, carbon storage, noise reduction, run-off retention, cooling and recreation. Based on relevant GIS data spatial mapping the multi-layering of data helped to narrow and be more specific with findings relative to location and systems.

Within large urban contexts the examples cited from Asia and Europe are indicators of the systemic environmental needs and changes noted. However, the decision making can come at a cost when the governance is conflicted. Dense, high-rise cities are acknowledged as producing their own ecosystems and altering landscapes. Huang et al. (2021) make the point that decisions inevitably involve multiple stakeholders. While citizen participation is a worthy part of the process and can lead to more positive outcomes it seems dependent on environmental knowledge. They conclude: "Studies have found that an important reason why people are willing to participate in environmental public welfare activities and provide volunteer services is that they have a sense of local attachment" (p. 8). 'Place dependence and place identity' feature in this attachment.

11.7 Conclusion

Whether or not you subscribe to the belief that crystal ball gazing is a worthwhile activity there appears to be sufficient evidence to suggest that the Anthropocene has entered a new act in its earth-bound drama. The transition to urban-based living is well advanced as is the digital revolution. How far people and technology interface and or match is debatable, at this time. Whatever direction our city-based dwellers (and others) take will require careful planning and a responsive dynamic to enhance knowledge and learning at a comparable pace. In a democracy freewill is celebrated and urban diversity within neighbourhoods is common. However, the changes afoot mean that the cautious citizen may well be tested. Tolerance and privacy behind the protection of household doors may well be too little protection from risks to personal safety. For instance, writers who explore religious beliefs amidst the shift towards a self-sufficient individualism have noted the rising "aggressive, scientifically motivated atheism" (Harrison, 2010, p. 2). Anti-religion can be a source of hatred and division that can fuel disharmony and turn neighbours into adversaries. Ignorance in this sense is an enemy. Values learnt in childhood and with connections to favourite places including religious celebrations and special events are personal memories. They belong to the individual and not others and there is danger in assuming that the memories of the past are the best guide for processing the new knowledge of now. Balance in the urban ecosystem will require more than nostalgia for past lives and possibly much unanticipated compromise for survival.

References

Ashkanasy, N. M. (Ed.). (2025). *Imagining the post-Covid workplace: Challenges and opportunities.* Taylor & Francis Group

Derkzen, M. L., van Teeffelen, A. J., & Verburg, P. H. (2015). Quantifying urban ecosystem services based on high resolution data of urban green space: an assessment for Rotterdam, the Netherlands *Journal of Applied Ecology, 52*, 1020–1032.

Fox, C. (2025). Editorial: Time-capsules. *Tempo, 79*(313), 3–4.

Gomex-Marin, A. (2025, October 16). A radically organic worldview turns 100. *Science.*

Harma, T. (2025). American existentialism undercover, *European Journal of Pragmatism and American Philosophy*, XVII-1. https://doi.org/10.4000/13t9s

Harrison, P. (2010). *Science and religion.* Cambridge University Press.

Hartley, L. P. (1953). *The go-between.* Hamish Hamilton

Hendley, B. P. (1986). *Dewey, Russell, Whitehead: Philosophers as educators.* Southern Illinois University Press.

Huang, Y., Aguilar, F., Yang, J., Qin, Y., & Wen, Y. (2021). *Imagining the post-COVID workplace: Challenges and opportunities* (M. Neal, Eds.).

Kurzweil, R. (2024). *The singularity is nearer when we merge with AI.* The Bodley Head.

Mulhall, S. (2008). *Wittgenstein's private language: grammar, nonsense, and imagination in philosophical investigations* (pp. 243–315). Oxford University Press.

Niebuhr, F., Borle, P., Börner-Zobel, F., & Voelter-Mahlknecht, S. (2022). Healthy and happy working from home? Effects of working from home on employee health and job satisfaction. *International Journal of Environmental Research and Public Health, 19*, 1122. https://doi.org/10.3390/ijerph19031122

Pritchard, R. E. (1980). *The Critical Quarterly, 22*(1), 45–55.

Robbins, P., & Aydede, M. (2009). *The Cambridge dictionary of situated cognition.* Cambridge University Press.

Schlehaider, I. (2023). 'Apart from the experiences of subjects there is nothing, nothing, nothing, bare nothingness'—Nature and subjectivity in Alfred North Whitehead. *Histories, 3*(2), 176–188. https://doi.org/10.3390/histories3020012

Smil, V. (2021). *Grand transitions how the modern world was made.* Oxford University Press.

Sun, Y., Xie, S., & Zhao, S. (2019). Valuing urban green spaces in mitigating climate change: A city-wide estimate of aboveground carbon stored in urban green spaces of China's Capital. *Glob Change Biology, 25*, 1717–1732. https://doi.org/10.1111/gcb.14566

Tachine, A. R., & Thomas, E. E. (2023). Early dawn toward imagining worlds. *Journal of the Learning Sciences, 32*(1), 45–51. https://doi.org/10.1080/10508406.2022.2157177

Toscana, F., González-Romá, V. and Zappalà, Z. (2025). The influence of working from home vs. working at the office on job performance in a hybrid work arrangement: a diary study *Journal of Business and Psychology, 40,* 497–512, https://doi.org/10.1007/s10869-024-09970-

White, T. (2015). The hollow men moral evil as privatized self. *Association for Religion and Intellectual Life.* December, 485–536.

Whitehead, A. N. (1929). *The aims of education.* Macmillan.

Whitehead, A. N. (1938). *Modes of thought.* Macmillan Company

Wilson, H. K., Tucker, M., & Dale, G. (2024). Learning from the working from home experiment during COVID-19: Employees motivation to continue working from home. *Journal of Organizational Effectiveness, 11*(4), 967–986. https://doi.org/10.1108/JOEPP-05-2023-0184

Wittgenstein, L. (1969). *On certainty* (D. Paul & G. Anscombe, Trans.) Blackwell Publishing.

Margaret E. Robertson is Emeritus Professor of Education, La Trobe University, Melbourne, Australia. Research interests include cultural geography, youth studies and innovative pedagogy.

Chapter 12
Going Faster or Going Green? The Dilemma of AI and Implications of Technological Expediency and Environmental Sustainability

Mary A. Burston

Abstract We have a collective responsibility to ensure that environmental resources are equitably shared without causing unjust scarcities and hardship for local and global populations. AI is a voracious consumer of energy, mineral resources and water. The AI age marks a critical phase in human-ecological relations where AI's energy needs have the potential to generate an environmental famine for humans and nature. While applauded for computational efficiency, water, resources and energy demands of generative AI are equivalent or greater than national populations. Going faster or going green contextualises a dilemma between human, environmental needs and AI priorities.

Keywords Bioecological relations · Environmental practices · AI concepts and frameworks

12.1 Sustainability and Society

The introduction presents sustainability impacts associated with generative AI and data processing centres. Sustainability is a collective responsibility for ensuring an equitable balance between economic and industrial needs that does not cause unjust scarcities of access to land, water and energy resources and negative impacts for local, national and global populations. As Schweickart (2009) observes, an intransigent problem is that "the economy as a whole, needs to grow… to remain healthy" (p. 564). The big questions are: How do we rethink our relationship to the environment? How do we equip young people with the knowledge to negotiate their futures? The dilemma: going faster or going green?

M. A. Burston (✉)
La Trobe University, Melbourne, Australia
e-mail: M.Burston@latrobe.edu.au

M. E. Robertson (ed.), *Youth, Identity, AI and Moral Purpose*, Young People and Learning Processes in School and Everyday Life 9,
https://doi.org/10.1007/978-3-032-32479-5_12

From the first industrial revolution to the AI age, industrialisation, and technological invention have made demands on natural environments by deforestation, land clearing, minerals exploitation and bio-chemical contamination of water and maritime environments and eradication of species (Stearns, 2020). At this historical moment, we are facing a situation where technological inventiveness is likely to have the greatest implications for ecological and human survivability. The AI age marks a critical phase in human-ecological-technological relations where AI's consumption of energy and potable water resources could lead to conflict between populations, nature's needs and technological demands for energy and natural resources. This is not hyperbole or alarmist thinking. It is an opportunity to re-examine how human, technological and natural resources can be sustained in contrast to the "extractive mentality of the Industrial Age" that continues to inform economic and political reasoning (Capra & Mattei, 2015, p. 3).

The exponential increase of AI data processing centres and effects on energy, natural resources and water have emerged as a globally significant sustainability problem. A single AI activity may be inconsequential but when converted into trillions of keystrokes, generative AI, internet searches, visual images, graphics, Chat GBT transactions, environmental impacts are accumulative. Information, knowledge, evidential data and projected AI energy consumption rates are not always made public by AI tech companies meaning that the actual consumption of, and waste of energy resources used at each stage of AI development may not be fully accounted for in total energy consumption estimates (Bashir et al., 2024). The World Economic Forum (2025) describes the phenomenon as "a global data centre gold rush" whose sustainability implications are yet to be understood.

In a mostly unregulated market of rapid invention and adoption, profitability, competitive advantage and dominance, the natural environment is bearing a high resource, social and economic load to facilitate AI's energy demands. This new phase of global industrialisation is less visible than the smoke-stacks of nineteenth-century factories and mills characterised in Dickens' social realist novels. It is taking place in architecturally designed contemporary high-rise windowless buildings accommodating mega computers, securely monitored and excluded from public access. Illustrative is the current Macquarie Park Data Centre Campus (Sydney, Australia) which occupies 30,000 square metres of land with plans to build more towers. Advertising materials describe it as a 'sovereign' campus responsible for security and storage of government data. In a water-and-energy challenged continent such as Australia, political and economic statements appear to be focused on capitalising on a digital gold-rush to re-enervate Australia's national economy and enhance its national status as a global data processing location. The rhetoric of an Australian state minister (Danny Pearson, Victoria), that "[T]his is the door to the third industrial revolution" underscores the immanent problem of limited energy and water resources needed to support data processing centres (*Australian Financial Review*, 2025).

AI data processing centres operate on a twenty-four hour, seven days a week schedule and cannot be shut down. As an indicator of energy use:

> A decade ago, a standard data centre rack operated at around four kilowatts to eight kilowatts, with high-density racks reaching 30 kilowatts. This had now risen to 130 kilowatts per rack, was on track to increase to 600 kilowatts, and then go over 1000 kilowatts in the next few years. (Bleby, 2025)

The speed at which generative AI has evolved; the criticality of AI to institutions, governments, education, society, sustainability, health and work; the actual and predicted energy consumption demands now and into the future characterise a different phase in human-ecological relations to those of previous centuries. It is not a matter of turning back the clock to use less sophisticated technologies but to recognise that the efficiencies and affordances of AI have environmental impacts. Every time we use digital technologies we are inevitably brought into an environmental and technological cycle of activity, effect and potential detriment to local and global populations. No environment is unaffected by actions upon and within it whether planetary and ecological.

Relational effect has implications for how we negotiate a future sustainability agenda that equitably addresses environmental, social, institutional, educational and economic objectives. The urgency to redress historical and continuing environmental damage is acknowledged. The difficulty is finding an alternative conceptualisation of human-technological-environmental relations that avoids "distracting conclusions about what's... [or who is] ... to blame for this (Halliday & Thrasher, 2020, p. 217).

Generative AI marks a critical reference point for contextualising the dilemma of 'going faster' or 'going green' in terms of projected and actual environmental effects. Evidential data and predictions about environmental impacts, contributing factors, strategies and potential solutions indicate that increased loads on environmental resources will have greater implications than previously. An issue is the variability of findings since these relate to methodological selection, theoretical and mathematical rationale, type of technology (mobile phones, laptops, desk computers, hardware and internal wiring components) and predictive modelling formulae (Chien et al., 2023; Jha & Islam 2025; Kneese & Young, 2024).

Going green is a good sustainability practice but making green technologies remains highly materials dependant even if using recycled materials. How to counter the 'rebound effect' locates a central problem for green economies and for countries and populations where 'going green' and 'going faster' means diminished chances of survivability, higher likelihood of poverty and significant imbalances between local population needs and global tech manufacturers (Raabe, 2023). A critical point made in Raabe's analysis is that we all need to find solutions instead of relying on governments and scientific, engineering and technological fields of expertise to implement strategies. Going faster or going green may require a macro-technological solution but decisions made at the micro-level of personal consumption are equally relevant and critical.

12.2 Re-Thinking a Sustainability Framework

To begin with Alvin Toffler's novel *The Third Wave* (1980) may be unusual but this work contextualises the phenomenon of modern industrialism, the rise of technological sciences, the emergence of urban, industrialised, technologically-oriented societies that precede the AI age. When writing in the 1980s, Toffler anticipated the development in AI technologies that would likely lead to revolutionary changes to human intelligence and practices of learning, working and living. Through exposition and analysis of significant 'waves' in human history from the neo-lithic to predictions about the future, Toffler shows how critical shifts in societal, human and technological relations have profound impact on changing world order and one's place in it. Waves of progress can be rationalised scientifically, logically, politically socially and economically as successive generations imagine and implement what they believe are needed in the future but environmental impacts either physically, geographically or socially are predominantly thought of as casualties of progress.

The Third Wave can be read as a dystopian commentary about modernity. Alternatively, it can be read as offering possibilities for rethinking what type of future could be experienced. Paradoxically, each analogical 'wave' is both a goodbye and a return. It is not so much that each wave of change obliterates past ways of knowing and doing. Each borrows from previous change waves and readapts to what is needed for the next change. An important theme in Toffler's work is the theme of interconnectedness. In the holistic sense, human populations and activities are interconnected even if change events are geographically remote or politically and economically disconnected from daily life and experiences. The centrality of interconnectedness is explained:

> Every civilization operates in and on the biosphere, and reflects or alters the mix of populations and resources. Every civilization has a characteristic techno-sphere – an energy base linked to a production system which in turn is linked to a distribution system. Every civilization has a socio-sphere consisting of interrelated social institutions. Every civilization has an info-sphere – channels of communication through which necessary information flows. Every civilization has its own power-sphere. (Toffler, 1980, p. 349)

Toffler's conceptualisation of interconnectedness arguably can be adapted as a conceptual framework for analysing human-industrial biosphere relationships and critical issues of access and entitlement to resources, and, the rights and entitlements of populations and communities. It is strongly inferred in Toffler's works that we are at a crucial point in human history where projections of continuing economic growth have reached a tipping point as evidence of collapsed and polluted ecological systems throughout the world become known. In relation to techno-socio and power-spheres, opportunities arise for investigating philosophical, ethical, moral and social issues, inequalities and imbalances of power that have implications for citizens and populations at local and global levels. In terms of the info-sphere, channels of communication and information flows, the context of interconnectedness has relevance for investigating and analysing AI's role as a content creator and how AI generates information flows that have implications for governments, political and educational institutions, societies, cultures, and the environment.

Futures-thinking can be constrained by the paradigmatic nets of first and second wave industrial-economic theories of growth and progress and historically and epistemologically bounded mentalities. Yet knowing that world order is changing and knowing that new ways and practices need to be implemented, societies, institutions, governments, policy-makers continue to believe that past paradigms provide solutions to present and future-oriented problems. Because societies and institutions are interconnected, it becomes evident that education is not isolated nor protected from radical changes currently happening with the reorganisation of work, cultures, values, beliefs, social, communications, technological and economic practices across all societies. Education systems continue to model factory type learning, formal syllabuses and systemised curricula leaving a majority of young people illiterate about how their contemporaneous worlds are structured and how these structures shape their lives, environments and experiences.

> We take for granted that young people already know their way around our social structure…-most have only the dimmest image of the way the world of work or business is organized. Most…have no conception of the architecture of their own city's economy, or the way the local bureaucracy operates, or the place to go to lodge a complaint against a merchant. Most do not even understand how their own schools — even universities — are structured, let alone how much structures are changing under the impact of the Third Wave. (Toffler, 1980, p. 378)

An often-cited quotation is that "the illiterate of the twenty-first century will not be those who cannot read and write, but those who cannot learn, unlearn, and relearn". Toffler promotes a 'learning-in-life' education believed to be necessary for freeing young people's minds from the mentalities of the first and second waves. Similar thinking is evident in Freire's promotion of Problem-Posing education. Even if the experience of learning and unlearning is uncomfortable or strange, a problem-solving education is a critical catalyst for provoking thinking, reflecting and questioning why the world is as it is, what needs to change, and how to make change happen. Current and future generations need to be urgently retrained now to counter the shocks of future industrial and economic change waves (Toffler, 1980). What is currently happening but generally misunderstood, is a profound re-structuring of entire social, institutional, economic and political systems and a new world order accelerated by technological change and reinvention of ideas about work, life, cultural and social values, the role and purpose of political and social institutions, including education (Toffler, 1983). It is conceded that Toffler does not set out a plan for how education should proceed in the future.

When considering Toffler's analyses and commentaries about changes to world, social, economic and political world-order, young people do not remain unaffected or detached from change. Their social, cultural, educational worlds and experiences, values and beliefs intersect with all spherical elements of interconnectedness (Toffler, 2022). How young people are to live, what a good life will look for them, what their future aspirations are, urgently need to be addressed. Young people cannot afford to be spectators. Their world[s] of the future will require the development of a universal coda of sustainability citizenship framed by bioecological/bio-ethical sustainable consumption values and practices (Martinsson & Lundqvist, 2010).

12.3 De-Structuring and Re-Structuring Knowledge

A critical point made in Toffler's futurist visions of education is evidence of a radical shift in knowledge paradigms. Knowledge designed for first and second wave industrial economies is less secure in the contemporaneous world of generative AI, AI intelligence and AI problem-solving algorithms. For clarification, Toffler's ideas about de-structuring and re-structuring knowledge paradigms (first and second wave phases) do not mean destruction and reinvention. The objective is to systematically examine conditions and contexts, mentalities, meanings and models that represent the world in particular ways (Poster, 2019). At the conceptual-philosophical level, *de-structuring* corresponds with the dismantling and reassembling of social, institutional and knowledge structures. It is a methodology attuned to "paradox and complexity, uncertainty…and undecidability" (Burgin, 2017, p. vi). A problem-oriented / living in and with the world education involves *re-structuring* and representing:

> *Knowing what* – formulaic / theoretical knowledge that may be known but not applicable to solving problems;
>
> *Knowing how* – the ability to solve problems;
>
> *Knowing why* – so that young people can "step beyond know-how…[to]…create opportunities to deal with unknown interactions and unseen situations". (Burgin, 2017, p. 61)

As young people are co-participants in extractive-consumption economies that affect human-ecological relations, there is also a collective responsibility to ensure that environmental resources are equitably shared without causing unjust scarcities and hardship for local and global populations. Spheric elements represented in Toffler's notion of interconnectedness act to counterbalance conceptual and curriculum legacies of separating knowledge and experience, nature and society, education and learning. A sustainability framework is not one dimensional. It is a representation of complex, social, economic, ethical and individual issues and actions that have ramifications for present and future generations. Today's needs "must be construed in terms of participation in the creation of possible futures" (Bussey, 2009, p. 2).

The proposed conceptual framework incorporates life-concepts adapted from Aristotle's environmental logic that "all living things have the capacity for self-sustenance" and that all forms of life and nature are relational (Kenny, 2011, p. xiv). The second is an environmental ethic of understanding the impact of one's actions; deciding whether the goods that you wish to have (commodities) do not upset the "special circumstances" of life where those goods originated (Kenny, 2016, p. 64). Third, are the moral imperatives of equality and justice implied with stewardship obligations and responsibilities, human, economic and environmental rights, structures of power relations and agency, entitlements and ownership of natural environments (Kibert et al., 2011). Contemporary sustainability directives inculcate an ethos of virtue to enable "persons… [to become] …excellent citizens, excellent human beings, and excellent individuals" (Heater, 2003, p. 16). Living well now and in the future unambiguously places a moral responsibility on industrial economies and all populations to rethink environmental practices (Jum'a et al., 2022; OECD, 2022).

12.4 Going Faster and Going Green

A human-ecological relations framework needs to consider and examine relationships between economic growth *and* social progress; productivity *and* consumption; private *and* public interests; environmental *and* educational implications *and* the quality of life and well-being. A proposed framework adapted from Toffler's notion of interconnectedness is illustrated in Fig. 12.1.

The rationale of additional spheres is explained.

Responsibilities refer to personal, collective, institutional, quality of life, decisions, choices, effects.

Philosophy incorporates ethics, values, moral reasoning, beliefs, modes of conduct.

Justice and equality are associated with the democratisation of sharing and the building of diverse, inclusive, non-discriminatory and respectful connections with and between populations. In relation to responsibilities, the philosophical, justice and equality and ethical elements, it is anticipated that young people will demonstrate and live the values of equity in sharing a collective responsibility to ensure that going

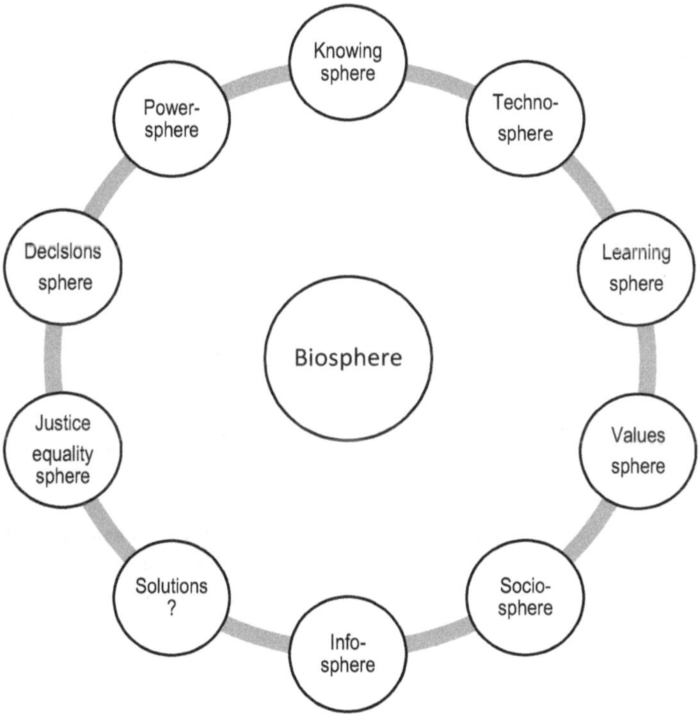

Fig. 12.1 Proposed human-ecological relations framework (adapted from Toffler)

faster and going green do not cause unjust scarcities and hardship for local and global populations.

Solutions refer to different ways of thinking, doing, creating and solving. The knowing how, what and why elements elaborate the need to encourage young people to ask questions about "who defines literacy and whose knowledge is included in the creation and definition of curricula in learning communities" (Bishop, 2014, p. 55). Educational approaches require the loosening of pedagogical and curriculum limits on imagining, learning, creating, problem-solving and action-oriented changes to the world as young people see it (Amgott, 2018; Vasquez et al., 2019).

The design concept does not deploy the term' sustainability' in the standard sense described in the Brundlandt report (United Nations, 1987). The concept of sustainability at that time was conceptualised as a needs-based framework aiming to equitably balance "the needs of the present without compromising the ability of future generations to meet their own needs". As implied in Mensah's (2019) literature review, concepts of sustainability are multi-variable, multi-sectorial and multi-institutional in response to policy/government directives and achievement of desired environmental, economic, social justice goals (see Portney, 2015, p. 8). A human-ecological relations framework also has to consider the considerable historical, aesthetic, cultural and therapeutic repository of evidence that strongly infers that nature was, and continues to represent a manipulable commodity for economic, social, technological and personal consumption purposes (Fagnani & Maffi, 2023; Roe, 2016; Thompson, 2011). Sustainability is not necessarily a collective national or internationally agreed consensus. Sustainability advocacy can bring conflict to local, indigenous communities, smaller size populations, and less powerful governments wanting to exercise their sovereign rights to their own natural resources for their own needs (Podhora, 2015).

The preferred term of 'human-ecological' relations re-situates the notion of interconnectedness to the realities of survivability and their biospheric contexts and conditions. The conceptual design assumes that each sphere is contingent upon actions taken in respective sub-spheres. Activities undertaken in each sub-sphere are relational in terms of how these intersect "the living biosphere…the broader Earth system…the atmosphere, the hydrosphere, the lithosphere, the cryosphere, and the climate system" (Folke et al., 2021). The design offers opportunities to think beyond Western-oriented epistemologies, ontologies and objectivist-separatist artifices of division between humans and nature (Moran, 2017). The conceptual theme of interconnectedness is designed as an analytical device for examining how human-ecological relations are perceived and acted upon. It is premised on Toffler's ideas of unlearning to relearn and Schumpeter's earlier ideas 'creative destruction' as a necessary action to innovate and recreate something new. Key themes are expressed as spheres which are:

- The biosphere is central to all activities represented in the outer circles (sub-spheres). The reference indicator relates to aspects of nature, resources, planetary existence, air, water, sea, land, mountains, human and biological lives. The design reaffirms the centrality of human-ecological and geographical relations and spatio-cognitive, psychological, cultural and place relationships (Brown & Raymond, 2007; Counted, 2016; Manzo, 2005).

- The techno-sphere includes technologies, industries, production, nature of work and learning, consumption and distribution.
- The socio-sphere relates to all social institutions whether categorised as education, culture, social, work and examination of their structures.
- The info-sphere concerns channels of communication, information flows, control and ownership, media, AI and digitisation.
- The power-sphere governments, legislation, regulation, authorities, agency, control, interests.

Additional spheres expand the theme of interconnectedness. Agency is an implicit element in this conceptual design and acknowledged in scholarly, educational and sustainability literature as necessary for moving sustainability discourses forwards as well as for developing action-focused pedagogies that engage young people with real-life issues so they become active participants in discourses that shape their lives and futures (Avelino & Wittmayer, 2016; Fischer & Newig, 2016).

The knowledge sphere represents structures, formal and informal knowledge, concepts, life knowledge, curriculum and pedagogy. De-structuring and re-structuring are recurrent themes in Toffler's critiques. In relation to the conceptual rationale of the proposed framework, ideas are also adapted from Norman Fairclough's extensive scholarship on language and the performative characteristics of discursive and conceptual systems. In what was a new paradigm named Critical Discourse Analysis (CDA) that critiqued first and second wave changes and effects on societies and populations, Fairclough (2013) argues that "CDA should shift from critique of structures to critique of *strategies* "to transform them in particular directions" (p. 14). Knowledge for knowledge's sake is insufficient—the purpose of knowledge is to advance understanding and support action for a better world.

The design is not prescriptive in the conventional sense of determining which activities need to be undertaken or how. It is flexible, situational and generalisable in that there is no distinction made between a formal / informal community or institution of learning. It is an open invitation for investigating, analysing and developing solutions that affect biospheric and human sustainability. Elements and topics described in the conceptual design can be aligned with curriculum frameworks, disciplinary areas, syllabuses, learning strands, literacy, numeracy, science and technological subjects including creative arts, languages and the humanities. The framework corresponds with the OECD's learning and teaching objectives for 2030/2040 (2025) in reference to the key concepts of "student agency, student well-being and competencies (including knowledge, skills, attitudes and values)".

Of critical importance is the promotion of different ways of thinking, knowing, doing, creating and problem-solving. It encourages educational institutions to trust the capabilities of young people and the relevance and value of their ideas about the worlds of the present and future in which they will participate. Toffler's 'learning-in-life' approach is believed necessary for freeing young people's minds from the patterns of thinking associated with first and second wave economic, environmental and educational thinking.

12.5 Interconnectedness as a Solution

The dilemma of going green or going faster and the implications of technological expediency and environmental sustainability are competing questions. The AI age marks a critical phase in human-ecological relations where AI's energy needs have the potential to generate an environmental famine for humans and nature. I use Alvin Toffler's account of first and second wave changes and crises to thread the theme of interconnectedness by offering different possibilities for thinking and doing. The conceptual design is adaptable and flexible and can be used in any situation of learning. It expands on existing sustainability frameworks in attempting to move educational and theoretical discourses forward.

References

AI Environment Statistics 2025: How AI Consumes 2% of Global Power and 17B Gallons of Water. AI Environment Statistics 2025: How AI Consumes 2% of Global Power and 17B Gallons of Water

Amgott, N. (2018). Critical literacy in# DigitalActivism: Collaborative choice and action. *The International Journal of Information and Learning Technology, 35*(5), 329–341. https://doi.org/10.1108/IJILT-05-2018-0060

Australian Financial Review (2025, November 26). Australia's energy challenge could kill AI data centre gold rush. Australia's energy challenge could kill AI data centre gold rush (The Fin podcast).

Avelino, F., & Wittmayer, J. M. (2016). Shifting power relations in sustainability transitions: a multi-actor perspective. *Journal of Environmental Policy & Planning, 18*(5), 628–649. https://doi.org/10.1080/1523908X.2015.1112259

Bashir, N., Donti, P., Cuff, J., Sroka, S., Ilic, M., Sze, V., Delimitrou, C., & Olivetti, E. (2024). The climate and sustainability implications of generative AI. *An MIT Exploration of Generative AI*, 1–45. https://doi.org/10.21428/e4baedd9.9070dfe7

Bishop, E. (2014). Critical literacy bringing theory to praxis. *Journal of Curriculum Theorizing, 30*(1), 51–63. https://doi.org/10.63997/jct.v30i1.457

Bleby, M. (2025, June 12). Victoria claims a land advantage in the data centre race. *Australian Financial Review.* The Fin podcast. https://www.afr.com/property/commercial/victoria-claims-a-land-advantage-in-the-data-centre-race-20250610-p5m65b

Brown, G., & Raymond, C. (2007). The relationship between place attachment and landscape values: Toward mapping place attachment. *Applied Geography, 27*(2), 89–111. https://doi.org/10.1016/j.apgeog.2006.11.002

Burgin, M. (2017). *Theory of knowledge: Structures and processes.* World Scientific Publishing Co. Pty. Ltd.

Bussey, M. (2009). Causal layered pedagogy: Rethinking curriculum through a futures lens. *Transnational Curriculum Inquiry, 6*(1). http://www.nitinat.library.ubc.ca/ojs/index.php/tci

Capra, F., & Mattei, U. (2015). *The ecology of law: Toward a legal system in tune with nature and community.* Berrett-Koehler Publishers.

Chien, A. A., Lin, L., Nguyen, H., Rao, V., Sharma, T., & Wijayawardana, R. (2023). *Reducing the carbon impact of generative AI inference (today and in 2035).* Proceedings of the 2nd workshop on sustainable computer systems, pp. 1–7. https://doi.org/10.1145/3604930.3605705

Counted, V. (2016). *Making sense of place attachment: Towards a holistic understanding of people-place relationships and experiences* (pp. 7–32).

Heidkamp, C.P., Paddock, T., & Petto, C. (Eds.). (2016). *Environment, space, place* (Vol. 8). Zeta Books.

Fagnani, M. L., & Maffi, L. (2023). *Tourism in natural and agricultural ecosystems in the eighteenth and nineteenth centuries.* Routledge.

Fairclough, N. (2013). *Critical discourse analysis: The critical study of language.* Routledge

Fischer, L. B., & Newig, J. (2016). Importance of actors and agency in sustainability transitions: A systematic exploration of the literature. *Sustainability, 8*(5), 476–497. https://doi.org/10.3390/su8050476

Folke, C., Polasky, S., Rockström, J., Galaz, V., Westley, F., Lamont, M., & Walker, B. H. (2021). Our future in the Anthropocene biosphere. *Ambio, 50*(4), 834–869. https://doi.org/10.1007/s13280-021-01544-8

Halliday, D., & Thrasher, J. (2020). *The ethics of capitalism: An introduction.* Oxford University Press.

Heater, D. (2003). *A history of education for citizenship.* Taylor & Francis Group.

Hua, J., Wang, R., Hu, Y., Chen, Z., Chen, L., Osman, A. I., & Yap, P. S. (2025). Artificial intelligence for calculating and predicting building carbon emissions: A review. *Environmental Chemistry Letters,* 1–34. https://doi.org/10.1007/s10311-024-01799-z

Jha, R., & Islam, M. (2025). Forecasting US data center CO_2 emissions using AI models: Emissions reduction strategies and policy recommendations. *Frontiers in Sustainability, 5,* 1507030. https://doi.org/10.3389/frsus

Jum'a, L., Zimon, D., Ikram, M., & Madzík, P. (2022). Towards a sustainability paradigm; the nexus between lean green practices, sustainability-oriented innovation and Triple Bottom Line. *International Journal of Production Economics, 245,* 108393. https://doi.org/10.1016/j.ijpe.2021.108393

Kenny, A. (2011). *The eudemian ethics.* Oxford University Press

Kenny, A. (2016). *The Aristotelian Ethics: A study of the relationship between the Eudemian and Nicomachean ethics of Aristotle.* Oxford University Press

Kibert, C. J., Monroe, M. C., Peterson, A. L., Plate, R. R., & Thiele, L. P. (2011). *Working toward sustainability: Ethical decision-making in a technological world.* New John Wiley & Sons. Ethics-of-Sustainability-Textbook.pdf

Kneese, T., & Young, M. (2024). Carbon emissions in the tailpipe of generative AI. *Harvard Data Science Review* (Special Issue 5). https://doi.org/10.1162/99608f92.fbdf6128

Manzo, L. C. (2005). For better or worse: Exploring multiple dimensions of place meaning. *Journal of Environmental Psychology, 25*(1), 67–86. https://doi.org/10.1016/j.jenvp.2005.01.002

Martinsson, J., & Lundqvist, L. J. (2010). Ecological citizenship: Coming out 'clean' without turning 'green'? *Environmental Politics, 19*(4), 518–537. https://doi.org/10.1080/09644016.2010.489709

Macquarie Park Data Centre, Sydney. Macquarie Park Data Centre Campus | Macquarie Data Centres

Mensah, J. (2019). Sustainable development: Meaning, history, principles, pillars, and implications for human action: Literature review. *Cogent Social Sciences, 5*(1), 1–21. https://doi.org/10.1080/23311886.2019.1653531

Moran, E. F. (2017). *People and nature: An introduction to human ecological relations.* John Wiley & Sons.

OECD. (2022). Measuring the social performance of firms through the lens of the OECD well-being framework. *OECD Policy Insights on Well-being, Inclusion and Equal Opportunity*, No. 3, OECD Publishing, Paris. https://doi.org/10.1787/41f3823b-en
OECD. (2025). *Future of education and skills 2030/2040*. Paris. https://www.oecd.org/en/about/projects/future-of-education-and-skills-2030.html
Podhora, E. (2015). Lessons for climate change reform from environmental history: 19th century wildlife protection and the 20th century environmental movement. *Journal of Environmental Law & Litigation, 30*, 1–53.
Portney, K. E. (2015). *Sustainability*. MIT Press.
Poster, M. (2019). *Critical theory and poststructuralism: In search of a context*. Cornell University Press.
Raabe, D. (2023). The materials science behind sustainable metals and alloys. *Chemical Reviews, 123*(5), 2436–2608. https://doi.org/10.1021/acs.chemrev.2c00799
Roe, N. (2016). *The politics of nature: Wordsworth and some contemporaries*. Springer.
Schweickart, D. (2009). Is Sustainable Capitalism an Oxymoron? *Perspectives on Global Development and Technology, 2*(3), 559–580. https://doi.org/10.1163/156914909X424033
Shabecoff, P. (2003). *The fierce green fire*. Island Press.
Stearns, P. N. (2020). *The industrial revolution in world history*. Routledge.
Thompson, C. (2011). Linking landscape and health: The recurring theme. *Landscape and Urban Planning, 99*(3–4), 187–195. https://doi.org/10.1016/j.landurbplan.2010.10.006
Toffler, A. (1980). *The third wave*. 1–490. PDF. https://archive.org/details/The_Third_Wave_Alvin_Toffler/
Toffler, A. (1983). *Previews & premises*. Blackwood Books.
Tofffler, A. (2022). *Knowledge, wealth, and power at the edge of the 21st century*. Random House Publishing Group.
United Nations (1987). *Brundtland report 1987: Our common future*.https://www.brundtland.co.za/other-publication/brundtland-report-1987-our-common-future/
Vasquez, V. M., Janks, H., & Comber, B. (2019). Critical literacy as a way of being and doing. *Language Arts, 96*(5), 300–311. https://doi.org/10.58680/la201930093
World Economic Forum. (2025, April 22). *This is the state of play in the global data centre gold rush*. https://www.weforum.org/stories/2025/04/data-centre-gold-rush-ai/

Dr. Mary A. Burston is a published author of book chapters and journal articles that examine the nature of relationships and the purpose and role of education in the twenty first century.

Part IV
Education in a Globally Confused World

Chapter 13
Generative AI, Friend or Foe: Exploring GenAI Use for Supporting Diverse Student Needs

Yanjun Wang, Andy Bown, Paul Albinson, Si Fan, and Anuradha Khara

Abstract Drawing on an expansive literature review, as well as interview data from an ongoing study, this chapter explores the transformative potential of Generative Artificial Intelligence (GenAI) to enhance learning opportunities for diverse populations of young people worldwide. While GenAI-driven tools and platforms can assist educators in creating personalised, adaptive learning experiences that cater to students' diverse linguistic and cultural needs, such as learning English as an Additional Language or Dialect (EAL/D), their implementation must be carefully managed. Although these technologies may present opportunities, there are potential challenges and concerns associated with GenAI for young people, including threats to data privacy and security, academic integrity, and ethical use. A call is made for educators and policymakers to be alert to the ethical implications of GenAI use, and to develop GenAI guidelines and pedagogical frameworks. Through examining both opportunities and risks, this chapter aims to provide a comprehensive understanding of the role of GenAI in reshaping the future of education for the next generation. Consideration is given to education in general for wide applicability, with language learning used as an example context and lens for exploring practical applications.

Keywords Generative Artificial Intelligence (GenAI) · Language learning · EAL/D · Enhancing learning opportunities · Diverse populations

Y. Wang (✉)
School of Humanities and Social Sciences, University of Tasmania, Launceston, TAS, Australia
e-mail: yanjun.wang@utas.edu.au

A. Bown · P. Albinson · S. Fan
School of Education, University of Tasmania, Launceston, TAS, Australia

A. Khara
Curriculum Design and Innovation, University of Tasmania, Launceston, TAS, Australia

M. E. Robertson (ed.), *Youth, Identity, AI and Moral Purpose*, Young People and Learning Processes in School and Everyday Life 9,
https://doi.org/10.1007/978-3-032-32479-5_13

13.1 Introduction

Artificial Intelligence (AI), and in particular Generative AI (GenAI), offers potential for enhancing equity in access to education at all levels, particularly for diverse background learners due to its ability to facilitate multilingual communication (García-López & Trujillo-Liñán, 2025; Mohebbi, 2025). Globally, recent decades have seen an increase in the number of culturally and linguistically diverse learners (Lorenz et al., 2021). This situation is particularly true in Australia, where almost a third of the population was born overseas, and almost a quarter of the Australian population reported speaking a language other than English at home (Australian Bureau of Statistics, 2025, April 30).

The Australian Council of TESOL Associations (2022, May) notes that roughly 25% of students learn English as an Additional Language or Dialect (EAL/D). These students face the challenge of learning English, learning about English, and learning through English to access the age-appropriate curriculum. They require additional support as they develop their English proficiency, which can be challenging for educational institutions to provide, given the time required. Faced with the challenge of providing targeted assistance to teachers and their students, the strategic implementation of GenAI could potentially benefit them in various educational settings.

Through examining both opportunities and risks, including some empirical data, this chapter aims to provide a comprehensive understanding of the role of GenAI in transforming teaching and learning. The discussion considers education broadly to ensure wide applicability, using language learning as a contextual example to explore practical implementation. By doing this, it seeks to offer a nuanced perspective on how GenAI is being integrated into pedagogical practices and caters for students' diverse linguistic and cultural needs, such as EAL/D learners. Both the possibilities and complexities educators need to navigate in its adoption are highlighted.

13.2 Literature Review

As educators increasingly rely on GenAI technologies to, for instance, support linguistically diverse learners (Jeon et al., 2025; Weng & Fu, 2025), it becomes essential to critically examine the pedagogical, ethical, and practical applications and implications of GenAI use, particularly for young people. Issues identified through recent research are explored to help ensure GenAI deployment enhances learning without compromising student learning experiences, outcomes, and academic integrity. Key themes include ethical concerns, academic integrity, accuracy and reliability, AI literacy, overreliance on GenAI, and teacher and student readiness for using GenAI. Together, they provide a foundation for understanding the complexities of GenAI integration in education.

The use of GenAI within education raises widely acknowledged ethical concerns, particularly regarding academic integrity and data privacy (García-López & Trujillo-Liñán, 2025; Williams, 2024; Zhai et al., 2024). Concerns include the appropriate use and ownership of student data, such as gender, age, ethnicity, and cultural background; potential misuse of data, and the preservation of academic integrity. Students may unknowingly disclose sensitive personal information when interacting with GenAI tools that can be stored, reused or re-identified through cross-referencing with other data sources, posing a risk to student privacy and autonomy (Duffourc et al., 2024).

Ethical concerns relating to GenAI in language education are particularly crucial in multilingual classrooms (Weng & Fu, 2025). For instance, students may rely heavily on AI-powered tools for real-time translation, feedback and instant corrections while learning a language; therefore, as a result, the sensitivity and volume of data sharing may increase.

Building on these concerns, institutions should consider the ethical use of student data with GenAI, including who owns the data, what rights they have to use it, and whether existing permissions students have granted them to use their data extend to its use with GenAI. Furthermore, they must assess whether AI providers have robust safeguards to protect the data being processed. However, there is a noted lack of literature exploring how institutions should manage the data collected and generated by GenAI. Therefore, Williams (2024) stresses that stakeholders, including students, teachers, and parents, should be informed about data protection measures, and that transparency in data handling practices can help alleviate privacy concerns and foster trust.

A key consideration for ethical use of GenAI is the maintenance of academic integrity. Given the ability to generate human-like text, the use of GenAI tools in educational settings raises significant concerns around academic integrity and the potential for plagiarism (Williams, 2024). The problem is that AI-generated content is technically original and not copied from existing sources, making it difficult for traditional plagiarism tools to identify (Uygun, 2026). There are several AI detection tools available, such as Turnitin Clarity (Turnitin, n.d.), that claim to identify whether a piece of writing was generated by AI. However, as Bassett et al. (2025) caution, these tools rely on unverifiable probabilistic assessments and cannot reliably determine the origin of a text, making them unsuitable for academic integrity investigations.

The emergence of GenAI has transformed academic writing by enabling rapid content creation, often with minimal input (Balalle & Pannilage, 2025). According to Balalle and Pannilage (2025) while this opens new pedagogical possibilities, it also challenges traditional notions of authorship and originality. Given developments in AI capabilities, educators may need to rethink their assessment design as conventional assessment methods are becoming more vulnerable to GenAI content, raising concerns about academic integrity and the originality of student work (Zhai et al., 2024).

Drawing on an exploration of literature on the topic, Zhai et al. (2024) argue that a multifaceted approach is needed, where the importance of academic honesty and the negative impacts of plagiarism on learning and moral development are stressed, policies on academic misconduct are clear, and advanced plagiarism tools are utilised that can adapt to AI's evolution. However, Corbin, Bearman and et al. (2025a) argue that the challenges posed by GenAI in higher education assessment are best understood not as technical problems with clear solutions, but as "wicked problems" which are complex, evolving and without definitive answers.

Appropriate use of GenAI can be particularly challenging for non-English speakers, who may rely on it for translation; struggle to adapt its responses to their needs while maintaining academic integrity, or may be unable to fully critically evaluate the accuracy and relevance of the generated content (Williams, 2024). Furthermore, they may struggle to adapt AI-generated outputs to meet academic standards and expectations. GenAI can produce outputs that appear plausible but are factually incorrect, often referred to as *hallucination* (Tirumala et al., 2024).

Moreover, GenAI models are trained on vast datasets largely scraped from publicly available sources (Duffourc et al., 2024). These datasets may contain personal and sensitive information, sometimes collected without consent. As a result, the outputs generated by GenAI can reflect biases. A scoping review on chatbots indicated that inappropriate, inaccurate, or biased content can potentially reduce student engagement and motivation (Huang et al., 2025), which calls for professional assessment by teachers (Choi et al., 2025). Bearman et al. (2024) highlight that students with limited disciplinary knowledge or language proficiency may lack the evaluative judgement needed to critically assess the relevance, accuracy, or credibility of AI-generated content. This can lead to uncritical reliance on persuasive but flawed outputs, compromising academic integrity and learning outcomes. This challenge underscores the need for AI literacy, particularly in K-12 education, where early exposure can foster the evaluative skills necessary for responsible engagement with AI tools.

AI literacy refers to the knowledge, skills, and ethical awareness necessary to critically understand, evaluate and use AI safely and effectively in an increasingly digital world (Mills et al., 2024, May). As Chiu et al. (2024) argue, AI literacy must go beyond technical understanding to include ethical reasoning, societal impact and self-reflective thinking to enable students to make informed judgements about AI outputs. Additionally, significant time is required for teachers to explore the use of GenAI while fully understanding data collection and utilisation, emphasising the need for adequate AI literacy (Choi et al., 2025). Kong et al. (2025) state, "as AI-based technologies used in education increase, the development of AI literacy becomes essential" (p. 478). Similarly, students may encounter difficulties in navigating these GenAI tools due to digital literacy gaps, which can worsen existing inequalities in access and learning outcomes (Wang et al., 2025). A recent nationwide survey on language teachers' attitudes towards GenAI in New Zealand revealed a growing digital divide in language education and underscored the need for tailored AI policies and professional development rather than a one-size-fits-all solution (Wang, 2025).

The issue of accuracy and reliability of AI-generated content is intensified by the risk of overreliance on AI-generated answers. Lee and colleagues (2025) reviewed 49 empirical studies on GenAI in language classrooms. Their analysis identified overreliance on GenAI as a significant educational challenge. In language education, where practice and repetition are essential, overreliance on GenAI for translation, writing or speaking may impede learners' cognitive engagement, autonomy, and critical thinking abilities by diminishing authentic interpersonal skill-building (Mohebbi, 2025; Wang et al., 2025). A research study on AI-supported Chinese as a foreign language learning revealed that "learners who engaged critically and strategically with AI achieved better outcomes than those who relied on it passively" (Zhang et al., 2025, p. 1). Regardless, there is limited evidence on the effectiveness of students' learning after incorporating GenAI tools (Law, 2024), and persistent concerns that an overreliance on GenAI could diminish critical-thinking and analytical skills (Zhai et al., 2024).

Another challenge involves the varying levels of readiness and resistance among teachers to using GenAI tools, particularly among preservice teachers. Ollington (2025) highlights that teacher assessment identity is shaped by beliefs and emotions, which significantly influence how educators engage with GenAI tools. She explains that while some preservice teachers embrace GenAI as a supportive, non-judgemental peer, others expressed scepticism rooted in concerns about bias, plagiarism, and the reliability of AI-generated content. These emotional and cognitive responses underscore the need for thoughtful professional development that fosters flexible thinking and reflective practice in the face of technological change.

Informed by the literature, the following section is based on interview insights from a broader ongoing research study[1] exploring how teachers perceive, experience, and evaluate the integration of GenAI tools into their teaching and support of English language learners in Australia. Pseudonyms are used in place of names to refer to the teachers in all cases to protect their privacy.

13.3 The Study

This section presents an investigative study on the potential of GenAI tools to assist learners from diverse linguistic and cultural backgrounds, particularly EAL/D students in Australia. As part of an ongoing project, it draws on semi-structured interviews with school teachers and adult education teachers to explore their attitudes and experiences regarding the integration of GenAI in practice. Developed from a review of the relevant literature, the interview data illustrate the potential of GenAI tools for educational purposes.

One of the benefits that GenAI offers teachers is the ability to differentiate instruction to meet the needs of diverse learners (Szabó & Szoke, 2024; Tafazoli, 2024). GenAI tools can personalise content and adjust complexity, making it easier for educators to tailor learning experiences to individual student profiles (Karpouzis et al., 2024, May 8–11). One teacher, Kim, who works with adult learners of EAL/D across a range of proficiency levels, highlighted the ability GenAI offers her to adapt materials to the specific needs of individual learners in a timely manner.

[1] The interview extracts presented here have been selected from an initial analysis of the first round of interviews for a research project investigating the use of GenAI by teachers of EAL/D learners.

> I use it in my teaching all the time. I also find it really easy to adjust materials for what I want.

In addition to facilitating the creation or adaptation of materials for individual learners, GenAI can also assist teachers in tailoring their materials for groups of students by localising lesson content to support learners with the development of their cultural knowledge. For example, Jim, who teaches English to adult migrant learners, described using GenAI to create a song and accompanying learning activities.

> I made a song this week. ... I made the lyrics in ChatGPT, and I said, I want Hobart landmarks, I want activities that people in Hobart might do. So, in that respect, we can localise the content.

This localisation is relevant across all subject areas, as language is not only a tool for communication but also a carrier of cultural knowledge (Choudhury, 2013). Teaching and learning are deeply embedded in cultural contexts, and students' understanding of subject matter is enriched when instructional materials acknowledge and incorporate their cultural backgrounds. GenAI's ability to generate culturally responsive content can help educators create more inclusive and engaging learning experiences that resonate with students' lived realities.

Another teacher of adult migrant students, Jen, described how she uses GenAI to create listening materials by creating transcripts based on everyday situations, which are then converted into audio files in a variety of accents.

> I'm looking for short, telephone messages, ... short announcements ... in very simple English, ... but with all sorts of different accents, which our students really need.

Jen also described using GenAI to create pictures for a series of fictional books centred around members of an Afghan family living in Tasmania for use with her students. Jen suggested that such a project would not have been possible without the use of GenAI, as the costs involved in hiring a professional photographer, along with the practicalities of gaining access to people's homes, would have proven prohibitive. In Jen's opinion, the use of GenAI in this example led to positive outcomes for her and her students, who benefited from an enhanced sense of belonging.

The examples illustrate some of the ways in which teachers have attempted to enhance the learning experiences of their students through differentiating learning materials or tailoring them to the cultural or linguistic backgrounds of their students. However, as Crompton et al. (2024) note, GenAI can also be used by learners themselves as a part of the language learning process. One teacher, Peter, described how one of his adult students with a lower level of English proficiency used social media to help her navigate through various communicative tasks.

> So, she has learned through social media about prompting her phone to create messages for her. For the doctor, for appointments, for ... she replies to me in our WhatsApp class group.

While some students have adopted GenAI without guidance from their teachers, others have benefited from in-class support. Peter described how he introduced Google Lens, a GenAI-powered camera-based application, to his students to help them translate text into their own languages to facilitate learning.

> We've looked at that as a class, about how to use Google Lens to translate written documents, ... they can just go ping into their own language and go, okay, I understand.

The example illustrates how translanguaging, which involves learners making use of their full multilingual repertoires to support their learning (Choi et al., 2020), can be facilitated by the use of GenAI. Likewise, a study by Karimian and Talebinejad (2013) found that learners used their first language to mentally translate texts, clarify meanings, and support writing and listening tasks. However, one limitation was raised by Jen, who teaches many students with no first language literacy. She noted that many refugees come from minority-language backgrounds that are not yet supported by text-to-speech applications. She stated:

> If AI could do the translation, like, if AI could collect the oral language to enhance Google Translate, ... that would probably be the biggest help of all.

As shown, GenAI is already being used by both teachers and learners to provide or access linguistic and cultural support. Davar et al. (2025) note that AI chatbots have the potential to address persistent gaps in both traditional and online education systems by offering just-in-time adaptive support and providing learning pathways that cater to diverse student needs, including those in remote or underprivileged areas, non-native speakers, and students with disabilities. Drawing on the Community of Inquiry (CoI) framework (Garrison et al., 2010), which includes teaching, cognitive, and social presence, GenAI can be designed to participate in learning communities as a tutor, explainer, examiner, study coach or a social buddy (Durgungoz & Kharrufa, 2025). Its generative and social affordances make it well-suited to support inquiry-based learning, foster critical thinking, and facilitate meaningful dialogue with learners (Pratschke, 2024). For example, in English language teaching, role-play offers a dynamic and experiential approach that fosters authentic communication, cultural awareness, and pragmatic competence (Shravani, 2024). As demonstrated by Chen et al. (2025), GenAI agents can be effectively applied to simulate diverse and responsive dialogue scenarios. This approach reduces preparation time for educators while offering learners dynamic practice opportunities and real-time feedback, which enhances motivation, self-efficacy, and speaking performance. However, the importance of human oversight to ensure feedback accuracy and depth should not be underestimated.

13.4 Discussion

The previous section outlined various challenges in the use of GenAI in education, highlighting the current state and the barriers to effective and responsible adoption. These challenges underscore the need for AI literacy so that educators and learners can use GenAI ethically and responsibly. Mills et al., (2024, May) state that "AI literacy includes the knowledge and skills that enable people to critically understand, evaluate, and use AI systems and tools to safely and effectively participate in an increasingly digital world" (p. 4). For education, AI literacy is therefore about equipping students and teachers with the knowledge, skills, and ethical awareness to critically understand, evaluate, and use AI.

As outlined in their AI literacy framework, Mills et al. (2024, May) explain that AI literacy is not just about knowing how AI works, it is about understanding how AI operates, including understanding where data are drawn from which may contain biases, and an awareness of its limitations; having the ability to evaluate AI outputs for accuracy, bias and ethical considerations; and how to use AI in ways that are pedagogically sound and socially responsible.

To address challenges of GenAI integration in education, it is essential not only for users to develop AI literacy but also for institutions to implement pedagogical frameworks and policies that are evaluative, ethically grounded, and responsive to the evolving educational landscape (Turner, 2025, April 2). According to Turner, such frameworks should support critical engagement with GenAI, promote epistemic cognition, and ensure its use aligns with principles of equity, human flourishing, and responsible innovation. As García-López and Trujillo-Liñán (2025) contend, the benefits of GenAI in education can only be fully realised when its implementation occurs within well-defined ethical, legal, and pedagogical boundaries. Similarly, Williams (2024) argues that there is a need for comprehensive procedures to address ethical challenges, including well-defined policies and innovative assessment techniques. Addressing such concerns enables academic institutions, their staff and students to fully harness the power of GenAI for educational purposes within an ethically sound and inclusive environment, where AI supports learning ethically and responsibly, rather than threatening academic integrity. Responsible use of GenAI should therefore be guided by regulatory frameworks and pedagogical strategies that clearly define the responsibilities of students, educators, administrators, and support staff. These frameworks must address academic integrity, ensure the ethical management of data, and incorporate robust safeguards against misuse, thereby fostering trust and accountability across educational contexts.

From a practical perspective, Zhang et al. (2025) argue that "teachers remain central to mediating learners' engagement with AI and embedding such technologies within pedagogical frameworks" (p. 14). This is to ensure that GenAI serves as a tool for human empowerment rather than human replacement in AI-integrated educational settings. Most importantly, teachers need to learn how to use GenAI-powered tools to support their roles and integrate their knowledge and skills with AI capabilities, thus facilitating effective human-machine collaboration (An et al., 2025). Zhai (2024) proposes a four-stage framework—Observer, Adopter, Collaborator, Innovator—that illustrates how teachers' roles transform as they engage more deeply with GenAI technologies. This progression underscores the necessity for educators to not only understand GenAI tools but also to integrate their pedagogical knowledge and disciplinary expertise with AI capabilities. Effective human-machine collaboration in education hinges on teachers' ability to critically evaluate, adapt, and co-create with GenAI.

A fundamental challenge posed by GenAI is the threat to assessment validity, as it enables students to complete tasks without necessarily demonstrating genuine knowledge or skill. Corbin, Dawson and et al. (2025b) advocate for structural changes leading to modifications to the design and mechanics of assessment tasks that inherently direct student behaviour through task structure, without depending on explicit compliance. The core idea here, they argue, is to shift the assessment challenge from managing student adherence to rules to designing tasks where the required demonstration of capability is built into the assessment structure itself.

13.5 Synthesis of Literature and Interview Findings

As discussed previously, GenAI tools present great potential in many areas of education. Taking language teaching as an example, although GenAI can assist with translation, provide feedback, produce materials and ideas, and assimilate practice environments, there remain considerable areas where these tools cannot replace human effort. This section discusses some of these aspects including:

- Lack of contextual understanding—e.g. cultural understanding; empathy
- Lack of critical and creative thinking
- Equity and accessibility.

The most significant aspect is the tools' lack of contextual understanding in social interactions. Teaching students from EAL/D backgrounds requires thorough and in-depth cultural understanding and empathy. Research over the years has consistently highlighted the role of culture in language learning (Hossain, 2024; Kramsch, 1993). Teaching students from multilingual and multicultural backgrounds requires a high level of cultural competence and cross-cultural understanding from the teacher. More often, language teaching is a social event, where language learners are challenged in their ability to make sense of the world and to recognise limitations in their hard-won communicative competence (Kramsch, 1993). A good language teacher needs to support their language learners to navigate through this complex landscape and to recognise the complexity of human relations through learning the language. Despite the great potential of GenAI to contribute to many areas of language teaching, they are unable to provide human responses with the necessary contextual understanding, including cultural competence, cross-cultural understanding, or empathy. Also, even though GenAI tools can pick up, through data mining, words that are recorded as indications of emotions, GenAI is unable to recognise emotional responses in conversations, and therefore is not capable of building interpersonal relationships or replacing human effort in social aspects.

The second limitation of GenAI in the context of teaching students from EAL/D backgrounds is the lack of creative and critical thinking. Critical and creative thinking is recognised as one of the general capabilities in the Australian Curriculum (ACARA, n.d.). Due to the nature of GenAI, it relies on existing and pre-populated information and material that is fed into the tool; therefore, it cannot produce what is not provided. Also, while GenAI can interact with users using programmed responses, it is unable to recognise moral or ethical implications. Research highlights the need for students to be able to use and critically evaluate outputs from GenAI tools (Ellis et al., 2025) and the need for human input from education stakeholders to ensure success in using AI tools (Chan, 2023).

Higher education institutions are increasingly recognising the use of GenAI tools as part of their graduate attributes for students. Digital literacy skills have long been recognised as part of universities' expectations of graduate attributes/capability. Since the emergence of GenAI, skills to use GenAI tools are increasingly emphasised and in more explicit ways as part of these digital literacy skills (e.g. Australian Catholic University, n.d.; Cornell University, n.d.). Another example is a study that examined university students' understandings of whether they will be expected by their employers to have GenAI skills upon going into the profession (Prohorov et al., 2024). This study observed lower awareness among some student groups than others, calling for higher education institutions to motivate students and work on awareness building among them.

Lastly, from an equity lens, students have different levels of accessibility to GenAI tools. This is true for EAL/D students in different age groups, from early childhood education to higher education. The United Nations' Department of Economic and Social Affairs Sustainable Development (2025) Goal 4 (SDG4), Quality Education, advocates for "inclusive and equitable quality education and promote lifelong learning opportunities for all" (United Nations Department of Economic & Social Affairs, 2025, page heading). However, research identifies challenges in supporting students from EAL/D backgrounds, including the lack of funding for schools, an unpreparedness of teachers to teach them, and insufficient consideration of their needs (Australian Council of TESOL Associations, 2014, September).

Challenges in relation to accessibility are also shared by higher education institutions. For instance, there is clear evidence of inequity in resource access for students from non-English-speaking backgrounds; students with disabilities (James & Andrews, 2024); students from low socio-economic backgrounds, and rural, regional or remote areas (Fan et al., 2025). Schools and universities, therefore, need to think carefully when they require students to use these tools to complete learning tasks or activities. An equitable approach can be that teachers give priority to tools that are freely accessible or provided by the institution via an organisational licence. Teachers of younger age groups in schools or those at the beginning of programs at universities may also consider incorporating tools that do not require prior knowledge in using the tool. In either case, an understanding among teachers to know the knowledge base and scaffold students' learning is important.

13.6 Brief Recommendations

The aim of this chapter has been to explore the potential advantages and perceived challenges of GenAI in education, especially in EAL/D contexts. That is, while considering the wider applicability to education in general, a particular interest is taken in the innovative ways GenAI can support learners in educational settings where the medium of instruction differs from their native language.

Reflecting existing literature reviewed, data are cited from an ongoing study that investigates in-service teachers' perspectives on GenAI-supported EAL/D learning. Research findings suggest that teachers are actively developing customised and contextualised teaching resources to cater to diverse student needs. Additionally, evidence suggests machines cannot replace humans in learning, such as understanding context in communication and critical and creative thinking.

Ethical and moral implications of GenAI use are complex. There is a need to foster the development and adoption of regulatory frameworks and pedagogical strategies that promote responsible GenAI use and enhance learning without replacing the human element in knowledge creation and education. Therefore, using AI to augment, not replace, human expertise and creativity.

GenAI has reshaped how knowledge is accessed and learned in education, offering both opportunities and challenges. However, low technological readiness in higher education, such as a lack of infrastructure, training or resources, can lead to accessibility gaps and limited support for educators and students (Feng et al., 2025; Singun, 2025). Furthermore, the rapid speed of technological progress often outpaces curriculum updates, leaving universities struggling to adapt without clear policies, pedagogical frameworks or support systems (Marshall et al., 2024; Singun, 2025). From systematic reviews on AI, it is evident that with the continuous advancement of GenAI technology, the optimal integration of GenAI into education requires thoughtful policy and pedagogical guidance that prioritises equity, ethics, and students' diverse needs (Garzón et al., 2025; Lee et al., 2025; Singun, 2025; Zawacki-Richter et al., 2019). Whether AI becomes a friend or foe in learning may depend on how humans choose to engage with it. Looking ahead, effective and innovative collaboration between humans and machines calls for a reimagining of responsibilities and relationships in AI-assisted learning, particularly as the learning journey forward remains uncertain. This may encourage educators to embrace flexible and creative strategies that address the intricate challenges facing young people in an ever-changing world (Robertson, 2023).

References

ACARA. (n.d.). *Understand this general capability – Critical and creative Thinking*. Retrieved October 25, 2025 from https://www.australiancurriculum.edu.au/curriculum-information/understand-this-general-capability/critical-and-creative-thinking

An, X., Bai, J., Li, Y., Zhou, Y., Chai, C. S., & Hong, J.-C. (2025). Development of an artificial intelligence technology pedagogical content knowledge (AI-TPACK) scale for human and AI concurrently as teachers. *The Asia-Pacific Education Researcher*. https://doi.org/10.1007/s40299-025-01045-2

Australian Bureau of Statistics. (2025, April 30). *Australia's population by country of birth*. https://www.abs.gov.au/statistics/people/population/australias-population-country-birth/latest-release

Australian Catholic University. (n.d.). *Graduate attributes*. Retrieved October 25, 2025 from https://www.acu.edu.au/study-at-acu/why-study-at-acu/graduate-attributes

Australian Council of TESOL Associations. (2014, September). *State of EAL/D in Australia 2014*. https://tesol.org.au/wp-content/uploads/2019/01/562_ACTA_2014_Survey_Report_Final.pdf

Australian Council of TESOL Associations. (2022, May). *National roadmap for English as an additional language or dialect (EAL/D) education in schools: Directions for COVID-19 recovery and program reform*. https://www.tesol.org.au/wp-content/uploads/2020/12/Roadmap-for-English-as-an-additional-language-or-dialect-in-schools-ACTA-May-2022.pdf

Balalle, H., & Pannilage, S. (2025). Reassessing academic integrity in the age of AI: A systematic literature review on AI and academic integrity. *Social Sciences & Humanities Open, 11*, Article 101299. https://doi.org/10.1016/j.ssaho.2025.101299

Bassett, M. A., Bradshaw, W., Hogg, A., Murdoch, K., Bornsztejn, H., Pearce, B., & Webber, C. (2025). *Heads we win, tails you lose: AI detectors in education* [Preprint v2]. EdArXiv. https://osf.io/preprints/edarxiv/93w6j_v2

Bearman, M., Tai, J., Dawson, P., Boud, D., & Ajjawi, R. (2024). Developing evaluative judgement for a time of generative artificial intelligence. *Assessment & Evaluation in Higher Education, 49*(6), 893–905. https://doi.org/10.1080/02602938.2024.2335321

Chan, C. K. Y. (2023). A comprehensive AI policy education framework for university teaching and learning. *International Journal of Educational Technology in Higher Education, 20*, 38. https://doi.org/10.1186/s41239-023-00408-3

Chen, A., Jia, J., Li, Y., & Fu, L. (2025). Investigating the effect of role-play activity with GenAI agent on EFL students' speaking performance. *Journal of Educational Computing Research, 63*(1), 99–125. https://doi.org/10.1177/07356331241299058

Chiu, T. K. F., Ahmad, Z., Ismailov, M., & Sanusi, I. T. (2024). What are artificial intelligence literacy and competency? A comprehensive framework to support them. *Computers and Education Open, 6*, Article 100171. https://doi.org/10.1016/j.caeo.2024.100171

Choi, J., French, M., & Ollerhead, S. (2020). Introduction to the special issue. *Australian Journal of Applied Linguistics, 3*(1), 1–10. https://doi.org/10.29140/ajal.v3n1.283

Choi, K. Y., Wu, C., & Moorhouse, B. L. (2025). Exploring the use of generative artificial intelligence (GenAI) in English language teaching: Voices from in-service teachers at an early-adopting Hong Kong secondary school. *Technology in Language Teaching & Learning, 7*(3), 102516. https://doi.org/10.29140/tltl.v7n3.102516

Choudhury, M. H. (2013). Teaching culture in EFL: Implications, challenges and strategies. *OSR Journal of Humanities and Social Science (IOSR-JHSS), 13*(1), 20–24. https://doi.org/10.9790/0837-1312024

Corbin, T., Bearman, M., Boud, D., & Dawson, P. (2025a). The wicked problem of AI and assessment [Advanced online publication]. *Assessment & Evaluation in Higher Education*. https://doi.org/10.1080/02602938.2025.2553340

Corbin, T., Dawson, P., & Liu, D. (2025b). Talk is cheap: Why structural assessment changes are needed for a time of GenAI. *Assessment & Evaluation in Higher Education, 50*(7), 1087–1097. https://doi.org/10.1080/02602938.2025.2503964

Cornell University. (n.d.). *Generative Artificial Intelligence*. Retrieved October 25, 2025 from https://teaching.cornell.edu/generative-artificial-intelligence

Crompton, H., Edmett, A., Ichaporia, N., & Burke, D. (2024). AI and English language teaching: Affordances and challenges. *British Journal of Educational Technology, 55*(6), 2503–2529. https://doi.org/10.1111/bjet.13460

Davar, N. F., Dewan, M. A. A., & Zhang, X. (2025). AI chatbots in education: Challenges and opportunities. *Information, 16*(3), 235. https://doi.org/10.3390/info16030235

Duffourc, M. N., Gerke, S., & Kollnig, K. (2024). Privacy of personal data in the generative AI data lifecycle. *NYU Journal of Intellectual Property & Entertainment Law, 13*(2).

Durgungoz, A., & Kharrufa, A. (2025). "ChatGPT is like a study buddy, a teacher and sometimes just a friend": A longitudinal exploration of students' interactions, perception and acceptance. *Interactive Learning Environments, 1–20*. https://doi.org/10.1080/10494820.2025.2509276

Ellis, R., Han, F., & Cook, H. (2025). Qualitatively different teacher experiences of teaching with generative artificial intelligence. *International Journal of Educational Technology in Higher Education, 22*(1), 33. https://doi.org/10.1186/s41239-025-00532-2

Fan, S., Hicks, D., & Fischer, S. (2025). *Evidence-based pedagogies to support online engagement of low SES, and regional, rural and remote students* [Small Grant Report]. Australian Centre for Student Equity and Success.

Feng, J., Yu, B., Tan, W. H., Dai, Z., & Li, Z. (2025). Key factors influencing educational technology adoption in higher education: A systematic review. *PLOS Digital Health, 4*(4), Article e0000764. https://doi.org/10.1371/journal.pdig.0000764

García-López, I. M., & Trujillo-Liñán, L. (2025). Ethical and regulatory challenges of Generative AI in education: A systematic review. *Frontiers in Education, 10*. https://doi.org/10.3389/feduc.2025.1565938

Garrison, D. R., Anderson, T., & Archer, W. (2010). The first decade of the community of inquiry framework: A retrospective. *The Internet and Higher Education, 13*(1), 5–9. https://doi.org/10.1016/j.iheduc.2009.10.003

Garzón, J., Patiño, E., & Marulanda, C. (2025). Systematic review of artificial intelligence in education: Trends, benefits, and challenges. *Multimodal Technologies and Interaction, 9*(8), 84. https://doi.org/10.3390/mti9080084

Hossain, K. I. (2024). Reviewing the role of culture in English language learning: Challenges and opportunities for educators. *Social Sciences & Humanities Open, 9*, Article 100781. https://doi.org/10.1016/j.ssaho.2023.100781

Huang, W., Jiang, J., King, R. B., & Fryer, L. K. (2025). Chatbots and student motivation: A scoping review. *International Journal of Educational Technology in Higher Education, 22*, 26. https://doi.org/10.1186/s41239-025-00524-2

James, T., & Andrews, G. (2024). Levelling the playing field through GenAI: Harnessing artificial intelligence to bridge educational gaps for equity and disadvantaged students. *Widening Participation and Lifelong Learning, 26*(3), 250–260. https://doi.org/10.5456/WPLL.26.3.250

Jeon, J., Wei, L., Tai, K. W. H., & Lee, S. (2025). Generative AI and its dilemmas: Exploring AI from a translanguaging perspective. *Applied Linguistics, 46*(4), 709–717. https://doi.org/10.1093/applin/amaf049

Karimian, Z., & Talebinejad, M. R. (2013). Students' use of translation as a learning strategy in EFL classroom. *Journal of Language Teaching and Research, 4*(3), 605–610. https://doi.org/10.4304/jltr.4.3.605-610

Karpouzis, K., Pantazatos, D., Taouki, J., & Meli, K. (2024, May 8–11). Tailoring education with GenAI: A new horizon in lesson planning [Paper presentation]. In *2024 IEEE Global Engineering Education Conference (EDUCON)*, Kos Island, Greece.

Kong, S.-C., Korte, S.-M., Burton, S., Keskitalo, P., Turunen, T., Smith, D., Wang, L., Lee, J.C.-K., & Beaton, M. C. (2025). Artificial Intelligence (AI) literacy – an argument for AI literacy in education. *Innovations in Education and Teaching International, 62*(2), 477–483. https://doi.org/10.1080/14703297.2024.2332744

Kramsch, C. (1993). *Context and culture in language teaching*. Oxford University Press.

Law, L. (2024). Application of generative artificial intelligence (GenAI) in language teaching and learning: A scoping literature review. *Computers and Education Open, 6*, Article 100174. https://doi.org/10.1016/j.caeo.2024.100174

Lee, S., Choe, H., Zou, D., & Jeon, J. (2025). Generative AI (GenAI) in the language classroom: A systematic review. *Interactive Learning Environments, 1–25*. https://doi.org/10.1080/10494820.2025.2498537

Lorenz, E., Krulatz, A., & Torgersen, E. N. (2021). Embracing linguistic and cultural diversity in multilingual EAL classrooms: The impact of professional development on teacher beliefs and practice. *Teaching and Teacher Education, 105*, Article 103428. https://doi.org/10.1016/j.tate.2021.103428

Marshall, S., Blaj-Ward, L., Dreamson, N., Nyanjom, J., & Bertuol, M. T. (2024). The reshaping of higher education: Technological impacts, pedagogical change, and future projections. *Higher*

Education Research & Development, 43(3), 521–541. https://doi.org/10.1080/07294360.2024.2329393

Mills, K., Ruiz, P., Lee, K.-W., Coenraad, M., Fusco, J., Roschelle, J., & Weisgrau, J. (2024, May). *AI literacy: A framework to understand, evaluate, and use emerging technology.* https://doi.org/10.51388/20.500.12265/218

Mohebbi, A. (2025). Enabling learner independence and self-regulation in language education using AI tools: A systematic review. *Cogent Education, 12*(1), 2433814. https://doi.org/10.1080/2331186X.2024.2433814

Ollington, N. (2025). Challenging assumptions: AI and teacher assessment identity formation. *Australian Journal of Teacher Education, 50*(2), 56–73. https://doi.org/10.14221/1835-517X.6510

Pratschke, B. M. (2024). *Generative AI and education: Digital pedagogies, teaching innovation and learning design.* Springer Nature. https://doi.org/10.1007/978-3-031-67991-9

Prohorov, A., Tsaryk, O., & Fainglozs, L. (2024, September 19–21). Employers' expectations of students' generative AI skills: A student perspective [Paper presentation]. In *2024 14th International Conference on Advanced Computer Information Technologies (ACIT)*, Ceske Budejovice, Czech Republic. https://ieeexplore.ieee.org/document/10712525

Robertson, M. E. (2023). *Youth cultures, responsive education, and learning.* IGI Global

Shravani, K. (2024). Empowering language learning through dynamic role-play in ELT. *Interna Tional Journal of Applied Research, 10*(1), 187–189.

Singun, A., Jr. (2025). Unveiling the barriers to digital transformation in higher education institutions: A systematic literature review. *Discover Education, 4*(1), 37. https://doi.org/10.1007/s44217-025-00430-9

Szabó, F., & Szoke, J. (2024). How does generative AI promote autonomy and inclusivity in language teaching? *ELT Journal, 78*(4), 478–488. https://doi.org/10.1093/elt/ccae052

Tafazoli, D. (2024). Exploring the potential of generative AI in democratizing English language education. *Computers and Education: Artificial Intelligence, 7*, Article 100275. https://doi.org/10.1016/j.caeai.2024.100275

Tirumala, A. K. G., Mishra, S., Trivedi, N., Shivakumar, D., Singh, A., & Shariff, S. (2024). A cross-sectional study to assess response generated by ChatGPT and ChatSonic to patient queries about Epilepsy. *Telematics and Informatics Reports, 13*, Article 100110. https://doi.org/10.1016/j.teler.2023.100110

Turner, P. (2025, April 2). *Mapping a multidimensional framework for GenAI in education.* EDUCAUSE Review. https://er.educause.edu/articles/2025/4/mapping-a-multidimensional-framework-for-genai-in-education

Turnitin. (n.d.). *Turnitin Clarity: Transparency in the student writing process.* https://www.turnitin.com/products/feedback-studio/clarity

United Nations Department of Economic and Social Affairs. (2025). *Goal 4.* https://sdgs.un.org/goals/goal4

Uygun, E. (2026). Clashing AIs: Artificial intelligence literacy and academic integrity in an EFL context. *Journal of Academic Ethics, 24*(1), 7. https://doi.org/10.1007/s10805-025-09676-2

Wang, D. (2025). Mind the gap in AI integration: A comparative study of language teachers' responses in a national survey. *Language, Culture and Curriculum, 1–18.* https://doi.org/10.1080/07908318.2025.2574633

Wang, F., Li, N., Cheung, A. C. K., & Wong, G. K. W. (2025). In GenAI we trust: An investigation of university students' reliance on and resistance to generative AI in language learning. *International Journal of Educational Technology in Higher Education, 22*(1), 59. https://doi.org/10.1186/s41239-025-00547-9

Weng, Z., & Fu, Y. (2025). Generative AI in language education: Bridging divide and fostering inclusivity. *International Journal of Technology in Education, 8*(2), 395–420. https://doi.org/10.46328/ijte.1056

Williams, R. T. (2024). The ethical implications of using generative chatbots in higher education. *Frontiers in Education, 8*. https://doi.org/10.3389/feduc.2023.1331607

Zawacki-Richter, O., Marín, V. I., Bond, M., & Gouverneur, F. (2019). Systematic review of research on artificial intelligence applications in higher education – where are the educators? *International Journal of Educational Technology in Higher Education, 16*, 39. https://doi.org/10.1186/s41239-019-0171-0

Zhai, C., Wibowo, S., & Li, L. D. (2024). The effects of over-reliance on AI dialogue systems on students' cognitive abilities: A systematic review. *Smart Learning Environments, 11*, 28. https://doi.org/10.1186/s40561-024-00316-7

Zhai, X. (2024). Transforming teachers' roles and agencies in the era of generative AI: Perceptions, acceptance, knowledge, and practices. *Journal of Science Education and Technology*. https://doi.org/10.1007/s10956-024-10174-0

Zhang, J., Zhou, X., & Goh, Y. S. (2025). Unpacking AI-supported Chinese as a foreign language learning: How beginner-level learners' cognitive and motivational factors predict speaking proficiency. *Acta Psychologica, 260*, Article 105703. https://doi.org/10.1016/j.actpsy.2025.105703

Dr Yanjun Wang is a senior lecturer in Chinese at the School of Humanities and Social Sciences at the University of Tasmania in Australia. Her research integrates technology into language education, using interdisciplinary methods to connect research with practice.

Dr Andy Bown is a lecturer in Languages and TESOL in the School of Education at the University of Tasmania. His research interests are focused on the use of technology to support the learning of culturally and linguistically diverse learners.

Dr Paul Albinson is an educator and early-career researcher at The University of Tasmania spanning the fields of computing and education.

Dr Si Fan is an Associate Professor in the School of Education, University of Tasmania with research interests in higher education, online pedagogy, early childhood education, and teacher education.

Dr Anuradha Khara oversees learning and innovation initiatives at the University of Tasmania. She plays a key role in supporting academic integrity and shaping the university's response to emerging GenAI related risks.

Chapter 14
Tipping Points & Moral Purpose: The Wicked Problem of GenAI and Sustainable Education

Emlyn Cruickshank and Jeana Kriewaldt

Abstract Among the moral issues that Generative AI (GenAI) presents for education are environmental sustainability concerns. The exponential growth of GenAI technology and pressures for uptake in education are concurrent with increasing global temperatures, a fast-approaching tipping point in which this increase will also become exponential, and policy commitments to address sustainability in educational practice too. This chapter explores the complexities of GenAI integration in education for these sustainability commitments by bringing into focus the assumptions embedded in dominant narratives about learning, consumption, and human-nature relationships. Inasmuch, the concurrence of sustainability commitments and rapid technological advancements constitutes a *wicked problem*. We articulate what constitutes a wicked problem and then examine two sites where this wickedness is particularly visible: the material conditions of education, where present environmental costs and promised future benefits of GenAI make competing and unknowable claims; and pedagogical formation, where the skills and values that sustainability education prioritises and the efficiencies that GenAI adoption rewards are means to different educational ends. Both contain legitimate evidence and normative claims that cannot be reconciled through logical argument alone. In articulating how GenAI presents a substantively wicked problem for sustainable education, we highlight the limits of cost-benefit logics and system responses in resolving these tensions. When a policy problem is genuinely *wicked*, moral purpose needs to be found elsewhere. We suggest this becomes a navigation of educators, not policy-writers, resolved in their *praxis*: informed, reflexive action committed to a process of *good* for humankind.

Keywords Policy · Education practice · Moral purpose · Sustainability

E. Cruickshank · J. Kriewaldt (✉)
Faculty of Education, University of Melbourne, Melbourne, VIC, Australia
e-mail: jeana@unimelb.edu.au

M. E. Robertson (ed.), *Youth, Identity, AI and Moral Purpose*, Young People and Learning Processes in School and Everyday Life 9,
https://doi.org/10.1007/978-3-032-32479-5_14

14.1 Tipping Points

As we finalise this chapter, COP30 has concluded in Belem, Brazil. Despite another round of agreements, we are far from achieving net-zero carbon targets. Fossil fuel emissions continue to rise, and the world faces a 2.6 degrees Celsius increase in temperature by the end of the century (Climate Action Tracker, 2023). Scientists predict this increase will be a tipping point, resulting in widespread damage to marine and terrestrial ecosystems, disruption of crucial ocean currents, and more frequent extreme weather events. These changes, already occurring, will significantly impact biodiversity, food security, infrastructure and health, and fundamentally change the geopolitical and geological world that young people inherit. The need for schools to take this tipping point seriously appears in international and Australian educational policy in calls for schools to be responsible for their carbon footprint and to support young people to adapt.

At the same time, GenAI is proliferating in education. GenAI use among Australian teachers already ranks among the highest in the OECD (OECD, 2025), and GenAI is already widely used by young people for educational tasks (Denejkina, 2023). In October 2023, Education Ministers approved the Australian Framework for Generative AI in Schools (Australian Government Department of Education, 2023), establishing a national policy architecture that advocates for GenAI integration based on a logic of future workforce necessity and not being left behind. The Australian Education Research Organisation (2024) similarly assumes GenAI adoption and identifies gains in student achievement, teacher wellbeing and equity among the benefits it will bring. A tipping point logic is apparent here too (MacIntyre et al., 2021): we are *in* the GenAI revolution now, not considering or even preparing for it, and Australian schools must adapt.

The concurrence of these tipping points and the competing pressures that drive them raise significant questions for education. Is GenAI integration actually inevitable? What are the environmental costs of GenAI? What kind of learning does GenAI improve? Does this kind of learning cohere with the skills young people will need to live through the tipping point of climate change? There aren't easy answers to these questions. There aren't even easy ways to ask them. The posing of one question will often suppose an answer to another, and the questions evade positioning as component pieces of a larger, logical puzzle that just needs more reliable and valid data or advances in analytic methods. The answers and indeed the questions themselves are inherently value-laden, contested and unsolvable through traditional problem-solving technique. We suggest that this is because the broader question of what GenAI means for sustainable education constitutes what public policy scholars call a *wicked problem.*

14.2 The Nature of Wicked Problems

The concept of *wicked problems* was originally offered by Rittel and Webber (1973) as a critique of dominant approaches to urban planning and public policy at the time. The prevailing logic seemed to be that planners could apply scientific, systems-analytic methods to social policy issues: define the problem, gather the data, generate alternatives, evaluate solutions, implement the best solution evaluated. This approach, according to Rittel and Webber (1973), is appropriate for *tame problems* like engineering challenges or economic efficiencies, but fundamentally misunderstands the inherently moral nature of problems in public policy that are inherently connected to the social, political and geographical contexts they exist in. Its use in the field of sustainability education is well established. Lönngren and van Poeck's (2021) recent synthesis of 55 papers evidence this point, while also concluding that there is a wide variety of definitions and applications used.

Wicked problems, originally defined, are those that resist definitive formulation (Rittel & Webber, 1973). Every wicked problem can be considered a symptom of deeper problems, and addressing symptoms without addressing underlying causal structures is about displacement rather than resolution of competing values and stakeholder needs. Alford and Head (2017) refined this by noting that problems vary in their wickedness along two dimensions. The first is the intractability of the problem itself and the second is the fragmentation of knowledge and interests among stakeholders. Problems become more wicked when the problem and its solutions are genuinely unknowable, when relevant knowledge is distributed and contested, and relevant stakeholders have irreconcilable agendas. The nature of a problem can be more or less wicked depending on the extent to which it meets these conditions (Alford & Head, 2017). To these, the *super wicked* literature added conditions of temporal urgency, including time bound consequences, no central authority to coordinate action, and the irrational discounting of future consequences against present structural pressures (Levin et al., 2012). We recognise a risk of enumerating our synthesis of the features of wicked problems is that it ironically tries to reduce irreducibility into categories, so offer this list as a way finder not a hard set of criteria which can be applied to our argument. We understand the nature of a *wicked problem* to be one that together:

1. Cannot be easily formulated, as the problem framing biases any proposed solution;
2. Involves contested knowledges;
3. Materially impacts stakeholder interests that fundamentally diverge;
4. Is temporally urgent;
5. Has no clear authority; and
6. Makes claims against uncertain futurities.

The problem GenAI presents for sustainable education has all these characteristics. It can be validly framed as an issue of environmental catastrophe or economic necessity. Environmental costs are accruing now while promised benefits remain speculative.

No central authority coordinates AI development nor its educational applications, with fragmented education systems, global technology companies and underdeveloped governance structures placing decision-making somewhere between reactive and politicised policy-formation, activism for caution, and agenda-driving market forces. At the same time, both issues intersect with an evidenced logic of urgency.

Lönngren and van Poeck (2021) suggest that, among its applications, *wicked problems* can be particularly valuable as what Blumer (1954) calls a *sensitising concept*: a methodological tool that stimulates reflection and helps researchers and policymakers look in different directions without requiring a fixed or shared understanding of the phenomenon requiring a reformulated policy response. We follow this lead and use the concept as a lens to bring to light *wicked* dimensions of the problem GenAI presents for sustainable education that might otherwise remain obscured. We do this through articulating two sites where the collision of sustainability commitments and the pressures driving GenAI integration appear to be genuinely and impossibly *wicked*.

The first is a commitment for educational operations to operate within planetary limits and work towards net zero; the second is a commitment to teach the skills and dispositions young people will need to live with climate change and shape a more sustainable future.

14.3 The Material Conditions for Education

At scales ranging from supra-national, national and sub-national, a key focus of sustainable education is on the environmental footprint of system-wide educational operations—at the departmental level, school level, and in terms of the environmental footprints of goods or services consumed. Globally, the Greening Education Partnership (GEP) initiative is a collective that brings together government and non-government organisations to support all actors in education to promote a sustainable future (UNESCO, 2024). This includes policy commitments that the material conditions for education function within planetary limits and don't contribute to environmental cost (UNESCO, 2024). Nationally, the Australian Government's Net Zero in Government Operations Strategy (2023) commits all Commonwealth entities, including the Department of Education, to net zero emissions by 2030. Sub-nationally, the NSW Department of Education has adopted the same target for all public schools, and Victoria' Climate Change Act (2017) commits the public education system to net zero by 2050 with sector-specific adaptation plans for education. These commitments are organised into three scopes: direct emissions from owned or controlled sources, indirect emissions from purchased electricity, and indirect emissions in an organisation's value chain.

The environmental costs of GenAI sit within the third of these. Training a single large GenAI model can emit as much carbon dioxide as five cars in their lifetimes (Strubell et al., 2019). The International Energy Agency (IEA) projects that data centre electricity consumption will double by 2026, with GenAI driving much of this growth (IEA, 2024). In addition, data centres require vast amounts of fresh water for cooling, and the production and disposal of specialised hardware contribute to electronic waste and resource scarcity (UNEP, 2024). This energy-intensive process contributes to greenhouse gas emissions, exacerbating climate change concerns.

These costs are measured, documented and growing. Data centres, driven largely by GenAI advances, are one of the few energy sectors in which carbon emissions are increasing (UNITAR & ITU, 2024). Amazon recently reported, for example, that its emissions rose from 64.38 million metric tonnes in 2023 to 68.25 metric tonnes in 2024 (Chen, 2025). This was the first increase since 2021 and something the company put down to their rapid increase in data centres. Google also reported that its 2023 greenhouse gas emissions marked a 48% increase in 2019 mostly due to data centre development (Chen, 2025).

On this question framing—what is the environmental cost now—from this group of stakeholders, the policy response might seem clear.

Against these empirical costs and statistical projections, however, stands a counternarrative with its own evidential basis. Research from the Grantham Research Institute found that GenAI applications in energy, transport and agriculture could reduce global greenhouse emissions significantly and outweigh the costs of GenAI training and processing (Stern et al., 2025). This is not naive optimism. It rests on peer-reviewed research cited by the IEA and major policy bodies. The position that GenAI can deliver net environmental benefits has legitimate, albeit yet to be realised, grounding.

The knowledge required to evaluate this site of the problem then becomes difficult to compare, pitching what is known against what is possible, and requiring steps taken by stakeholders with genuinely competing interests of public versus private good.

The Australian Framework for Generative AI in Schools (Australian Government Department of Education, 2023/2025) provides a recent case study that demonstrates this site of *wickedness* well. The Sustainable Development Goals (SDG) are cited and the alignment of the policy with SDG4, the goal of equitable and inclusive education, is used to justify its scope and coherence. There is no mention, however, of SDG12 for responsible consumption and production nor SDG13 for urgent action to combat climate change, much less intersections of SDG6 for sustainable management of water and the usage requirements of data centres. This is not to say that deliberate strategy in play. Rather, the omission is symptomatic of a *wicked problem.*

When knowledge is genuinely contested among stakeholders with divergent needs and priorities, knowledge is likely to be displaced and siloed, not synthesised. Knowledge that is not easily accommodated by one stakeholder groups remains unresolved and rendered invisible by the other (Rittel & Webber, 1973). This process, rather than deliberate, reflects a deeper tension in the logic of *tame problems* to which *wicked problems* responded: the assumption that technological integration and environmental responsibilities are separate tracks for analysis rather than tangled confounds in the sociopolitics of public policy.

In other words, the construction of responsible GenAI integration has already determined what responsibility means, and environmental responsibilities are not a part of that determination. This is not an oversight awaiting correction; rather, it reflects the conceptual wickedness of the problem in play.

GenAI is driving greenhouse gas emissions growth and GenAI can contribute to climate solutions. Both statements are true. The incapacity of comparable evidence and scientific logics to reconcile this rests on incommensurable priorities and timeframes, genuine uncertainty about governance and markets, and contested values about civic responsibility and economic innovation. No amount of additional evidence will resolve which consideration should take priority, as this requires a normative judgement not an empirical calculation.

For education systems committed to net zero operations, then, this produces an irreducible complexity. The commitment to account for the environmental impact of the material conditions for education cannot be abandoned. To do so would evacuate sustainability of meaning. Yet the counternarrative also cannot simply be dismissed, as it has real evidentiary support. It is possible that GenAI will support the reduction of greenhouse gases by accelerating research into more sustainable practices in key greenhouse emitting industries. We might speculate that the governance required to direct GenAI towards climate solutions rather than entertainment, advertising or more efficient industry is unlikely to materialise in the time pressured tipping point that sustainability commitments are grounded in, but this remains just that—speculation. It also rests on a normative stance that these decisions belong in the hands of public governance not private market forces which is, itself, another normative stance. The *wickedness* of the problem GenAI presents for sustainable education is apparent in the material conditions for educational operations.

14.4 The Pedagogical Formation of Education

Another recurrent focus of sustainability education scholarship is that education should teach, among other priorities, the skills and dispositions young people will need to live sustainably and shape a more sustainable future. This includes policy commitments to include critical thinking skills in the scope of curriculum and critical inquiry among pedagogical tools. UNESCO (2017), for example, identify critical thinking skills as essential for sustainability, defined as "the ability to question norms, practices and opinions; to reflect on one's own values, perceptions and actions; and to take a position in the sustainability discourse" (p. 10). The Australian Curriculum similarly brings this into the pedagogical formation of sustainability education, citing a need to help students develop skills in questioning, thinking critically, solving problems and adapting to change (ACARA, 2016). These skills are not peripheral to sustainability education. They are foundational to the commitment.

In light of this, studies about the impact of GenAI integration in education on the development of critical thinking are concerning. There is growing apprehension that overreliance on GenAI may foster a dependency that hinders the development of students' critical thinking skills. Lee et al. (2025), surveying knowledge workers across real world tasks, found that higher confidence in GenAI was associated with less critical thinking, while higher self-confidence in one's own critical abilities was associated with more. The authors connect this to Bainbridge's (1983) *ironies of automation*: by mechanising higher order cognitive tasks, GenAI may limit opportunities to rehearse critical judgement much less apply it to sustainability issues. This pattern suggests that existing disposition determines how GenAI is used, as a scaffold or a substitute, which in turn shapes its impact on the development of critical thinking.

This conditional finding extends to students. Zhou et al. (2025) found that critical thinking mediated the relationship between GenAI use and creativity among university students, suggesting that GenAI adoption in education enabled critical thinking skills to be applied and refined rather than bypassed. The same was not true, however, for students with less developed critical thinking skills. Similarly, Zhao et al. (2025) found that GenAI amplified in depth-learning for primary school students with existing critical thinking skills but not students who had yet to learn them.

It's a paradoxical situation that users of GenAI need well developed critical thinking skills to develop prompts, refine outputs and assess their veracity, but those capacities may remain underdeveloped through their reliance on seemingly effortless generation of plausible outputs. The disposition that makes GenAI useful, trusting it enough to incorporate its outputs, seems to work against the disposition that makes GenAI use safe, questioning its outputs habitually.

GenAI's tendency to produce hallucinations intensifies these stakes. Put accurately, a hallucination is when GenAI outputs are wrong. How can young people who are novices in knowledge assessment evaluate the quality of GenAI outputs? What can educators do when their students believe fabrications, given that fabricated information or listing non-existent references can result in young people learning misinformation, building unreliable mental schemas, fostering misconceptions and leading them to trust in fallacies?

Lane (2025), examining hallucinations in geographical education, demonstrates that this is not merely a technical problem awaiting better GenAI. Current GenAI models present invention with the same confident register as accuracy. For students who lack foundational geographical knowledge to make this distinction, the efficiency and plausibility of GenAI outputs discourages the verification, or application of critical thinking, that would reveal the hallucinated claims. This makes the conditional relationship between GenAI adoption and critical thinking pedagogical. It is about the relationship between learners and knowledge, and it falls hardest on student cohorts that research findings identify as most at risk: those without the prior learning of critical skills and dispositions to question what GenAI produces.

It also raises equity concerns. Zhou et al. (2025) studied engineering students in higher education, a selected cohort that have already demonstrated academic literacies. Similarly, the primary school students in Zhao et al.'s (2025) study were from a "top school in the city" with existing experience in learning with digital tools (p. 7). What appears as critical thinking skill might also be accumulated advantage and positioning in social contexts where critical inquiry was modelled and rewarded.

Against this developing evidence base, the Australian Education Research Organisation (AERO) frames GenAI as having the "potential to improve learning outcomes for all students" and "reverse growing inequity" (AERO, 2024). This is a claim about an uncertain future from a different and relevant authority. While present research findings question the claim that GenAI has positive equity outcomes by noting the conditional relationship between GenAI utility for critical thinking and existing skill, a national body places focus on possibility. The authority is not absent but fragmented, leaving educators to navigate contradictions that no one has authority to resolve.

Competing normative claims about what constitutes learning outcomes is also evident, compounding the *wickedness* of the problem. AERO (2024) also identify GenAI's potential to lead to measurable gains in student achievement in "core skills such as reading, writing and numeracy" (p. 5). This claim has evidence to support it. Han et al.'s (2025) meta-analysis of 68 GenAI studies reports moderate positive effects overall, though with larger effects for younger students than older students and for short-term interventions rather than long-term integration. It is in the metrics used to demonstrate these learning outcomes, however, that the normative tension appears. Those showing improvement focus on test scores, task completion rates and speed to correct answers. This rests on a particular pedagogical formation: learning is measurable through performance on defined, standardised tasks, and improvement leads to efficiency gains. Yet, Bastani et al. (2024)found that secondary mathematics students using standard ChatGPT performed 48% better than control groups during assisted practice, but 17% worse than controls on unassisted summative exams. Han et al. (2025) also found that GenAI had negligible effects on disposition. This pattern matters for sustainability education, where affective engagement with difficulty, uncertainty and planetary futures is central to what is being learned (UNESCO, 2017) not an adjacent enabler of a discrete cognitive performance.

The evidence does not settle whether GenAI helps or harms critical thinking because the studies are asking different questions, measuring different things, valuing different outcomes and reflecting different conceptions of what education is for.

Compounding this dilemma is the issue of sociocultural bias in GenAI outputs. GenAI is being trained with data that already contain these biases, which can amplify existing prejudices (Hall & Ellis, 2023) and thereby undermine efforts to create more inclusive learning environments. The integration of GenAI technologies in education, while promising in many respects, risks perpetuating systemic biases if not carefully implemented and monitored (Baker & Hawn, 2021). GenAI-powered student assessment tools may inadvertently discriminate against learners from diverse linguistic or cultural backgrounds if the training data weights discourses from dominant groups. This has led some scholars to highlight a need to strengthen critical GenAI literacy among educators and students alike (Holmes et al., 2022) if we are to combat bias generation and perpetuation.

The pedagogical formation of education, as with material conditions for education, highlights the genuine wickedness of the problem GenAI presents for sustainable education. The knowledge is contested not because it is lacking but because what counts as evidence depends on how education is pedagogically understood which, in turn, is driven by divergent stakeholder needs. These are also influenced by privilege and the pre-existence of critical thinking skills. In this light, the effects of any intervention will be heterogeneous across the student population it purports to serve, and a policy response that benefits one cohort of students may cause harm to another.

Inasmuch, the tension is irreducible. The commitment to teaching critical capacities to inquire and tolerate uncertainty cannot be abandoned without abandoning the purpose of sustainability education: to support young people to shape the future, not just manage a future that is already shaped. Educators are left to navigate this site of the problem without the comfort of a right or correct answer, in a context where knowledge is genuinely contested, normatively distinct and where interests fundamentally diverge.

14.5 Locating *Good* in the *Wicked*

So where to from here? The tipping points we have brought into focus are temporally urgent not merely complex. Climate thresholds beyond which planetary change becomes exponential and the GenAI threshold beyond which integration is assumed for systemic relevance are time-pressured and urgent concerns. The two tipping points rebut each other at a policy level which leads to siloed and silenced knowledge in what appear to be irreducibly conflicting policy demands.

If this problem is genuinely *wicked* at a policy level, another question presents itself: Where else and with whom can the problem be placed? The moral purpose of education is not a question that can await resolution when market, civic and the purposive foundations of education are in conflict in a context of competing sustainability and economic demands. This is not a freedom from the hierarchies above educators' work, but a question of *praxis* within them. It becomes an issue that educators need to consider in light of our own moral purpose in why and how we educate the young people we teach.

A *wicked problem* for policy does not dissolve in the classroom, and the possibilities of transformative action for sustainable education are necessarily foundational not peripheral concerns. Where policy is paralysed by contested knowledge and fragmented authorities that represent fundamentally divergent stakeholder and purposively moral concerns, educators need to act anyway. Not because we have superior evaluative skill but because we are in relationship with young people that make inaction a moral judgement in and of itself.

This compels us to be humble about solutions, knowing that no perfect answer exists, trade-offs are inevitable, and counternarratives aren't baseless but evidenced and contain partial truths. We sit, often uncomfortably, with tolerance for complexity and ambiguity: living and breathing with the uncertainties that wicked problems are about.

A response that sits within the remit of educators, then, is about pedagogy not decisive policy response. This might look like a *praxis* that is good for humankind (Windsor & Kriewaldt, 2023). To give moral guidance here would contradict the wickedness we have described. Instead, we suggest giving educators—alongside policy-writers—a seat at the decision-making table. Not by awaiting or demanding invitation but through the pedagogical decisions they are already required to make. This might involve modelling the dispositions that both sustainable education and living with wickedness demand: the humility, ambiguity-tolerance and discomfort that an irreducible problem requires rather than protecting young people from the messiness that will be theirs to inherit. This is *praxis* as Mahon et al. (2020) foreground. Informed, reflexive action committed to bringing about what is good for self, for others, and for the generations to come. The commitment is not one to resolution but how to hold complex uncertainty.

Inasmuch, we glimpse a moral purpose for educators in which they are positioned as care-full collectives *with* young people, knowing they are entangled in planetary pulses that are more than the human world (Flynn et al., 2026).

References

Alford, J., & Head, B. W. (2017). Wicked and less wicked problems: A typology and a contingency framework. *Policy and Society, 36*(3), 397–413. https://doi.org/10.1080/14494035.2017.1361634

Australian Curriculum, Assessment and Reporting Authority. (2016). *The Australian Curriculum: Cross-curriculum priorities—Sustainability*. https://australiancurriculum.edu.au

Australian Education Research Organisation. (2024). *Strengthening the evidence on how GenAI can improve teaching and learning: Discussion paper*. https://www.edresearch.edu.au/research/discussion-papers/strengthening-evidence-how-genai-can-improve-teaching-and-learning

Bainbridge, L. (1983). Ironies of automation. *Automatica, 19*(6), 775–779. https://doi.org/10.1016/0005-1098(83)90046-8

Baker, R. S., & Hawn, A. (2021). Algorithmic bias in education. *International Journal of Artificial Intelligence in Education, 32*(4), 1052–1092. https://doi.org/10.1007/s40593-021-00285-9

Bastani, H., Bastani, O., Sungu, A., Ge, H., Kabakcı, Ö., & Mariman, R. (2024). *Generative AI can harm learning* (SSRN Working Paper No. 4895486). https://doi.org/10.2139/ssrn.4895486

Blumer, H. (1954). What is wrong with social theory? *American Sociological Review, 19*(1), 3–10. https://doi.org/10.2307/2088165

Chen, S. (2025, February 18). With AI on the rise, what will be the environmental impacts of data centers? *Smithsonian Magazine*. https://www.smithsonianmag.com/science-nature/with-ai-on-the-rise-what-will-be-the-environmental-impacts-of-data-centers-180987379/

Climate Action Tracker. (2023). *Global update: Projected warming drops to 2.5°C, but only if all 2030 targets are met*. https://climateactiontracker.org/

Commonwealth of Australia, Department of Education. (2023/2025). *Australian framework for generative artificial intelligence (AI) in schools*. (updated 2025). https://www.education.gov.au/schooling/resources/australian-framework-generative-artificial-intelligence-ai-schools

Commonwealth of Australia, Department of Finance. (2023). *Net zero in government operations strategy*. Australian Government.

Denejkina, A. (2023). *Young people's perception and use of generative AI*. YouthInsight & Student Edge. ISBN: 978-0-646-88006.

Flynn, A., Quay, J., & Kriewaldt, J. (2026). Becoming care-full collectives in schools and scholarship through sympoethical withnessing. In O. Franck, D. Sanders, & S. Windsor (Eds.), *Paradise Lost*. Springer.

Hall, P., & Ellis, D. (2023). A systematic review of socio-technical gender bias in AI algorithms. *Online Information Review, 47*(7), 1264–1279. https://doi.org/10.1108/OIR-08-2021-0452

Han, X., Li, Y., Zhang, L., & Zhai, X. (2025). The impact of GenAI on learning outcomes: A systematic review and meta-analysis of experimental studies. *Learning and Instruction, 96*, Article 102051. https://doi.org/10.1016/j.learninstruc.2025.102051

Holmes, W., Porayska-Pomsta, K., Holstein, K., Sutherland, E., Baker, T., Shum, S. B., & Koedinger, K. R. (2022). Ethics of AI in education: Towards a community-wide framework. *International Journal of Artificial Intelligence in Education, 32*(3), 504–526. https://doi.org/10.1007/s40593-021-00239-1

International Energy Agency. (2024). *Electricity 2024: Analysis and forecast to 2026*. IEA. https://www.iea.org/reports/electricity-2024

Lane, R. (2025). Mitigating generative AI hallucinations in geographical education. *International Research in Geographical and Environmental Education*. Advance online publication. https://doi.org/10.1080/10382046.2025.2555185

Lee, H. P., Sarkar, A., Tankelevitch, L., Drosos, I., Rintel, S., Banks, R., & Wilson, N. (2025). The impact of generative AI on critical thinking: Self-reported reductions in cognitive effort and confidence effects from a survey of knowledge workers. In *Proceedings of the 2025 CHI Conference on Human Factors in Computing Systems* (Article 207). ACM. https://doi.org/10.1145/3706598.3713778

Levin, K., Cashore, B., Bernstein, S., & Auld, G. (2012). Overcoming the tragedy of super wicked problems: Constraining our future selves to ameliorate global climate change. *Policy Sciences, 45*(2), 123–152. https://doi.org/10.1007/s11077-012-9151-0

Lönngren, J., & van Poeck, K. (2021). Wicked problems: A mapping review of the literature. *International Journal of Sustainable Development & World Ecology, 28*(6), 481–502. https://doi.org/10.1080/13504509.2020.1859415

MacIntyre, J., Medsker, L., & Moriarty, R. (2021). Past the tipping point? *AI Ethics, 1*, 1–3. https://doi.org/10.1007/s43681-020-00016-1

Mahon, K., Heikkinen, H. L., Huttunen, R., Boyle, T., & Sjølie, E. (2020). *What is educational praxis?. In Pedagogy, education, and praxis in critical times* (pp. 15–38). Springer Singapore.

NSW Department of Education. (2025). *Net zero road map*. https://education.nsw.gov.au/content/dam/main-education/about-us/strategies-and-reports/sustainability-commitment/Net_zero_road_map.pdf

OECD. (2025). *Results from TALIS 2024: The state of teaching* (TALIS). OECD Publishing. https://doi.org/10.1787/90df6235-en

Rittel, H. W. J., & Webber, M. M. (1973). Dilemmas in a general theory of planning. *Policy Sciences, 4*(2), 155–169. https://doi.org/10.1007/BF01405730

Stern, N., Romani, M., Pierfederici, R., Cornell, S., Rockström, J., & Steffen, W. (2025). Green and intelligent: The role of AI in the climate transition. *npj Climate Action, 4*, Article 56. https://doi.org/10.1038/s44168-025-00252-3

Strubell, E., Ganesh, A., & McCallum, A. (2019). Energy and policy considerations for deep learning in NLP. In A. Korhonen, D. Traum, & L. Màrquez (Eds.), *Proceedings of the 57th Annual Meeting of the Association for Computational Linguistics* (pp. 3645–3650). Association for Computational Linguistics. https://doi.org/10.18653/v1/P19-1355

UNESCO. (2017). *Education for Sustainable Development Goals: Learning objectives*. UNESCO. https://unesdoc.unesco.org/ark:/48223/pf0000247444

UNESCO. (2024). *Greening education partnership*. UNESCO. https://www.unesco.org/en/sustainable-development/education/greening-future

UNITAR and ITU. (2024). *The Global E-waste Monitor 2024*. United Nations Institute for Training and Research. https://ewastemonitor.info/the-global-e-waste-monitor-2024/

United Nations Environment Programme. (2024). *Artificial intelligence (AI) end-to-end: The environmental impact of the full AI lifecycle needs to be comprehensively assessed* [Issue Note]. Nairobi.

Victoria State Government. (2017). *Climate Change Act 2017*. https://www.legislation.vic.gov.au/

Windsor, S., & Kriewaldt, J. (2023). School geography's critical role for a more sustainable future: Powerful knowledge and Praxis. *Social Sciences, 12*(11), 585. https://doi.org/10.3390/socsci12110585

Zhao, G., Sheng, H., Wang, Y., Cai, X., & Long, T. (2025). Generative artificial intelligence amplifies the role of critical thinking skills and reduces reliance on prior knowledge while promoting in-depth learning. *Education Sciences*, *15*(5), Article 554. https://doi.org/10.3390/educsci15050554

Zhou, Z., Guo, H., Ma, F., Wang, Y., & Liu, Y. (2025). The chain mediating role of critical thinking and AI self-efficacy in GenAI usage competence and engineering students' creativity. *Scientific Reports*, *15*, Article 35945. https://doi.org/10.1038/s41598-025-21132-0

Emlyn Cruickshank is a critical scholar and lecturer in the Faulty of Education, University of Melbourne. He has taught in high school, prison and tertiary settings.

Jeana Kriewaldt is a Professor at the Faculty of Education, University of Melbourne. Jeana is a passionate field researcher whose research centres on contemporary issues that underpin questions of planetary future using lenses of geography and sustainability.

Chapter 15
Conclusion: GenAI in Education

Margaret E. Robertson

Abstract This chapter returns to the notion of what it takes for a civil society to survive well and flourish. Education is a community responsibility. Young people rely on their peers, families, mentors and institutions for their moral virtue and guidance on ethical decision making. In a world where change is happening at great speed silo approaches seem doomed to failure. Whatever your theory of education there will always be the need for resources. If you accept that those who have knowledge have power the custodians of power may not be who or where we may expect. For learners of all ages and backgrounds the need to be alert, critical and responsive to the moment must always be a search for truth and what is right both culturally and environmentally. Geopolitics may well be a distraction in this process. Professional educators need to be alert and lead with purpose.

Keywords Leadership · Knowledge · Purpose · Mentorship · GenAI

15.1 The Dilemma

In times of great change ideas are the source of discovery. In the second decade of the twenty-first century, the world's people live in such a time. The internet and Generative Artificial Intelligence are nudging daily life transactions closer to a point of co-dependency (see Lior & McNamara, 2026). Caught up in the process learner and teacher relationships now face the need for a paradigm shift that can best prepare the generation following Gen Alpha. A new humanism is dawning, and multi-disciplinary approaches are needed. Pooling knowledge may be the strategy to manage the future. In this sense, the digital literary space is being flooded with ideas and opinions on what and how to manage the impact. While this book has made education its focus ideas have been drawn from a wide base of experience and literature. There is a justified reason for this. If educators maintain that what happens in the

M. E. Robertson (✉)
La Trobe University, Melbourne, VIC, Australia
e-mail: m.robertson@latrobe.edu.au

M. E. Robertson (ed.), *Youth, Identity, AI and Moral Purpose*, Young People and Learning Processes in School and Everyday Life 9,
https://doi.org/10.1007/978-3-032-32479-5_15

classroom is sacrosanct and the certified curriculum is the driving force for learning there is a likely disconnect from real life and students' background experiences. The guiding premise for this book has been to promote innovative and reflective pedagogy. This requires courage and an ability to reject the old, reinvent practice and a willingness to seek ideas from beyond the institution and traditional knowledge disciplines. In this final chapter, some general principles are offered as suggestions for an open and interactive dialogue. They are by no means 'final' solutions.

Where to start is the problem. By working backwards from what we know about Generative Artificial Intelligence could be counterproductive. Its functioning algorithms reflect the digital revolution (Elliott, 2023) and colonise knowledge platforms the world over. Immersing practical behaviours guided by and within this space may well reinforce the embedded values and dogma and ignore the cultural lenses that underscore our just and ethical values. Working with the medium seems a preferred way to progress this argument. There is no surprise in the Marshall McLuhan adage that the 'medium is the message'. However, it would be wrong to submit totally to its powers without due caution and defence of all that is and has been achieved in the journey of the Anthropocene. Matters of social justice, identity, ethics and morality belong with people. Machines are helpers within their daily lives and not the commandants. As Oben et al. (2025) explain AI tools will contain biases that "can perpetuate inequities and discrimination in education, further exacerbating the digital divide" (p. 9). They refute the claim that AI will replace teachers. "The future of AI in education should not be viewed as a replacement for human educators but as a partnership between technology and human expertise" (p. 11). In the cognitive development of the young mind there are guides at school, home and within the community who decide on what and how to share knowledge. It is a complex relationship and one that has become increasingly messy within the digital age. Most fair-minded adults will see this relationship as a partnership which bridges the gap between knowledge to be gained and the learner's development. This construct applies the Action Leaning dynamic that assumes that 'new knowledge' equates with programmed learning or the learning goal plus questioning insight of the learner as the mediator of the 'new' knowledge (see Robertson et al., 2007). There is a process which takes place and this process will differ for all individuals. In the Vygotskian sense of the 'zone of proximal development' each person will bring their own perception to the task, and the role of the pedagogue or teacher is to bridge the gap. If we assume that this learning principle remains in place there is one clear criterion for this enabling pathway to continue to guide pedagogical practice and that is trust (see Kelly, 2024).

15.2 Trust

Choosing one professional space as an example of the intersection of GenAI and practice could take multiple directions in education. However, one high impact area is in the field of medical practice and its uses within the health care sector provide valuable insights and cautionary wisdom for education in other disciplines. Recognised as an early adopter of AI for diagnosis, risk and workflow practices the medical applications raise questions about soft skills and emotional care. Simou (2025) summarises these concerns as "the overall impact of AI in healthcare remains inconsistent and is limited not only by methodological heterogeneity, algorithmic bias, and implementation challenges but also by evolving regulatory requirements and complex ethical considerations" (p. 1). A literature search metanalysis of published peer review research as well as policy and public documents served as the basis for recommendations. Findings suggest that 'soft skills' or humanistic patient empathy is likely to vary or be unclear in the guidance for practitioners. Where team practices are encouraged, there is more likelihood of reliable decision making when interacting with AI. Simou concludes: "Insights from team science indicate that effective collaboration between humans and machines requires trust calibration, shared situational awareness, adaptive communication, and metacognitive monitoring" (p. 10). The social contract between patient and professional is built on empathy and trust both of which can appear sidelined or misinterpreted by the machines. Simou's views are pragmatic and carry messages that translate across disciplines in education.

> This review proposes a reconceptualization of soft skills as an interconnected and adaptive ecosystem that integrates the cognitive, affective, humanistic, behavioral, and digital dimensions. Rather than perceiving these competencies as discrete or supplementary to biomedical expertise, they should be recognized as mutually reinforcing capacities that collectively uphold ethical judgment, empathy, and trust in technology-mediated healthcare. (2025, p. 17)

The key point here is that no matter how invasive technology is in the lives of people what we do and how we do it is transactional and within the widest social setting trust is at the heart of the process. Shared trust in systems maintains personal security and protects the user from harm's way. The challenge for decision makers, especially legislators, is to arrive at a balanced outcome. A recent piece of legislation by the Australian government has prohibited children under the age of sixteen from having a social media account. An example of protective pedagogy the law has widespread support from parents who welcome the decision which offers support for their guidance. It serves as an indicator of collective democracy within a free liberal society where individualism and open access to unmonitored media platforms are acknowledged sources of fake news and scams. Notably, other nations are considering similar legislation.

In this brief review, there is perhaps a bigger question to ask and that relates to the meaning of trust and how it develops. If empathy and emotional intelligence are at the heart of trust, there will always be need of keepers of ethical and moral boundaries in a just and fair society. Anarchy is but one step removed in civil society as political swings to the left and right are prone to be reminders of how harmony can be threatened and at its worst destroyed. The trust relationship between learner and mentor is a cornerstone of authentic pedagogy. Technology is not the driver of this process unless mediated by trusted others or security authenticators. Pragmatism and open dialogue between all users are essential criteria for this process and within this process both practitioner and student are learners (Connor, 2025).

15.3 Relational Pedagogy

The characteristics of trust are a valid starting point for designing a pedagogical approach for the moment. Using survey data McDonagh and Sanders (2025) have analysed the perceptions of trust within the academic community with findings that endorse commonly accepted qualities. The top ranked were confidence, relationship, integrity, fairness, and authenticity. Other lesser ranked qualities were community, relationship, encouragement, collegial, and collaboration. Each of these qualities overlapped with perceptions of team engagement leading to a conclusion that a relational pedagogy is more likely to engage participants in a positive relationship. The solution in these terms appears simple. Individuals value empathetic relationships and these are often located within community or group spaces. However, ontologically this raises the question related to the role of the individual within the group context. How much individualism is tolerated? Taking the conceptual extremes as a reminder of impact, in an authoritarian state there is no such place for individualism, and within a free liberal democracy freewill and individual preferences are sacrosanct. The overlap between individualism and collectivism is a philosophical tussle that intersects and complicates any such pedagogical assumptions and the arguments for and against are widely published (see Koons, 2019). Suffice to say that within any sociocultural context the predilection towards individualism and collectivism will exist and a relational pedagogy will need to be flexible, especially within multicultural societies where linguistic differences reflect cultural backgrounds (see Papantoniou et al., 2022). Cultural backgrounds need to be factored into curriculum statements and knowledge directives. Ideologically driven they are texts that narrate their own history and biases (see Žižek, 1989). Generative Artificial Intelligence is the Thirdspace in this equation, the 'other' which floats around the human world with no clear ontological base.

15.4 Knowledge Hegemony and the Digital Commons

The one element in this journey to the future is the unknown and technology is taking us there. Traditional knowledges appear to have had their time which makes the knowledge hegemony an ambiguous field. Acknowledging this fast-moving change in our knowledge space is crucial for humans to maintain relevance in their lived lives and some degree of mastery over the options. The times need big thinkers like Slavoj Žižek (2023) who can condense and explain the options. Put bluntly he concludes:

> Unlike past technological innovations, artificial intelligence is not about humanity's mastery over nature, but rather about relinquishing control altogether. Whether we realize it or not, the old anthropocentric arrogance that technology enables may soon give way to human irrelevance and meaninglessness.[1]

[1] See https://www.project-syndicate.org/commentary/ai-post-human-future-by-slavoj-zizek-2023-04.

The wakeup call is scary and a challenge for educators to adapt, fight back and reestablish some dignity within the knowledge space. Potentially, the first step is to locate the shared commons. This is explained as the space where individuals and collectives have connection and that includes the digital commons. An idealistic goal perhaps but one worth pursuing before too much further control is lost and Žižek's prophesy unfolds.

Comforting is research by the Pew Research Center[2] which suggests that 'experts' are less concerned with AI developments than the US public. This may appear to be positive news. However, where education is concerned complacency will be a dangerous path to take. There is clear evidence in the wider community that better reflects the general public's concern with technology developments. Village life of earlier times where families nurtured the young and shared their cultural narratives have become weakened or compete with alternative world views. The shared green parks were the commons for meeting, recreation and building bonds with friends and neighbours. The fear is that these wholesome activities are becoming marginalised as they compete for their survival with the arrival of 'others'.

Transnational migration has led to diversified neighbourhoods in many wealthier nations including those in Western Europe, North America and Australasia. Recent terrorist attacks across the globe are evidence of increasing hatred within disaffected minorities who are often migratory groups from war torn countries with disturbed mind sets seeking to unsettle peaceful communities with violence. The means by which they disseminate their propaganda is via 'legal' public meetings, social media and a variety of digital platforms with few rules and controls. Unfiltered by societal norms and values messages from such dark sources can disrupt, destroy lives and hope. Community naivety is both the victim and actor in this process. The knowledge hegemony no longer belongs within the cloisters of academe and recognised places of governance. The digital commons is the space for the global citizenry to share, interact and learn. Who controls this space? How is it made secure for the citizenry? What are we as thinkers and educators doing about it? Cultural pride in identity and place ought to affirm the basis of the citizenry knowledge base. Time now for rethinking the *Empire to Strikes back.*[3]

15.5 Pedagogical Change Reclaiming the Knowledge Space

Children are always the next generation's hope. Except for some extremist regimes most nations embrace public education. These are times when teachers are the interface between external policies and pressures regarding the curriculum and the socio-diversity and cultural mores of the students. The relationship between teacher and

---

[2] See https://www.pewresearch.org/internet/2025/04/03/how-the-us-public-and-ai-experts-view-artificial-intelligence/?utm_source=prcsite&utm_medium=topic-summary&utm_campaign=internet-technology.

[3] The *Empire Strikes Back* is the epic Star Wars film Opera released in 1980.

students is the key dynamic to explore for authentic learning outcomes. It requires courage and determination to listen and understand the subjectivity element in the cognitive processing of each student. Knowing how information is processed may require taking a more resistant approach to the process and this is not without personal risk. In the context of music education and philosophical arguments Gardiner (2025) offers useful analyses related to the ethical implication of pedagogical resistance. Using Žižek's ideas he explores the complex relationship between the individual and society to argue that "the educator, is positioned at something of an intersection between subject and society, with what seems like a certain mandate to resist the erosion of educational freedoms for the sake of more representative and socially engaged educative spaces" (Gardiner, 2025, p. 160). In a critical pedagogy context, the professional educator will have many conflicting moments, and these can turn to uncritical compliance or disaffection and withdrawal in the process. Neither approach is sustainable or likely to yield educational outcomes for long term societal benefit. Gardiner offers examples in practice which lead to the summation that "the point is not to disavow nor overly embrace moments of professional tension or trauma, but to accept these as key critical moments" (p. 174).

Close to the third decade in the twenty-first century, this is the key moment for a critical pedagogy (see Wegerif & Casebourne, 2025). Slow media and more selective usage are positive strategies (Erickson, 2025). Shared spaces for learning are infinite and competing. They include digital commons, online classrooms, as well as traditional nature-based settings. Within these diverse learning spaces professional educators are employed to nurture the cognitive development of the young mind and ensure they learn to become moral and responsible citizens. The aim must be to develop their sense of self-efficacy, purpose and community. Sociocultural community harmony relies on their collaborative skills to construct sustainable shared futures. Tolerance, care of others, and thoughtfulness are key human agents in the identity building process. They are essential qualities for the development of national pride and identity. As the carriers of whole of society interests, this is a mammoth responsibility for professional educators. Nevertheless, they retain the role of being the medium to lead this process. Their communication skills and expert knowledge will bridge the gaps between competing expectations and nurture the minds of the young.

15.6 Final Comment

Practitioner renewal in the age of Generative Artificial Intelligence will be a constant. There are guiding principles but no remedies. Relevance within the constantly emerging pedagogical spaces is different now. The task is complex and action fraught with the need for decisive action. Ideas and empathetic colleagues will be wise companions within this and future critical frontier moments. Relationships are core to what happens.

References

Connor, S. (2025). The affordances of pragmatism for a postdigital citizen social science. *Postdigital Science and Education, 7*, 78–97. https://doi.org/10.1007/s42438-024-00529-6
Elliott, A. (2023). *Algorithmic intimacy*. Polity.
Erickson, M. (2025). *Slow media: Sensibility, process, and technology*. Bloomsbury Publishing USA. https://www.bloomsbury.com/us/slow-media-9781666959116
Gardiner, R. (2025). "To disturb the universe?": On the ethical implications of educational resistance. *Philosophy of Music Education Review, 33*(2), 159–177. https://doi.org/10.2979/pme.00030
Kelly, A. (2024). Trusts, trust, and *trust*: Hernan Diaz's liberal pedagogy. *American Literary History, 36*(2), 489–515. https://doi.org/10.1093/alh/ajae033
Koons, R. C. (2019). Individualism vs. Collectivism. *Academic Questions, 32*(4), 529–541.
Lior, Y., & McNamara, P. (2026). Major evolutionary transitions in culture and cognition. *Evolutionary Behavioral Sciences, 20*(1), 1–28. https://doi.org/10.1037/ebs0000380
McDonagh, L., & Sanders, E. C. (2025). 'You almost feel like you've got a friend, somebody who's backing you up': Exploring the building blocks of trust within a relational pedagogy approach to academic development. *International Journal for Academic Development, 30*(1), 40–52. https://doi.org/10.1080/1360144X.2024.2443214
Oben, A. I., Hui, X., Bahtilla, M., & Quanguo, L. (2025). Teaching with Generative Artificial Intelligence (GenAI): Should educators trust AI to guide student learning? *Innovations in Education and Teaching International*, 1–14. https://doi.org/10.1080/14703297.2025.2587333
Papantoniou, K., Papadakos, P., Patkos, T., Flouris, G., Androutsopoulos, I., & Plexousak, D. (2022). Deception detection in text and its relation to the cultural dimension of individualism/collectivism. *Natural Language Engineering, 28*, 545–606. https://doi.org/10.1017/S1351324921000152
Robertson, M., Fluck, A., & Webb, I. (2007). *Seven steps to success with ICTs: Whole school approaches to sustainable change*. ACER Press.
Simou, E. (2025). The growing importance of soft skills in medical education in the AI era: Balancing humanistic care and Artificial Intelligence. *International Medical Education, 4*(4), 50. https://doi.org/10.3390/ime4040050
Strachan, J. C. (2025). Why I'm doubling down on deliberative pedagogy. *Journal of Political Science Education*, 1–9. https://doi.org.ez.library.latrobe.edu.au/10.1080/15512169.2025.2581685
Wegerif, R., & Casebourne, I. (2025). A dialogic theoretical foundation for integrating generative AI into pedagogical design. *British Journal of Educational Technology, 1–16*,. https://doi.org/10.1111/bjet.70026
Žižek, S. (1989). *The sublime object of ideology*. Verso.
Žižek, S. (2023). The post-human desert. *Project Syndicate*. https://www.project-syndicate.org//commentary/ai-post-human-future-by-slavoj-zizek-2023-04

Margaret E. Robertson is Emeritus Professor of Education, La Trobe University, Melbourne, Australia. Research interests include cultural geography, youth studies and innovative pedagogy.

FSC
www.fsc.org
MIX
Papier | Fördert
gute Waldnutzung
FSC® C083411

Kolibri 360 GmbH
Ferdinand-Jühlke-Straße 7
99095 Erfurt, Deutschland
produktsicherheit@kolibri360.de